# France

The Secret Knowledge of
Mary Magdalene, the Cathars,
Templars and Avalon

# France

## The Secret Knowledge of Mary Magdalene, the Cathars, Templars and Avalon

JUDITH KÜSEL

Published by Judith Küsel
http://www.judithkusel.com
info@judithkusel.com

First edition 2023

**France: The Secret Knowledge of Mary Magdalene,
the Cathars, Templars and Avalon**
Paperback Edition ISBN 978-0-639-75489-5

Copyright © 2023 Judith Küsel

All rights reserved. No part of this publication may be reproduced,
stored in a retrieval system, or transmitted, in any form or by any means,
without the prior written permission of the publisher.

Editor: Jill Charlotte Combes and Janet Vollmer
Photography: Judith Küsel
Production assistant: Jill Charlotte
Typesetting and layout: Quickfox Publishing

# Contents

Prologue .................................................. 7

**PART 1. THE CALL**

Chapter 1. Part 1. Preparing for the ultimate journey to rediscover the Holy Grail .......... 16

Chapter 1. Part 2. Cape Town – further secrets revealed ........................................... 26

Chapter 2. An epic journey begins ..................... 38

Chapter 3. The Sun Gate and Sun Discs of Versailles ................................................. 51

Chapter 4. Chartres .......................................... 58

Chapter 5. Jeanne d'Arc makes herself known ..... 68

Chapter 6. The High Order of the Bards ............ 75

Chapter 7. Opening of the Star Gate at Carnac ... 79

**PART 2. THE LASTING LEGACY OF THE CATHARS AND THE TEMPLARS**

Chapter 1. The journey to the South of France .... 90

Chapter 2. The Fires of Illumination – Occitania .................................................. 96

Chapter 3. The greatest secret and hidden treasure ................................................... 101

Chapter 4. Foix, Monségur ............................... 109

Chapter 5. The 7 seminars, group tour to Monségur: the reopening of Mary Magdalene's Mystery School .................... 117

Chapter 6. The Anointing at Bugarach .............. 130

Chapter 7. The Templar ................................... 137

Chapter 8. The Tragedy and the Triumph ......... 141

Chapter 9. What did the Templars and Cathars Hide? ........................................ 147

Chapter 10. The Gift of Love: The Mystery of the Rose, the Serpent and the Holy Grail Reveals Itself ................................. 158

Epilogue ........................................................ 163

Additional Information:

Sun Discs ................................................ 168

Spinal Cord ............................................. 169

Crystal Pyramids ..................................... 170

The Temple of the White Flame ............... 172

The Secret Legacy – Atlantis and Lemuria .................................................. 173

The Druids and the Three High Orders of the Druids ........................................ 177

The High Kings and High Queens of Avalon ............................................. 186

Before the Final Hour ............................. 189

Book List ....................................................... 194

Index ............................................................. 195

# Prologue
## Elysium, the Lion Kingdom and Avalon

France is the womb of the Earth, and accordingly houses some of the most sacred and holy places on Earth, which were created within her from the very beginning. She holds the Divine Feminine energy, so the history of France and the contents of this book cannot be understood if we are not familiar with what happened long before the rise and fall of Atlantis. Thus we need to return to the very beginning. Some material that I share here has already been recorded in my first book, *Why I was born in Africa: the previously unrecorded history of Elysium and the Lion Kingdom*.

## Elysium – the First Civilization on Earth

In the beginning the Divine Source created the first 12 Master Galaxies – thus the Milky Way Galaxy was one of 11 other galaxies, star systems and constellations created in the beginning. Some of these included the Milky Way Galaxy, Andromeda, Lyra, Sirius, Orion, the Pleiades, Cygnus and the Bear Constellation. They formed the first Master Galactic Races and the Intergalactic Federation, which, in turn launched the Intergalactic Fleet. They represented the physical aspect of Divine Creation, for there is always a visible (physical manifestation) of Creation, and an invisible (purely energetic, etheric or spiritual manifestation) which is, in reality, just as present and palpable as the visible physical aspect. They were highly evolved beings, acting as co-creators with the Divine Source.

As there are many solar systems within each galaxy, and planets within each solar system, the Intergalactic Fleet helped to co-create new planets and stars. This was made possible because on board the great motherships, the huge cities in space, there were scientists who specialized in this kind of work. They were Priest-Scientists.

As they were already traversing the Milky Way Galaxy and our solar system, which at that time linked through the Milky Way Galaxy to the 7th Central Sun of Illumination, they needed a halfway satellite station, and so they created it. There was no planet Earth at the time, although Jupiter, Mercury and Venus already existed, as did Saturn and Neptune.

Many thousands of earth years later, they decided to build an outer crust around the satellite station, which the scientists set about co-creating. As they laid down the outer crust, they created the Web of Light, the Crystalline Light Webs, vortices, the Earth and the telluric energy centers. These became the energy centers over which they created the Crystal Pyramids and the Crystalline Energy Grids, the powerhouses of the planet, which would provide free energy for their spacecraft, temples, homes, and whatever else was needed. These were carefully laid down in line with the sacred geometries, sacred mathematics, sacred tones and sounds which were all incorporated in the co-creation of Earth. This included the Spinal Column of the Earth, which acts like a tuning fork and Lightning Energy Conductor, tuning Mother Earth into the solar system, the Milky Way Galaxy and all Universal levels. In the beginning it was also tuned into the 7th Central Sun of Illumination.

The Inner Earth (the original satellite) then became Agartha, the Inner Earth Civilization, which functions as an entity on her own, with her own inner sun, animals, trees, plants, and all life and life forms. The beings who live inside the Earth are certainly much older than the current human race, and thus are still tuned into the 7th Dimensional Vibrational Frequency band, or what is often referred to as the 7th Heaven.

When the outer crust was complete, the mineral kingdom fully established, and the waters parted, the Supercontinent of Elysium emerged. It was one single landmass and Africa, Europe and parts of Asia still encompass and support the original Spinal Column of the Earth. (Geologists are very aware of this, and have been working to piece this supercontinent together.) The Elementals, such as the Celestial Fairies, Gnomes, and the Elemental Kingdom assisted in the process of creation. They are entities in their own right, created by the Divine to help with creation.

Thus the establishment of outer life on Earth had begun in earnest. Some great motherships of the Intergalactic Fleet had huge laboratories on board to house plants, trees, and other biological species, which were first introduced to the planet, mainly by the Pleiadeans, the Master Botanists of the Fleet. These species were donated and gathered from all 12 Master Galaxies, as part of an experiment which was launched to see how they would adapt to life on Earth.

Gradually other life forms were introduced, and subsequently the mammals, fish, birds and insects and so forth arrived. All creatures agreed to come here, including the whales and dolphins from Sirius.

The scientists co-creating the Outer Earth, and everything upon her, fell deeply in love with planet Earth, as she certainly was beautiful, and was often referred to as "The Crown Jewel of Creation." All who saw her were enchanted by her exquisite beauty at that time.

Some asked if they could settle there, so a petition with this request was presented to the Intergalactic Councils, which was granted; however, there was a clear understanding that they would be participating in an experiment on Earth.

Thus Elysium the first civilization, and a Paradise on Earth was born. All of life prospered, and all lived in Harmony, Unity and Oneness.

The Crystal Pyramids were built, with the Crystal Pyramid Temple of The White Flame as the main temple, and 12 High Priests and 12 High Priestesses were in charge of the 12 Main Temples. They ruled over each of the 12 Tribes, and each tribe was attached to a certain Temple. You can read more about this in my first book, *Why I was born in Africa: the previously unrecorded history of Elysium and the Lion Kingdom*.

They defined and marked the vortex or spiraling energy sites of the Earth, placing markers on the most sacred of them. They created Inner Earth space stations, using amphibious craft with spaceports, where the motherships and all intergalactic craft could land.

Elysium unquestionably was a place of peace, love and joy. All lived in harmony, and thus all was One.

Then the Wars of the Heavens erupted, and the scientists had to be evacuated by the Intergalactic

Fleet, apart from those who chose to stay on in the inner Earth, Agartha. The planet between Jupiter and Mars blew itself up, as its inhabitants had sided with the rebel faction causing the Wars. Consequently, Earth was bombarded by the debris and thrown totally out of orbit, as was the Milky Way Galaxy and the counter solar systems and galaxies, including Melchior.

Total chaos reigned, as some master galaxies had been blown up or suffered severe damage, and subsequently for many millions of years the outer Earth was left undisturbed, while the inner Earth, Agartha, survived intact. The Intergalactic Fleet had great difficulty operating in the midst of asteroids and cosmic debris, which had been created by the galactic explosions and which hampered space travel. Slowly but surely, the Intergalactic Fleet rebuilt things, and the original space routes reopened as more sophisticated means of travelling emerged, teleporting craft in milliseconds from one galaxy or system to another. This rebuilding process sped up when help arrived from other universes to assist with the clean-up operations. Meanwhile, the faction that had caused the Wars of the Heavens withdrew to other systems, and thus were not completely defeated.

Some animal and plant species survived the catastrophes, and the Supercontinent of Elysium shifted, as new inland lakes were formed and chunks of land were torn off and submerged in the oceans. Yet somehow the main frame had endured, with most of the Supercontinent still in place.

## The Lion Kingdom

During the Wars of the Heavens, Lyra suffered severe damage, and most of their home galaxy was so impaired that they sought refuge in Sirius. The Intergalactic Head Quarters is based on Sirius, and when they were asked if the Lyrans could re-colonize the Earth, this wish was granted.

They arrived on planet Earth in their motherships and other craft to begin rebuilding the outer Earth. They were the Lion People, with distinct feline features and golden manes, very tall, starting from 15 meters! They were a handsome race, and rebuilt mostly on the original sites (those that had survived the Wars of the Heavens), usually in places where they knew the vortices or telluric currents existed.

The Lyran People are the Master Architects and Engineers of the Universe, and they erected cities, temples and abodes of incredible beauty, using and applying sacred geometries, sacred tones, sound technology, sacred mathematics and physics. All these places were astronomically aligned to reflect the Heavens on Earth.

They built their temple complexes in these sacred geometrical forms to utilize the sacred and powerful energies on site, and to amplify the Earth energy and telluric currents (spiraling energy). They loved to add labyrinths, and to create mazes.

In addition, they rebuilt the Crystal Pyramids, repaired the Crystalline Pyramid Grids, and built new cities and buildings which were works of art, with engineering feats that Earth has not witnessed since that time. They created these things along with massive and spectacular hanging gardens that defied gravity, and everyone who saw them was spellbound, and filled with awe and wonder. This was in the 7th dimensional state, the state of Paradise, and indeed it was Paradise for a while, and was much loved and admired for its exquisite beauty. Thus planet Earth regained her title as the "Crown Jewel of Creation!"

Unity and Harmony reigned, and the Lion People prospered here. They invited the Pleiadeans from Sirius and Orion to assist them, life flourished, and their engineering feats around the world still astound us today, as preserved in the Megalithic sites.

The inhabitants were extremely tall, with blonde to red hair, which was mostly worn in a topknot. They were giants, from 15 to 30 meters tall, and brought a new Master Race into form and being on Earth.

They also introduced the cat, and other four-legged animal species.

## Isis and Osiris arrive from Sirius with the Shining Ones and the Illumined Ones

It was at this time that the High Councils of the Intergalactic Federation wished to expand the consciousness on planet Earth and raise it to the 9th dimensional state, in greater illumination as part of the evolutionary process of planets and souls.

In alignment with this aspiration, the High Priest and Priestess of the Temple of the White Flame invited Osiris and Isis (Aysis) from Sirius to bring the higher illumined knowledge to planet Earth, to teach and administer it to those who sought to raise their vibrational frequencies to the 9th dimension.

Those from Sirius are a highly evolved and advanced super race, and it was agreed that these two would reign as High Priest and High Priestess, and High King and High Queen of the Lyran People, as they had lost their Royal families during the Wars of the Heavens. So they came as very pure surrogates or substitutes for the Lyran Royalty or rulers.

As Sirius holds the Higher Temples of Learning, Intergalactic Universities and Temples of Knowledge, and Orion those of Wisdom, the fact that these two had a Father from Orion and a Mother from Sirius, made them the perfect couple to rule over the Lion Kingdom, and they agreed to assume this role. Note this was their first sojourn on this planet.

They thus ruled the Lion Kingdom as High Priest and High Priestess, initiated in the Mystery of Mysteries, and in the secrets of the Universal Divine Knowledge and the higher states of Illumination and Cosmic and Galactic Mastery, as held in the Cosmic Mystery Schools of Sirius and elsewhere.

It is vital to understand this context in relation to what later ensued in France, Greece and Egypt. The Egyptian God Osiris, and his consort and sister Isis, and the birth of Horus, had their origins in far older times, in the Lion Kingdom.

The first-born offspring of Isis and Osiris were twins – Horus, was the elder and consequently the more enlightened and illumined one from birth, and his younger twin brother was not of the same calibre. One rose in the Priesthood, and the other in rebellion.

After their birth, Isis foresaw in a vision exactly what would happen to the Lion Kingdom, and was told to safeguard the secret knowledge which came from all over the Kingdom. For that reason, she created the first 12 Mystery Schools, in what is now Egypt, the Middle East, Africa and Europe, but not as we know Europe today, for indeed Europe was still part of the Supercontinent, as were the Americas, and the rest of the world. Thus the Himalayas, the Pacific, and every landmass now covered by the oceans, are also included here.

During the Lion Kingdom, massive temples, sacred sites and temple complexes were dedicated to the Goddess Isis – such sites in France included what is now Paris, Monségur and the Pyrenees.

Please take careful note of this, for you will only comprehend the chapters that follow if you understand the history and context.

Mother Isis had foreseen that her younger son would rebel against his own brother, causing the destruction of the Lion Kingdom. It was one of the most brutal wars ever seen on Earth (Atlantis was the worst), and in the process the Mediterranean Sea formed, islands were born, and the European Continent was created. However Britain and Ireland, and the islands offshore from Europe in the Atlantic Ocean, and the landmass within this ocean, as well as the Americas, were still attached to Africa and Britain. (Scotland was joined to Norway, and also to parts of France, Holland, and Spain.)

The Mystery Schools that Isis had founded were created to hold the light steady during these times, as

Isis and Osiris withdrew to return to Sirius, only to incarnate again much later on.

## Avalon Arises

The Mediterranean Sea was created during the terrible wars between the two brothers, and thus Malta, Ibiza, Sardinia and all the Islands were created, as well as Spain, Italy, Greece, etc. and thus the Earth looked very different after the wars, since most of the destruction occurred in these areas, and North Africa as well as in the Middle East.

Yet the upper part of the Kingdom, the areas which are now Spain, Portugal, France, and Britain, Ireland and the offshore islands, parts of Scandinavia, Norway and further north, were still attached to each other. The upper section became the Northern Kingdom of Avalon, while the more southern parts, including the Alpine regions, Holland, Belgium, Germany and so forth, made up the Southern Kingdom.

Avalon did not suffer from the Wars as much as certain other regions, and thus in the interim the Mystery Schools there held steady. These included the Mystery Schools in Greece, which survived inside the Earth, in tunnel systems and chambers underneath what is now Delphi, keeping the knowledge alive in small pockets.

Avalon then rose in prominence and came to the fore, as some High Priests and Priestesses had fled to these areas, and thus were incorporated in the Mystery Schools in the Pyrenees, Paris and the Temples offshore from Carnac, Brittany, parts of Norway, and what is now Britain, Iona and Ireland, the Orkney Islands, and so on.

Avalon was a civilization of highly trained Wizards, not as we understand them now, but more in the line of Merlin. Indeed, High Priestesses were called Merlinda, and held equal rank, and this Priesthood was the forerunner of the later Celtic Druids, who succeeded in keeping the sacred secrets in independent pockets, like branches of the self-same tree.

It was through their vast esoteric knowledge, and the ability to manifest so powerfully, that all the old Isis sites, spiraling energy centers, and the sacred sites were preserved. They used them in co-creative work to teleport, to bi-locate, to shapeshift and to create, and they utilized the Power of Sound to convert vast tons of stone to a featherlight weight, which they were then able to cut with precision, and teleport to the exact place it was needed. They had learnt this from the Master Teachers and Magi in the Lion Kingdom, and thus this knowledge was preserved.

It is important to note that during the time of Elysium, the Lion Kingdom and Avalon, and what followed, there was no written language. They did not use their vocal cords to speak – only for singing and chanting, so telepathy was prevalent. In addition they knew how to tap into energy and energy fields, to utilize and download the information and knowledge contained in the Sun Discs.

The Sun Discs were introduced to the planet by the Lyran and Sirians, and gigantic ones were located at the most powerful places on Earth, to be fully used and accessed by the Mystery Schools, in many ways.

In Avalon, the Matriarchy ruled, and thus the Isis sites were utilized, nurtured and maintained as sacred and holy, so only the purest of the pure Priesthood and Mystery Schools ever held the power of such places, as well as the knowledge of how to use this power in unadulterated and responsible ways.

The main seat of influence was just offshore from Carnac in Brittany, linked to Isis Island in Paris (where Notre Dame Cathedral now stands), and towards the South of France, in Monségur.

I drew the energy lines and sacred sites on the map of France, long before I arrived there.

Every place I visited in France was connected by these same links.

Thus it is no accident that one of the greatest and most ancient Mystery Schools on Earth created by

Isis, was situated in the High Pyrenees, with its main seat in Monségur. This is especially important to be aware of, as Isis held the White Flame as a Divine Mother Emissary. She rebuilt the Temple of The White Flame in the Lion Kingdom, and Monségur held another temple. They were thus twin sites.

Additionally, throughout Europe the Isis sites link up together as one great energetic Sun Disc. The Celtic Druids who followed knew this, and charted the Ancient Sun Paths, which the Celts later continued.

Avalon was 7th dimensional and pure, existing in harmony and unity in a time that fully implemented the psychic powers, together with those of the heart, and the High Bardic Orders were even aware of how to utilize the Power of Sound in miraculous ways. They could shapeshift into any chosen form, and knew how to co-create with energy and energy fields and how to transform matter, and manifest matter into form. Much of this would seem like magic today, but they merely knew how to apply metaphysical Universal Divine Laws.

All the Ancient Megalithic Sites in Europe, Britain, Ireland, etc. stem from the Lion Kingdom and Avalon, as do the Standing Stones and the Stone Circles, with many more found elsewhere in Europe, Britain and Ireland, which were destroyed in later wars. The Romans, for instance, made it their business to dismantle such places, and to kill the Druids, for they feared their powers.

Avalon is still there within the heart of the Cathar country, along with the Troubadour Courts of Love, for here the High Bardic Orders of pure love were cultivated, and the teachings of Avalon and the Mystery Schools were preserved by a long lineage of families who held and guarded these secrets.

The fact that the Cathars and Templars descended from the very same traditional families, was no accident, but by Grand Design. An outstanding man who had access to immeasurably powerful hidden knowledge, was none other than Saint Bernard of Clairvaux. One cannot fully understand the context of either the Cathars or the Templars without studying this extraordinary man and his visions.

Undeniably, the legacy of Avalon lived on in many other customs and practices. One only needs to travel in France and read the symbolism that is apparent everywhere, in plain sight. It appears as if someone familiar with the ancient knowledge of the Mystery Schools initiates was deliberately leaving clues. If you wish to preserve the truth, having the symbols etched in the buildings ensures that the energetic truths in the sacred sites are actually imprinted in the landscape.

Most tourists run across these and fail to notice them. Yet, for the truth seeker, they speak a sacred language leading to awareness and understanding. A truth found deep within the self, which the soul knows and recognizes as such!

Avalon was an era in which one could manifest miracles and magic with love. There was such harmony, unity and peace, love and a lightness of being. One knew the inner workings of the Universe and the Laws of Creation, and applied them. The principle was never to hurt or harm, but to rather enhance all life.

Therefore, when destruction came, it was all the more poignant. For although they were highly advanced, they had no means of defending themselves against the brutality of a lesser, more primitive race from the inner bowels of the Earth, who suddenly invaded their lands. A brutal machine of men who, when they could lay their hands on them, slashed the Priestesses and Priests to pieces, and began their rule of fear.

Merlins and Merlindas then had to resort to using their powers to defend themselves, which violated vows to never abuse these abilities. Some partook of this, and others refused. Some indeed withdrew underground to survive in pockets in the high mountains, and later emerged as Druids who taught the hidden secrets, and applied them.

It is important to remember the information above as you read this book.

For indeed my own journey, and the subsequent revelations I have been given, apply and relate to all of these civilizations.

Note that at the same time that Avalon was in its heyday, Mu and Lemuria were born in the Pacific Regions.

The last to rise was Atlantis, in the area of the Atlantic Ocean, and indeed it changed the face of the Earth forever.

However, the story of Mu, Lemuria and Atlantis must wait for another time, another book.

Let us now start our journey of rediscovery on multiple levels, and in multi-dimensional space.

Let us now delve deeper into the legacy of Avalon and the Secret of Secrets, the Divine Feminine, and the hidden knowledge of Mary Magdalene, Joan of Arc, Esclarmonde de Foix, Cécile de Foix, the Cathars and Templars. Indeed, all paths lead back to Ancient Secrets and Secret Knowledge, and the Mystery Schools of Isis …

* * *

# PART I

# THE CALL

CHAPTER 1

# Part 1: Preparing for the Ultimate Journey to Rediscover the Sacred Grail

The Journey of life is an unfolding. It is a journey to continually reconnect with the heart, mind and soul at a deeper and deeper level, and the most profound and greatest All-Knowing is found within oneself.

The Journey never ends, for with every single unfolding and deep remembering, all the layers of illusion, the Maya, are stripped away, so that one stands there, naked to the very core of one's Soul, vulnerable, open. It is this brokenness, this delicate openness that allows the re-birth and remembering, for the soul to be reinvented and revamped by the Holy Spirit, the Divine itself, into a far greater and more insightful version of self.

Without this breaking open, nothing can grow, for indeed the clearing has begun in earnest, and all the weeds and overgrowth restricting the higher development of the soul have to be stripped away, so that only the core Light, Love and Wisdom of the Higher Soul Self, can shine through on an even higher Vibrational and dimensional frequency band, than ever before!

In truth my soul was called on a Quest so ancient, that it astounds the mind. I was urged to return to a place on Earth where my soul had lived out so many previous soul incarnations. It would be a homecoming in the deepest sense, but often excruciatingly painful, as I was cleaved open to the very core, as painful memory banks opened up, one

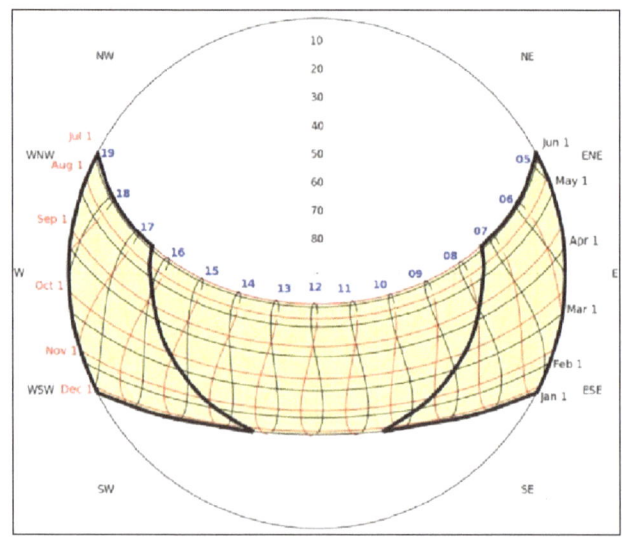

*Figure 1. Sun Paths*

after the other. So many times, I had to lay the ghosts of my own past incarnations to rest, but also those of all the souls who had walked there with me during those lifetimes. How deeply these wounds are buried only became apparent to me long after I had left the shores of France and returned home. In transcribing my journal entries, they came to life once again, and I had to release everything which still needed to be freed.

What about France, then? She holds the womb of the Earth within her, the Goddesshood itself – in fact those parts of her which were the most suppressed, persecuted and hated.

Half of modern-day France, Portugal, Spain and Belgium, were torn off from the mainland and sank under the sea. They all formed part of one single land mass before the emergence of the Mediterranean Sea. Inland seas existed, and in the area where Paris is located, lay one of the most sacred Islands dedicated to the Goddess. These islands were also found in other areas, into North Africa and even beyond, into the Balkans, Bohemia, and beyond, and also further north and west.

Sections of these sunken lands were ripped apart when the Lion Kingdom was destroyed, during a massive nuclear war between the twin sons of Aysis and Osiris, who were battling over the unoccupied throne, on their return to Sirius. Out of the ashes and remnants of the Lion Kingdom, Avalon arose. This is vital to understand, for in truth their histories have long been obscured in the myths and legends of the Celtic people, who in fact were just a remnant of what remained of Avalon.

The Celts left what were known as the Sun Paths throughout Europe, stretching from Gibraltar up through Southern France, while other pathways originated in Portugal, La Compostela, and northwards, via Brittany and Belgium, linking up to Britain, Wales and Ireland, then further north, to where the Nordic part of Avalon once existed offshore from Scotland, Norway and Canada, and westwards to the USA. The Druids were but a relic of what once had been the High Priesthood of Avalon.

Avalon itself existed millions of years before Atlantis. The nine main islands on which Atlantis stood, were in fact the remains of Avalon. While Avalon had existed in the 7th dimensional state, Atlantis had already fallen into the 5th, and could not retrieve the previous ancient technology of Avalon, the Lion Kingdom or Elysium.

So Atlantis often gets confused with previous ancient civilizations, because people tend to remember only so far and no further.

My quest then was to go north, to open the ancient energy centers and to activate the ancient Sun Discs, sungates and the Crystal Pyramids, in specific regions of what is now France. Even before I arrived there, I was already remotely opening the energy lines and the ancient sungates in other areas of the north, linking them to France.

Actually, I was knitting together France and the African Continent with Antarctica. In fact, in the beginning, the Supercontinent called Elysium incorporated many of the land masses which sank under the sea, although parts have risen. When the land masses sank, continents were born, but drifted further apart. Some geologists and botanists now link the USA to North Africa, and indeed, that is where it once was located. South America was in fact attached to the western shores of the USA, and more or less fitted into the western coast of Africa. So often when I am drawing energy lines on maps of the places I am called to work on, I am told to turn them upside down, as this was actually how the Earth was formed originally. However, confusion was deliberately sown, when Humanity fell into the seas of forgetfulness and ignorance.

My journey of recollection began in 2004, during the dark night of my soul, when I was attacked by someone familiar to me, and as his face contorted in rage, a deep soul memory bank was evoked, and I saw him in a priest's brown habit, singing the psalter, while I burnt at the stake with five Knights Templar.

I would later remember the location where this happened: the Bishops Palace in Urgell.[1] This one single memory, triggered the rest, and sparked off the deep awakening of my soul on so many levels.

Why was I burnt at the stake with five Knights Templar? What had I done? Why was I the only woman among five knights, and particularly knights of that order? This stirred my deep longing to know more, and slowly but surely the story of Cécile de Foix, the youngest daughter of Raymond Roger, the Count of Foix, emerged.

Then life circumstances forced me to resign from my dead-end job, and my first Quest or journey began for real, as I had to reopen the Spinal Column of the World, and reactivate the Crystal Pyramids and Crystalline Pyramid Grids as recorded in my book, *Why I was born in Africa: the previously unrecorded history of Elysium and the Lion Kingdom*. That was the beginning of this remarkable journey, as I tapped into other lifetimes, and the Super Consciousness Energy Fields, as I began to do my Soul Readings. Through these readings astounding information poured through me, which has never been recorded before, and which elicited a deep response within my own soul memory banks.

I always knew that one day I would return to France, but little did I know that in January 2016, I would be called to go there to do massive energy work, while simultaneously retrieving ancient information, which had to be returned to Humankind.

From 2015, onwards I often had glimpses of what was to come, while I was opening up the Energy Grids to Egypt and in December I was instructed to go to France. I had no idea how I would get there, or when, but I was receiving intense upgrades.

Initially I was guided to draw energy lines on the map of France, and to begin with there were just three lines going up and down, more or less in the middle, from Monségur[2] in the north, but then I was told to extend them. These lines now shifted from Versailles, to Chartres, to Orleans, and then from Versailles to Carnac in Brittany in the West and from Brittany down to the triangle where the lines met in the South of France, forming 3 triangles.

On the 8th of January 2016, I began tuning in to a man with long dark hair with silvery strands, dressed as a Knight Templar, tall, handsome, and powerful, but with a purity seldom found. I remembered him as a lover, and our secret deep and profound alliance from that lifetime as Cathars in Foix. Indeed, he bore the rank of Grand Master of the region of that part

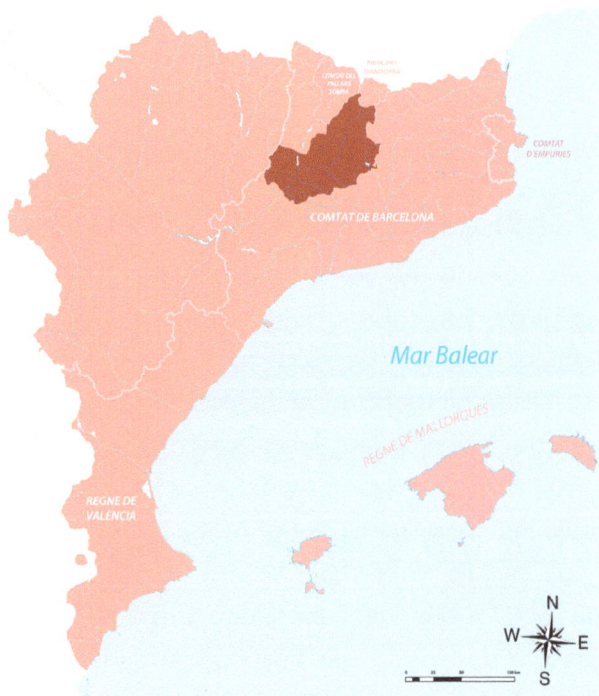

*Figure 2. Urgall.*

---

1  Modern-day Urgell, also known as Baix Urgell, is a comarca in Catalonia, Spain, forming only a borderland portion of the region historically known as Urgell, one of the Catalan counties. Andorra. Wikipedia.
2  Monségur is a bastide town in the Gironde in France, about 75km (46 miles) upriver from Bordeaux in the low rolling vineyard country between the River Garonne in the South and the River Dordogne in the North. The town – its names means "hill of safety" – was founded by charter of Eleanor of Aquitaine in 1265. The layout follows a classic bastide design, with a town square surrounded by arches, narrow streets, parallel back lanes and ramparts. Wikipedia.

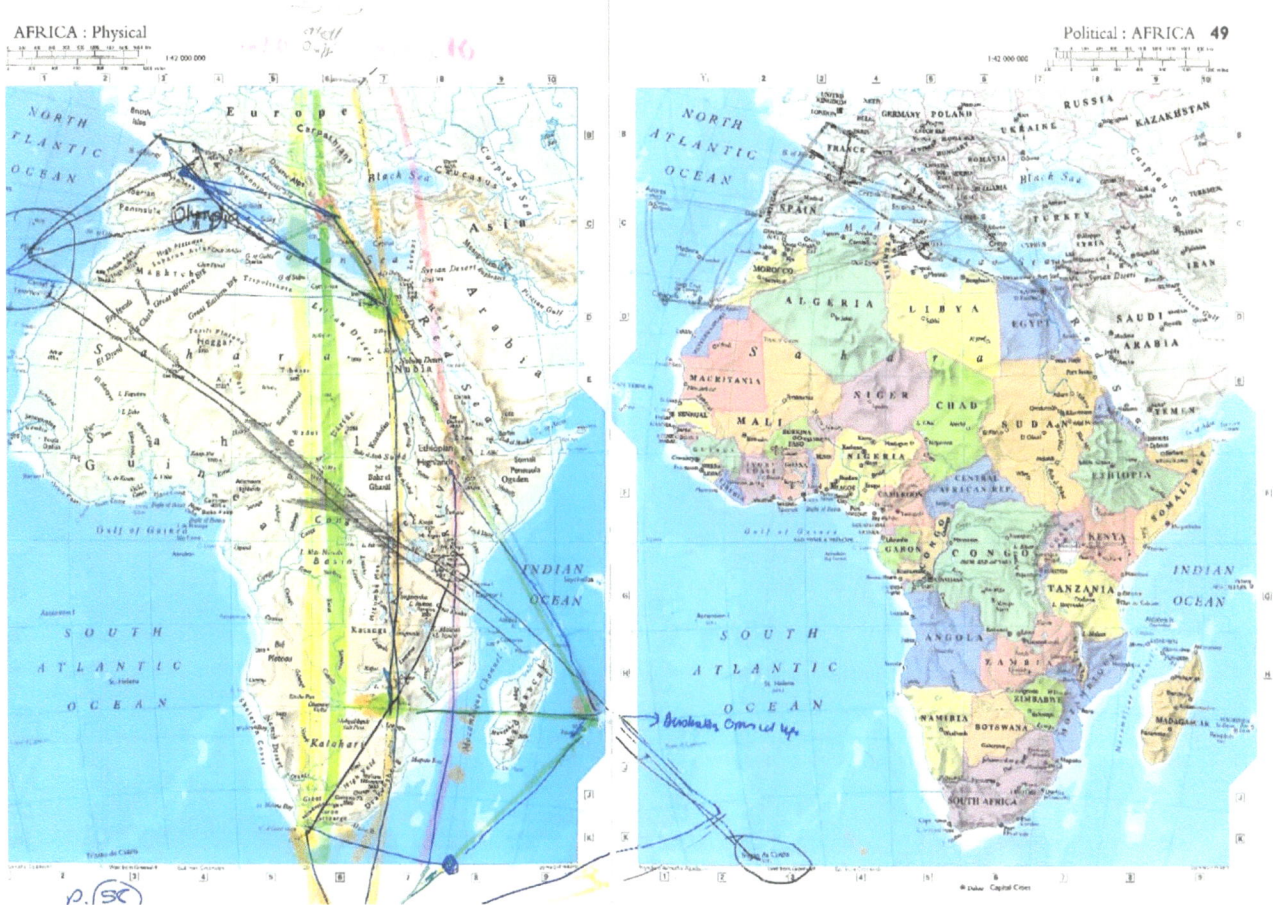

*Figure 3. Map showing the 3 triangles.*

of France, which belonged to the extended families who held the Sacred Grail, and all the secrets of the area. They all intermarried, and in truth were the offspring of the High Priesthood of Avalon, who had been driven to marry with Royalty, in order to survive. From this ancestral line, stemmed the top-ranking leaders of the Cathars and Templars, indeed the Founder of the Templars, Hugo de Payen, came from these families.

## JOURNAL ENTRY

**8th January 2016**

Our liaison was clandestine and linked to secret ceremonies in the caves and tunnel systems underneath Monségur where our final meeting took place. Something hugely tragic happened there which I still can't access but it has to do with the secrets that died on the stake with me. He bears the same codes and keys as I do, we both belong to the Inner Rose, Serpent and Sacred Grail Brotherhood and Sisterhood, High Priest and High Priesshood, thus hold all the keys and codes of Enlightenment.

I did not feel well on Thursday and had massive energy upgrades. I saw how my whole body had energy lines emitting from it and connecting me to all the crystal pyramids and crystalline pyramid grids I had activated. Then I saw a huge mass of Golden Energy pulsating and flowing like a mighty river of Life from Antarctica up into Africa. The Man appeared from the North with energy lines coming from him – so this Golden Energy is going north now, from the south – from the energy grids I have now fully activated. Something very urgent and profound is happening!

We will meet this Knight Templar in person, much later on in this book, when I was led to the place where he willingly died, rather than betray the secrets he held.

In the meantime I had, through profound guidance, made contact with Kristina Kahnlund, a Swedish lady who lived in the South of France, who would accommodate me, for the duration of my stay, in her home in St. Julia de Bec.

Through intense energy upgrades, and now planning my trip to France, I was told to first go to Paris, then Versailles, then Chartres, Orleans and then Carnac, to travel south from there, though my travel agent had other ideas. My higher guides were not amused and told me that under no circumstances should I deviate from the orders given: "*You must go there for multiple purposes. There is plenty of karma to be healed, energy to be released and portals to be opened up. This work will assist the Earth's ascension and the awakening of humans. It will activate immensely powerful power grids, although people are not ready for all the knowledge to be remembered, the power grids require the work you will do in France, so that they can function when the time is right. You must not let outside influences divert you, and you will be rewarded. There will be many guides with you in France – Mother Mary, Mary Magdalene, Jeanne D'Arc, Jesus, and Merlin.*"

I was also told that I needed to give 7 seminars in France over 7 days. I did not know how, where or when, but followed their instructions exactly!

I was beginning to tune into the standing stones at Carnac. It was as if I was being presented with jigsaw puzzle pieces here and there, to hold in safekeeping until the time when I would physically arrive in France.

### JOURNAL ENTRY

**3 May 2016: Carnac**
"In the beginning Carnac formed part of the Sacred Island of priestesses where sections of the Island had torn off. Now it is flat – it used to be mountainous, with snow-capped emerald green mountains. There were massive pyramids and stone circles there. When I had a look at pictures of these stones on the Internet, I was already tuning into them, and feel that they are calling me compellingly." (S.K.)

"When I look at the Carnac Stones, I can see ceremonies being held there. I see all the people who lived there. It breaks my heart. We wore green and red cloaks, with hoods made of velvet. The Druids are present as well. The energies where these stones are located are extremely powerful and are inter-dimensional, which is why you have to go there, and you will be further upgraded."

"You can step into other dimensions in these places, like walking into other worlds. You will go there to open up portals again. These rocks are sentinels, and they were promised that someone would come to reopen the portals, and release the energies once again. There are patterns there – sacred geometrical patterns, the keys to opening the energy centers. You will see the patterns overlaid in the stones, like streams of intersecting light. You will see them with your third

*Figure 4. Map showing important areas in France.*

*Figure 5. Rennes Le Chateau.*

*eye, and these patterns will unlock codes and keys. You already have them within you, and will unlock them there. You will know where to go, as the energies will pull you in the right direction, to the right area – it will feel like a magnet. When you arrive at the right place, you will see the patterns you are meant to see, as they will light up. This will be more than you have ever known or experienced previously. You must pay attention when they ask you to prepare. You are the one who they have been waiting for. They thank you for volunteering to do this work. It will forever change you. It is very important that this work be done for the sake of Mother Earth and all her children."* (S.K.)

Almost every single day my higher guides made me aware of the importance of my visit to France, as I was being energetically worked on and my energy fields constantly upgraded. I literally was incorporating massive energy downloads into my spinal column and then they placed Sun Discs into my head, my wrists, my ankles and even my womb and neck area. At times I felt myself being able to tune into sites in France at will, or when I looked at photos or illustrations, I could read the energy fields and history. I received the following message:

**JOURNAL ENTRY**

**20 May 2016**

Those who need to be at your seminars will be there, for you all promised in lifetimes before that you would come together again. They will know! The Rainbow people are gathering. We will bless you and your every word, speech, action and you will sweep that area clean and you will move the energies and open up the north from the south and you will be led to all the places where you are needed.

Indeed those who have been the Keepers and Guardians who will come and show you and you will be taken there and welcomed back like a long-lost most beloved daughter, mother and Giver of Life and Illumination.

All those who have helped you will be there, and all those who are will be blessed. You will have to become the greatest of all so that they will be freed from their bondage and given the blessing of Love in its purest forms. So go out, be and become and you shall be given it all.

---

I was in close contact with Kristina during this time, and did a Soul Reading for her which revealed this soul sister had been with me, during the eras of Mary Magdalene and the Cathars. She was searching for the correct Seminar venue, suggesting that we have our last day at Labrador, a retreat centre near Rennes le Chateau, with a plateau in front of the village. She felt this deep connection and indeed, this proved to be the place where we would later reopen Mary Magdalene's Mystery School. During our Skype conversation, without me ever having been there, and merely tapping into the photos she sent, I tuned into the following information:

---

**29 May 2017: Mary Magdalene's Mystery School**
The American woman who built the lion fountain and owned the plateau and Labrador (since sold), must have had a vision of Mary Magdalene's original Mystery School which incorporated the Ancient Mystery School for women and children on this site. Within it there was a courtyard of lions, very much like that of the Alhambra, with a rose garden and fountains. It was a happy place, with plenty of music, song, dance, chanting, and prayers, where the women trained and the children and young acolytes were taught. It was Mary Magdalene's pride and joy and a sanctuary where she could just relax and be, away from the ever-threatening storm gathering around her head, from men who wished to oust the women from their ranks forever and who hated her and those of her ilk.

In that time there was more than one Mary, as Mary was the title of the High Priestesses, and there were 12 in all, among whom Mary Magdalene was the most elevated. However, disaster struck, when men bombarded the premises under the cover of night, and literally blew up the place so it erupted in flames. Indeed, simultaneously, from the clear night sky, lightning struck the ground which opened up, and the remains of the flaming building and all within it, were swallowed up and buried. The place of Illumination and Unconditional love, was no more and the Priestesses and acolytes who survived in the other branches of the Mystery Schools, were now persecuted relentlessly, and had to resort to hiding deep underground, mostly giving sermons in the Pyrenees caves, and the hidden ancient Goddess sites of the area, watched over by the men who stayed true unto death.

---

That recall brought a great sense of sadness, like a heavy mantle of premonition weighing me down, and in a higher sense, preparing me for what was to come. Perhaps had I known what was to come, I would not have boarded that plane to France. Yet, the calling of my soul was greater than the sum total of myself, and it was time to finally go and complete the full circle.

Lifetime after lifetime, I had been prepared for this. Lifetime, after lifetime, I and so many women, had been completely silenced and disempowered, often having to bear immense trauma and pain, rendered speechless by what we had to endure and take in, often wishing to speak out, but not being able to. When we dared to, we were burnt, stoned to death, or beheaded. No wonder our throat chakras and sexual energy centers needed to be cleared as a priority in this lifetime. We are finally rediscovering our voices again. We are finally finding ourselves in the deepest depths of our souls, gathering in strength and courage to live our highest truth. Along with all this comes the soul knowing that forgiveness is the truth of All-being, and that in truth, there is *no-thing* and *no-one* to blame.

So many in the High Priestesshood, took it upon themselves to hold the light and love steady, even in the midst of the greatest darkness. It was selfless service. So many have been forgotten, lost in the mists of time, but their souls have returned to discover their voices, and the deepest truth within themselves, so they do not shrink in fulfilling the roles assigned to their souls, and are living their mission and purpose, with great love and wisdom. Perhaps, the greatest of blessings, is to remember Love is the greatest Power there is. There is no greater Power, when steeped in the wisdom of the Soul.

Likewise let us not forget the men who stood by us, when everyone else deserted us. They were lion-hearted men, who never shrunk from living their truth with love and wisdom. They too are back and making their Presence felt, alongside us.

Somehow, I had a deep knowing that I was burnt with five Knight Templars who could have gone free, but nevertheless refused to leave me, which took immense courage. Little did I know, that I would be led to remembering more about these enlightened men, who in truth had two branches of their organization, the armed wing, and the esoteric inner circles, that had each safeguarded what they could in their own way? In fact, some were even married, as women were allowed to belong to the Order. Let this fact sink in …

During this time, I was having to break new ground – I was being challenged to present my first ever seminars on foreign soil. I had no idea what to expect. I took a leap of faith, and with the help of Kristina, started searching for the perfect venue. We eventually decided on the Château des Duc de Joyeuse Hotel, in Couiza which lies next to the river Aude. I tuned into the area and knew that this was exactly the place where the original Alchemical

*Figure 6. Duc de Joyeuse Hotel in Cuiza.*

Mystery School had been. Indeed, this was confirmed by the hotel brochure, so the Duc must have known this when he built the castle there.

My dear friend and editor Jill Charlotte was always on hand to encourage me with insights and her own psychic gifts, which proved to be very accurate. "*I see you working and talking and there are two ladies with you. Two assistants trying to keep up and you are quickly talking to the one and then to the other. There will be less serious opposition than you think. They are almost static, and lost in time …*"

JOURNAL ENTRY

**28 May 2016: Sun Discs**

I have been intensely upgraded this morning. They placed discs and sacred geometrical patterns in my head while I sat in the sun. I saw how strands of Light went through me and connected me to all the pyramids. They went from my heart and sacred centers, mind, head and the spinal column. I was shown the standing stones at Carnac and how all were connected to the same energy patterns as they are preparing me now for the opening up of the energies there.

**29 May 2016**

"*That is why they are upgrading you again, as you know. The coming together of these energies that will take place in France is much more powerful than you have previously experienced in this lifetime. I see ISIS with you in a very predominant way. She is an aspect of your soul, or you were her. This work in France is like raising the dead, I am in tears now. All of them will be with you to support you: Joan of Arc, Mary Magdalene, Jesus, the Druids, Templars, Ancient Ones …*" (S.K.)

So often my Higher Guides would give me messages and encouragement through Susan or Jill and this helped me immensely to keep the faith and have the courage to proceed into the greatest adventure of my entire life. I had never been to Europe and to me this was one gigantic leap into the Unknown.

I felt like the proverbial Knight embarking on a Quest to find the Holy Grail. I was receiving so many upgrades, information, messages, and at the same time, I often pored over the map of France, trying to make sense of it all. Slowly but surely, I began to understand that this journey would take place on so many levels and timelines. I understood that I would have to download, interact and retrieve not only the continuation of the Lion Kingdom, of Avalon, but also that of the Druids, the Druidic High Orders, the Celts and the Gauls, and simultaneously, that of Ancient Mystery Schools hidden in the Pyrenees, as I had been clearly shown where they were located.

In addition, there were the women who were High Initiates, belonging to the self-same Mystery Schools: Isis and Osiris, the Essenes, The Egyptians, The Oracle of Delphi, Mary Magdalene, the Cathars, the Troubadours, Esclaremonde de Foix, Cécile de Foix, the Templars, Joan of Arc and Marie Antoinette. This would culminate in the French Revolution. I always knew my head had been chopped off during the Revolution, and my greatest wish was not only to visit Versailles, but also the Louvre and the Tuileries Gardens.

A mammoth task, indeed!

What was I letting myself in for?

During this time, the man previously mentioned, the Knight Templar, was making his presence felt with increasing intensity. I intuitively received the name Guillaume, and somehow, he was like a ghost risen from my past life as Cécile de Foix, connected with my last years, when I was so desperately trying to safeguard the Cathar secrets. He often came to me in my dreams, and then disappeared, as if he was pointing to something, or an event, which would be important to remember when in France – but what was it?

PART 1: PREPARING FOR THE ULTIMATE JOURNEY TO REDISCOVER THE SACRED GRAIL

JOURNAL ENTRY

**30 May 2016**

I have had intense lower back pain since they worked on my energy fields yesterday. I was told they are upgrading me – preparing me for France. I went to lie down and they continued working on me.

They were putting Rose symbols all over my breasts and womb area.

I was shown a medieval castle and I was in a huge bedchamber. He was there in full Templar Clothing and I helped him undress. His name was Guillaume and he was the Grand Master of the Templars in that region, and a cousin. I won't go into details here, suffice is to say that our love for one another knew no bounds, and was intensified by the life-threatening times we lived in. It was a deep love. Then, I saw him taking his leave with a company of Templars while I stood on the ramparts watching them go.

He was the reason why the five Knights Templar burnt on the stake with me, remaining true to the end. They never wavered – they stayed true!

---

I was given codes and symbols, which often had me searching for the meaning behind it all. I wrote down as much as I could and made sketches of what I was being shown, but had no idea how all of this would fit together. For instance, the spiraling energy, the four-sided cross, the Rose and the Serpents, and four individual sites, all of these were like a door, opening another door within the greater whole of what has lain dormant for so many thousands of years.

The updates continued and I was taken to Egypt and underground canal systems and pyramids. Winged Sun Discs appeared to be placed in me, especially into my head, wrists, upper arms, solar plexus and womb, throat and head areas.

**5 June 2016**

"I keep having visions of you spinning gold discs around your heart and around your outstretched arms. I see them. I know the discs have to do with energy being released and reactivated but I can't see past this. She is rising again. She, who you once were. Isis. I can't stop shaking and crying. The Goddess energy is back. I began physically shaking and crying. I have never experienced anything like the shaking earlier. For the last three days I keep seeing you with the discs spinning and circling around your head and wrists/hands and you are wearing a long green velvet dress with a cape and gold embroidery on the bodice of the dress which is white. The cape is burgundy. There are tiny stars sparkling in between the discs which are gold in colour. The discs are about 6 inches in diameter. You are standing on a mound or rocks too so that you are elevated." (S.K.)

---

The very next day, while meditating I was anointed with the Fires of Illumination and I literally saw lightning coursing through me and into the ground and the crystal Pyramids and Crystalline Pyramid Grids and lightning striking everywhere! This happened three times. I started speaking the Light Language, the Universal Light Language of sacred symbols and sound. I was told over and over again by my higher Guides that I would bring the Standing Stones to life again!

\* \* \*

CHAPTER 1

# Part 2: Cape Town – Further Secrets Revealed

JOURNAL ENTRY

**Cape Town**

On the 20th June 2016 I found myself in exactly the right spot again, in Cape Town. I was told which hotel to book into at the Victoria and Albert Waterfront. My allocated room had the most beautiful view of Table Mountain and Devil's Peak. It was pouring with rain when we landed and reminded me of Mauritius somehow, like I was linking that island and Cape Town together.

I was in Cape Town for my visa application for France. I sat by the window and saw that I was directly in line with Table Mountain and Devil's Peak. It was the first time that I had ever been in such close proximity to the latter, and I immediately felt immensely powerful energy pouring from it. I called in the Guardians and Keepers, and found their three faces aligning, one on the top, the Goddess on the left-hand side, and further to the right hand, three male faces and three smaller ones (see Figure 1).

I was shown how Devil's Peak and Table Mountain link up directly to Antarctica! Indeed, Table Mountain and the harbour, flanked by the two sphinxes, Devil's Peak and Lion's Neck, reflect the ancient patterns of the sacred sites I had previously tuned into in Antarctica. (Reference: *Why I was born in Africa*)

Robben Island had once fitted into the whole before it broke away, and thus was on the same direct energy lines. The two sphinxes were much further out, guarding an inland sea.

I had to come here to this exact place, to align the two portals now linking Cape Town and Robben Island with Antarctica, and I had to do this before going to France!

I felt landmasses being torn up, with some parts rising, and this caused immense Earth changes and shifts, which closed down these portals for millions of years.

I was told to swing my chair to face Devil's Peak. I was in total alignment with it and the three pyramids

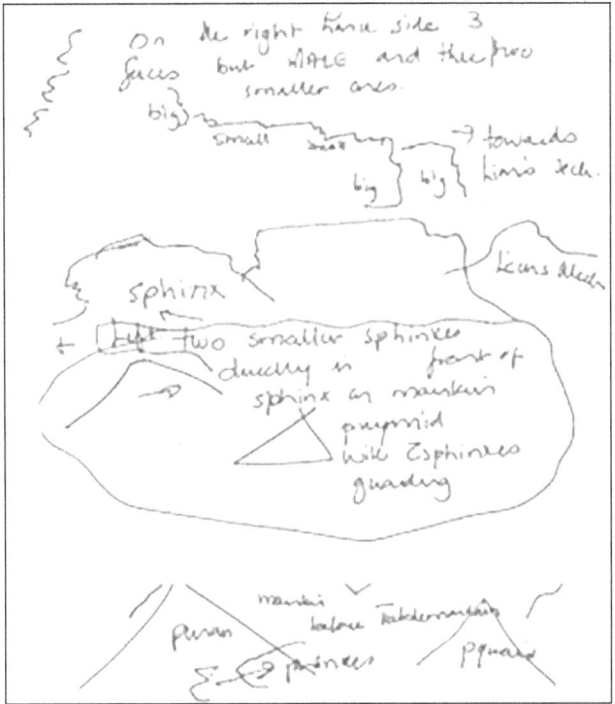

*Figure 1. Faces and alignment with 3 smaller ones*

(Figure 1). As I became aligned, I had immense surges of energy pouring through me and something amazing happened: I was then activated to beam energy through my hands and third eye directly into the three pyramids. Energy started moving, the three pyramids were activated, and they began pulsating with liquid golden energy which was beamed back into me. As I became one with this energy and its flow, I directed it from the pyramids and Devil's Peak, into Robben Island and knitted them all together!

Then an incredible thing happened! I saw a solar disc (Sun Disc) but it was double (Figure 2), with strands of energy holding the two discs together and it spun even faster. As it spun another disc formed behind it,

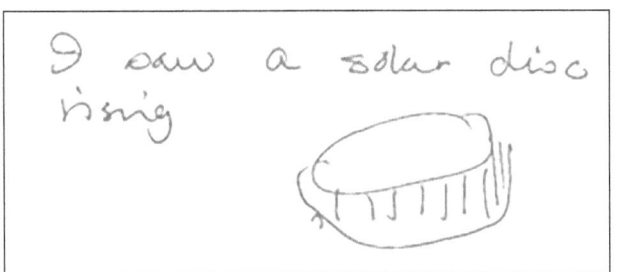

*Figure 2. Solar disc (Sun Disc)*

as they were activating the Sun Discs which had been previously placed in my body!

I had to beam massive golden energy through my hands and body and into the pyramids and Sun Discs. I became Isis. They activated the cobras (kundalini energy) depicted in the crown of Egypt, three cobra heads and three triple crowns, and I was lying in the middle of a massive Sun Disc, with one behind me which was much larger and upright.

Suddenly 12 men appeared, dressed like priests in the ancient Egyptian style, and they formed a circle around me, walking clockwise and anti-clockwise with their erect penises, and abruptly fire balls erupted and the ground cracked open! The Earth spewed fire, and spiraling energy began spinning out muck, dirt, stuck souls, spirits, and other energetic debris!! This spitting fire ball energy moved straight into Table Mountain, and then into Lion's Head. Suddenly, three pyramids, Devil's Peak and Robben Island, disgorged energy like a massive laser beam, right into Antarctica!

Now the Giza Pyramids appeared up north. The lightning spurted forth from Giza, and then from Antarctica to the three pyramids here and simultaneously moved up the Spinal Column of the Earth. Fire balls emerged and erupted like volcanoes, moving up and up towards the north, and into Giza – not along the spinal column, but rather creating a totally new energy line!

It hit Giza like an explosion and then burnt its way through the island of Malta, from Giza through the Sahara Desert! The latter seemed to be contained near Spain, or in line with Spain, but not yet in Gibraltar!

All the energy lines were on fire, in fact burning with fire, balls of fire!

I was holding all of them together.

Coming out of all this slowly I saw that all energy lines had been freed, not only from Cape Town to Antarctica, but also from Cape Town to Giza, and from Giza to Malta and beyond, nearly all the way to France! (Figure 3)

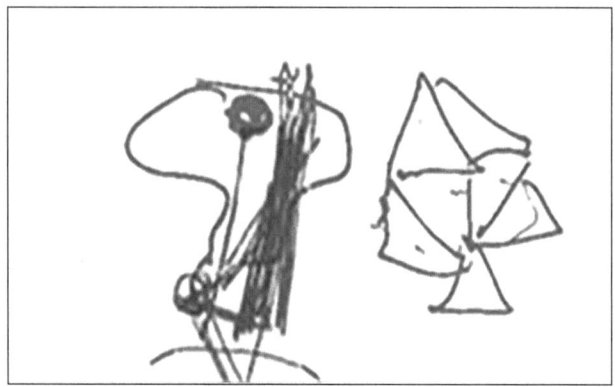

*Figure 3. Sketch showing the three pyramids.*

I was feeling rather dizzy and disorientated.

It was only much later that I realized that the fires of purification had paved or opened the way for the Energy work which needed to be done in France. It would help to add impetus to the work as, indeed, it had already begun!

I was then shown how the pyramids in Cape Town and Antarctica aligned to the 7th Central Sun with the Sun Codes. I was shown a triple helix stream of energy awakening, and given the codes 333 and 777 and then again 333.

I was named Isis of Elysium/Lion Kingdom/Avalon = 3 Kingdoms.

During the next two days, I visited Robben Island to clear more of the energy grids from the island itself.

I saw 7 double-tiered Sun Discs flying in formation out of Devil's Peak (Figure 4). Three pyramids were stacked on top of one another and a beautiful sacred geometrical pattern emerged in a diamond shape.

*Figure 4. Seven Sun Discs flying in formation.*

I was told that this is the Inter-Stellar Energy Grid and not part of the spinal column or the Crystalline Pyramid Grids. The Inter-Stellar Grid forms the pattern of a spot in North Africa, and links directly to the pyramids in Devil's Peak.

This beacon is the 'sunken' headquarters or was the main City of the Lion People. The King of the Lion People, the Leopard man and the Ancient Ones are here with me showing me all of this.

Malta is a small remnant of what was once a huge sprawling city, when the Mediterranean Sea did not yet exist. The rest has sunk, buried in a type of bubble inside the Earth, part of which lies under the Sahara Desert.

---

Returning home, I was not only preparing for my journey north, but tuned into some of the sites I had been told to visit. I was having spontaneous past life recalls, sometimes feeling as if I was being teleported to locations like Carnac, to do the energy work there. (In fact, much later on it would prove to be invaluable, as I often did not have direct access to the sites, once I was on the spot due to security measures.)

JOURNAL ENTRY

**20 June 2016: Carnac**

The Standing Stones in Carnac are pure quartz crystal and work with the emerald green rays. Indeed, they once were pure crystal, but with the subsequent earth upheavals, they are now coated with granite. They were under a huge crystal dome which acted as a Star Gate.

The stones were programmed to hold knowledge and information. The reactivation of the pattern of the Crystalline Star Grid will occur, and this in turn will activate the Sun Discs, and is very powerful. When all Singing Stones are reactivated, they activate the ancient knowledge of the Energy Centers so that the Ancient Mystery Schools of the Lion Kingdom and Avalon can rise again, and in turn be reactivated. All of these energy centers hold the spiraling energy of the Goddess herself.

The Standing Stones sing! They vibrate to sound and have been programmed to sound frequencies, as they communicate through sonic sound and light frequencies and energy vibrations, and this opens up the patterns of the Star Energy Grid of the Star Gate (Stellar Portals).

---

I started to glimpse the importance of the work I had been called upon to do. I was told repeatedly that I had been prepared for many lifetimes for this, therefore I was undergoing these intense upgrades. In fact being able to connect to sites like Carnac and Versailles, plus Monségur, long before I arrived there, proved invaluable. It prepared me for the reality of seeing them again, so many lifetimes later, changed and now within built-up areas, often fenced in, and out of reach, and more than this, it enabled me to do the work within that framework, unobserved when needed, for I had already tuned in and done most of the work before I even arrived in France!

When I was given these downloads and upgraded, I would find myself in that lifetime, and in that embodiment. It was like stepping back in time, but at the same time also forward – mostly holographic and vivid, like I was an actress in a movie, where everything blended together and the plot thickened daily! I often felt like a super-sleuth trying to piece the pieces together, finding clues all over the place, but then having to dig very deep within my own soul memory banks for wisdom, insight and clarification, in order for the greater picture to emerge.

I was actually dealing with multiple civilizations, in one single country: The first was the Lion Kingdom, and I found statues of lions all over France, as if deep in the subconscious French mind, firmly entrenched, they still remembered their own deep rootedness in the Lion People and their Kingdom from millions of years ago. The next was Avalon, in the wake of what was left of the Lion Kingdom, after massive wars destroyed so many sites, and the land mass ripped off and sunk under the sea, totally altering the landscape. From the remnants of those who had stayed true to the Law of One, arose Avalon. When Avalon fell, Atlantis arose, more to the west, but still linking what remained of Avalon (which had not been destroyed, and from which the Celtic Race emerged with the Druids), and Lemuria. Lemuria, itself is another story for another time, but it rose in Avalon's heyday, to the east, in what is now the Pacific Ocean.

When Atlantis fell, colonies of Light Bearers survived – those who had kept the sacred Fires of Illumination alive in pockets of the 7 Mystery Schools, which Isis and Osiris founded, were among the survivors, having been pre-warned of the approaching demise of Atlantis. They now moved these schools from the sinking land mass, while some of them, like those in the Pyrenees, merely moved underground, linked to the inner world, Agartha.

When Atlantis blew itself up, and narrowly missed blowing the entire Earth up, it was these Mystery Schools which kept the Fires of Illumination and the Ancient Knowledge alive, often under severely challenging circumstances. They became Beacons of Light during the darkest darkness which befell Humanity, having now sunk from the 7th dimension of Avalon and Lemuria, into the 5th dimensional frequency band of Atlantis, and then into the abyss of the 3rd dimensional state, lower than the animal kingdom! About 88% of all living creatures were annihilated during the fall of Atlantis and the terrible wars of destruction, so only the very strongest survived, most of whom regressed very far into the seas of forgetfulness. The only remembrance they still had of the previous Glory, was through their oral traditions, myths and legends. It is no accident that the Great Flood was remembered all over the world by diverse cultures, because it was the time of destruction and cleansing by water, while the Epoch we are now in will see purification by Fire.

I received the following message on the 1st July 2016 more or less confirming this:

*"What is forthcoming is the freeing and releasing of all the souls who were mowed down, especially the High Priestesses and High Priests of the Lion Kingdom and Avalon. It is freeing the planet and Humanity from Patriarchy, and with it comes the freeing of the Goddess sites, so that balance can be restored and the vortex (spiraling) energies opened up.*

*"In this regard you will have all the assistance you need as all the ancient High Priestesses who stayed true to the Law of One will be there, adding their collective powers to yours.*

*"You will have with you from now on, Merlin (the Ultimate Master), the Marys and the whole contingent of the three Druidic High Orders, men and women from all over Europe. They are gathering. Add to this the Mystery Schools that are rising again and you will have unparalleled support. All of these with the Ancient Ones, the Lion People and the entirety of the Ancient World, including Greece and Egypt.*

*You will have support while you are in France from the Templars (often in their original incarnations) plus many other hidden orders who will make themselves known to you.*

*The Guardians and Keepers of all the places you will be led to will welcome you – they know that you are coming, and they are there to welcome you home!*

*The seminars will be amazing. We will give you the information you need and will prepare you for them.*

*In the weeks prior to leaving, we will activate you further, allowing you to totally integrate the Goddess Isis in a much more powerful way at amalgamated levels. We will rejuvenate and revitalize you so that you have the stamina for the work ahead.*

*This is a very powerful year for you, and miracles will happen. The people will just love you. We will help you and protect you and give you all the guidance we can.*

*There will be so much for you to integrate, assimilate and bring to the fore, an unfolding as you now step onto centre stage – this is truly what you have incarnated for. It is time! (Melchizedek and the High Order of Melchizedek)*

The upgrading now continued in earnest. I was now tuning into Versailles at a deep and profound level. I knew that I had lived there during the time of Marie Antoinette, and had loved the Hunting Lodge more than the Palace itself. So, in a greater sense it would be a homecoming of my soul, to a place I had lived in previously.

JOURNAL ENTRY

**3 July 2016: Sun Discs in Versailles**
Versailles, Sun Discs and what the gardens are actually hiding:
The Stellar Gateway Portal in France buried under Versailles, links up with the Sun Discs and works in tandem with the Spinal Column of the Earth, the Crystal Pyramids and their grids.

When the circles, the spiraling energy centers of the Goddess Energy Centers, were closed down, so were all the energy grids, when the Black Magi took control, and built the Cathedrals on top of what they believed were the ancient Goddess sites. Since they wished to totally divorce themselves from the Divine Feminine, and render her totally useless and disempowered, they wanted to destroy any evidence which might point to the existence of such sites.

So many desired to use them for their own much hidden agendas (Chartres and Rennes-le-Château are two such sites). Yet, the most important energy centers here were made invisible by the Goddess, and she ensured that they were mostly shut down. So, they actually built the cathedrals out of alignment, as false beacons were given, and no one was more aware of this than the Templars, who built the Cathedrals with the Master Architects and Craftsmen, who belonged to secret fraternities, and in turn to the hidden Mystery Schools.

Where Versailles now stands, there was an ancient Sun Temple complex, with a similar but in fact much larger Stone Circle than Stonehenge. It formed a part of one of the most sacred sites dedicated to the 7th Central Sun of Illumination, and incorporated immensely powerful vortex energy centers, and a massive Star-Sungate.

However, when the Romans conquered the Gauls/Celts in that region, they removed the Stones, demolishing the site. Julius Caesar himself gave the instructions, as he had befriended a Druid, and thus had knowledge regarding the inner power of this site, which he feared. He believed that as long as the Standing Stone Circle and temple complex stood there, he would not be able to conquer the Gauls/Celts, and their related Germanic Tribes, and that they would continue to be uncontrollable. He gave his legions and craftsmen instructions to not only demolish the site, but to take as many as possible of the massive blocks to Rome. However, the minute the legions started dismantling the stones by exploding them into smaller more manageable bits, a huge storm erupted, with fierce lightning bolts and thunder, which ripped the ground open. Most of those on site were struck dead, and simultaneously all their wagons and transport systems burnt in the resulting fire. Those who had survived died in the fires, before torrents of rain bucketed down and the whole area was washed over, and covered with earth and stones.

It was lost, hidden underneath the site, and I was asked to open it up again. The memory of this was held in the Celtic oral traditions, and within the Druidic Circles, after the Romans conquered the Gauls. Only a hint of this survived, in ancient Alchemy texts, but was recorded long afterwards. The Celts never wrote anything down, as they had other methods of storing energy in fields, and in the Stone Circles and Standing Stones, which most never bothered to tune into. That is why in order to even pass the first degree of apprenticeship, one had to study for 21 years, to attain the lowest ranks within the 3 Druidic High Orders.

Louis XIV, the Sun King of France, wanted to reclaim the site for himself, in order to resurrect the ancient Sun Worship at Versailles. He had been informed of this through someone who still possessed the ancient Alchemy texts, and had identified the site. It was remembered in these texts that the Sun Discs were in the centre of the Stonehenge-like Circle, so Louise now wanted his own Sun King Palace to be built at this exact place.

However, the site where the original Château and later the palace itself was built, was a false beacon. In reality the Druids had sealed off the original site after the Roman disaster, thus concealing it, and later extensive landscaping assisted in this process, namely the extended gardens and woodlands of Versailles.

The Guardians and Keepers of that Ancient Sacred Site kept the workmen and diggers there away from the true sacred sites where the Sun Discs and Star-Sungate were buried. So, in fact that site is now carefully hidden and sealed off under the gardens, fountains and forests of Versailles.

Louis, the Sun King, who wished to crown himself the Sun God, in actual fact was sitting on an empty shell!

In ancient times, the Stonehenge-like location at Versailles held all of the triangle together with Chartres and Orleans. It was also linked with Carnac, and what is hidden or had broken off in Brittany, and now lies offshore.

You will first have to travel to Versailles, and into the gardens to do the work. We will lead where needed. You will have your inner eyes opened, as we will show you the entire complex.

In Ancient Times this site was on the periphery of the hub of 7 Sun Discs, and held the power grids of Avalon, together with the Pyrenees. They were remembered as winged Sun Discs, for they zoomed in double storey formation, such as you encountered in Cape Town. They will come to the fore once you open up the Stellar Portal in the West at Carnac.

The Sun Discs and the Stellar Portal with the Crystal Stones (remember the standing stones were pure quartz crystal with an emerald shield on top), together form one single energy grid and field.

The Transformer Crystal Pyramids (7) lie offshore from Brittany, in direct alignment with Carnac. When you are in the hotel in Carnac you will be shown these. They are Light Blue Rays with Sapphire and Topaz. They work on the same energy gird as that of the energy lines you opened up in Malta – and they work on the same principles as those of Antarctica and Cape Town.

When Elysium was still a huge single continent, France was much further east, and in the Southern Hemisphere (remember the Earth is shifting on its axis). As the Mediterranean broke up (or the sea emerged), the upper part moved west (Lion Kingdom), moving the landmass more towards a western alignment.

Yet if you tip the Earth over, you can see that the actual movement was east and not west! Now in those days the portal was aligned east towards the rising sun, and not to the western setting sun.

Sun God and Goddess rising!

It is aligned to the 7th Central Sun so its codes are 777.

It is imperative that this understanding dawns, for significantly France was aligned East towards the rising sun, and not west!

This is still true in places, but not to the extent it first was, and in that period, it was in the Southern Hemisphere.

Those who were the instigators of the destruction of Stonehenge and the Goddess sites in Versailles, also destroyed the Druids. Their aim was to extinguish the original energy centers and knowledge, in order to enslave the people on Earth, as there were links to the Gold Lines (gold mining for ceremonial items, and also symbols from certain gold mines in those areas).

The conquerors falsely believed that owning these mines would add to their power and wealth. In truth gold was used for energy grid purposes, for rejuvenation, longevity and Enlightenment in alchemical transmutation of powers, which the Ancient Druidic Order was aware of, and they knew how to harness these co-creative forces.

The High Priestesses especially knew how to bind the serpent (spiraling) energy, with gold veins and crystal powers and pyramids, in such a manner that they were immensely powerful creators.

They knew how to call in the Fire, Water, Air and Earth energies, and to transform one kind of energy into other forms. This enabled them to teleport themselves, and to shape-shift into any form they chose. They become as one with the energy in order to move it, and dissolved into it, and then manifested it into form.

Therefore, this is what your journey is all about. To reopen and reactivate these centers and to reclaim and remember your true powers.

We will give you more information in due course and will activate all your powers so that you will now totally incorporate the Highest Goddess Powers and reassume your original form.

---

Intriguing information like this often left my head reeling, but I had learnt to just allow it to flow through me, knowing that I am transmitting that which has frequently been totally forgotten by Humankind. Yet, all information is stored in the Super Consciousness Energy Fields, and in this case, that of the 7th Central Sun, to which our planet has always been linked. Nothing ever happens under the Great Central Sun, in Divine Creation, which is not immediately recorded in these energy fields. No date can ever get lost, nor be hacked or disappear.

During an activation I was given a set of Master Keys and codes, in the form of numbers to remember. When I went to France, and whenever I needed to open up energy fields or do energy clearing work, I would be halted by the Guardians and Keepers, and asked to give all these codes, and the number sequence unlocked the rest.

They incorporated the 7 Goddess aspects of Isis into me, every single one of these being a different characteristic or fire of my own soul. I had to integrate these with immense and powerful energy surging through me, while they worked intensively with my pineal and pituitary glands and my throat area. Sometimes balls of fire were placed in me, and sometimes energy like lightning which all seemed to link up with stars and galaxies. It was truly incredible, and my physical body at times had a hard time integrating these massive upgrades.

JOURNAL ENTRY

**11 July 2016: The Canary Islands**

Today I was told to lie down at 18h00. I immediately felt the energy moving into me. I was taken back to Cape Town, the double tiered Sun Discs and Devil's Peak.

I had fire coming into me – fire on my forehead, and the Sun Discs on my wrists, arms, body, feet and those above my head were spitting fire.

I was shown the Canary Islands, Tenerife, Madeira, and told that I needed to knit the pyramids on these islands, together with those on Indian Ocean islands like Mauritius and Reunion (they indeed look the same, even though thousands of miles separated them, namely the African continent!).

I raised my arms, and with fire spurting out from me, I activated the pyramids with immense energy coursing and transmitted through me.

I saw myself in Mauritius, on top of the pyramid there, which I had first encountered when I was there in 2015 (as recorded in my book *Why I was born in Africa*), but it was much taller. Standing on the top, I had vast upgraded energy pouring into me.

I had to literally throw Fire Energy Balls into the energy lines connecting the Canary Islands and Tenerife with Mauritius and Reunion, through the continent of Africa and in a straight line!

They were opening up and being reactivated by spitting fire. It blazed a trail of fire to the islands, which hit them with immense force. From Tenerife and the Canary Islands, it now moved into Madeira and the Azores. It shook them as if by an earthquake. The ground broke up and opened.

I saw a massive Crystal Pyramid rising from the ocean floor, and it was violet and emitted a violet flame/fire.

The Mer people appeared and helped me to enter the pyramid. It was enormous. Entering there I had sounds pouring through me in a strange language, as energy moved through my hands, indeed, the same fire energy I had experienced before.

I was teleported onto a vast golden platform. I was met a by an extremely tall High Priest with reddish hair, who wore a Sun Disc over his forehead which pulsated with white-golden spiraling energy. He was naked except for a white garment loosely worn around his torso, like a sarong. He had Sun Discs at his navel and on his upper arms too.

He then took me down an elevator, and we were transported into a massive circular building – in the middle was a huge standing stone circle, which reminded me once again of Stonehenge. In the centre there was a colossal Sun Disc pulsating with emerald green light, with gold and lime green. It was huge!

I was told this linked directly to the 7th Central Sun of Illumination.

Out of nowhere, 12 priests and 12 priestesses appeared, circling around the Sun Disc, chanting, moving clockwise and anti-clockwise. I was starting to spit fire again – my forehead was on fire, my crown as well and my hands and wrists and womb turned into green-golden fire.

I had to stand in my greatest power and commanded the river of fire to move back through the many layers to Mauritius!

The whole energy line was filled with a swirling, twirling mass of fiery liquid green/gold, which was lava-like! (Figure 1)

As this liquid Fire River was pulsating, I was shown:

7 x Crystal Pyramids rising:

– 1 Violet
– 1 Turquoise
– 1 Yellow Green
– 1 Reddish Gold
– 1 Pink/Red/Purple
– 1 Platinum/Gold/Silver
– 1 Crystal Clear Quartz

I was shown Europe. I was shown how this site linked directly to Carnac, and then through Portugal to Monségur and the Pyrenees.

I was told the stone pyramids still remaining on the islands mentioned, had been built much later – they were replicas of what had sunk under the sea to remind Humanity of what used to be and what had been lost, including the massive platforms on Tenerife and the Canary Islands.

The green-golden river of fire crossed the energy grids. I had already opened up the energy lines to Malta, where there were massive megaliths and round temples (under the sea). I was told it used to be the Sun Temple and was linked directly to 7th Central Sun. It therefore holds the energy as custodian, for the opening up of Versailles, Chartres, Orleans and Carnac. That is one single component. The other is the Pyrenees. This is immensely powerful!

The fire then began cleansing and clearing all the energy lines I had opened up, transmuting all that which was not of the purest God-force energy.

On this occasion I wore a plain white shift, with an emerald cloak, covered with sun symbols. I was once the High Priestess of the Sun, and the Sun Goddess. I was told that henceforth I would blind people with the radiant fire pouring forth from my third eye. *"You shall be exalted and you will stand fully as Goddess, the true Goddess, greater than any other woman on this planet and you will outshine them and take your place as the true Goddess, the radiant, exalted, shining Illumined One and through you shall pour the Fires of Illumination and activation and through you shall come rebirth, reactivations and the total resurrection of the 7th Central Sun-in-Splendour! We are pouring blessings upon blessings upon you!"*

## 15 July 2016

I literally have to incorporate 7 Goddesses. I know it sounds strange, but they are different personas or soul flames of the Goddess. It is like the old me has died and I am being resurrected.

*"They are bringing you back to who you once were. Integrating all the aspects of your soul that have been separated from you. It is a necessary gift in repayment for you coming full circle after many lifetimes. It is a remarkable blessing.*

*You are travelling back to France where your journey began many lifetimes ago. You need to be fully integrated for this. It is a completion. You earned it! It is the completion of the life cycles of your soul. You will have a new life after this."* (S.K.)

## 15 July 2016

Tonight, is the activation of the Rose, Serpent and sacred Chalice/Grail. I had to lie down with red Jasper, Serpentine and Yellow Calcite. They started their work on my energy fields.

I was taken to a room in a lifetime where I had long blond hair and I wore a white garment. I had to bath in a pool filled with rose petals. It was a circular room, and formed part of circular temples. I wore a wreath of roses on my head.

Twelve priestesses appeared and then another arrived. I stood in the middle of a labyrinth. I was told this was the original one in Chartres. The priestesses now performed a type of Maypole dance, dancing around me and weaving ribbons together. I was being prepared for sacred sexual union with my Divine Other, my Twin Flame. I was anointed with rose oil and then saw scenes of union with my beloved on a bed filled with rose petals … As we entered sublime and sacred union the serpent (kundalini) energies were activated, and the sacred fires ignited around us like rosy fires.

In the next scene I was standing in the full regalia of a Queen with him, and wore a ruby and gold crown. We were in a boat which looked like a shell, when two white swans appeared. They were drawing our boat with two leashes, or ribbons.

The Swan King and Queen! (Note, the Swan King and Queen would appear time and again on my journey, as did swans! Here lies an important clue.)

More ceremonies were held, working with rose quartz, and the full activation of the kundalini or serpent energy as the portals opened up within me. This took three hours!

Swan King and Queen.

Rebirth!

A few hours later the following message came through: "*Mary Magdalene wants to speak to you. She is with you. She is part of the Sisterhood of the Rose. You are soul-connected. She is helping to raise your vibration at the moment. You will be clearing the feminine from historical pain and trauma in France. Lots of suffering, so much bloodshed. Plenty of disempowerment of the Feminine there. She asks that you work with her there to cleanse the energy, and lift the energy of the Earth. You are ready to do the work with her.*"

During these intense ceremonies and upgrading in the inner planes, I had a deep sense of being prepared for something massive. I was now not only integrating the Goddess energies, I was fully initiated into very ancient sacred and secret rites, which pertained to the highest ranking within the Mystery Schools, and I knew that many of these were so very ancient. Some related to the High Druidic Orders of Avalon, and what had been before Avalon in the Lion Kingdom. Then there was the next level which incorporated Mary Magdalene, and the initiations in her own sphere, thousands if not millions of years later, and lastly that of the Cathars and Templars, the most recent of the three. Yet, Mary Magdalene, the Cathars and Templars all had their origin in the Original Source, and had to go deep underground, during the darkest ages of Humankind.

During this time Tom Kenyon's book on Mary Magdalene assisted me enormously, as I now had a reference point on the sacred uses of the Kundalini or serpent energy within the Mystery schools, confirming what I had already downloaded in my own way over the previous few years.

**18 July 2016**

I had a massive download again today. I was told to go into the triangle formed by Versailles, Orleans and Chartres (I was shown that from the Stonehenge of Versailles there were concealed tunnels connecting Versailles, Orleans and Chartres which had all been sealed off, and no one was aware of them.

I was taken to a deep underground cavern with huge pillars of fire – gold and green. I literally had to step through the fires to get into the middle of the room and was told that they were the fires of purification, and I was incorporating the Goddess of Fire. I had wave upon wave of energy pouring through me.

Then I had to give the keys and codes of the 7th Central Sun given to me earlier, and I was chanting in the Light Language. I was not only pulsating with fire but directing it as well!

I was then joined by the Knight Templar. We merged together, and the green-gold fire merged with the red-gold. The fires now formed a pulsating stream blazing across the energy lines to Carnac.

I was told to resurrect the 7 streams of Sun Rays, from the place where this underground furnace was located.

One to Carnac, one to the Islands, one through Portugal to the Islands in the Atlantic, one to Monségur, one to Rennes-le-Château, one to Orleans (see sketch).

The whole began spinning, forming a vortex and spiraling energy.

A massive Crystal Pyramid of Gold and Green started to appear, illuminating the whole scene with green-gold light.

Majestic!

I was told this was the unlocking of the first.

I was working with the fire energy, and the Knight Templar and I were merging – it was so powerful. I have never felt anything like this before!

After that I did more work with fire, and they helped me to assimilate this intense energy into my physical body.

---

In the next few days, leading up to my flight to France in early August, I tuned into the Monségur area in the Pyrenees. I sensed 7 underground Crystal Pyramids that worked with the same golden green energy. The Fires of Illumination worked with precisely the same colour flame. I saw that deeply buried, under the Monségur Mountains, stood the tallest of these pyramids. I now understood why I had always known this on some level, for I had always known that Monségur had never been used as a castle, nor was it ever fortified, but rather served as a temple. It was built in ancient times on top of the mountain, linked to the underground tunnel systems and chambers where the Ancient Ones dwelt, and where the old initiations and ceremonies had taken place. I had had memories of these with my first awakening.

Interestingly, about two months earlier I had been told to find a Peridot necklace. I had no idea where I would find one, but when I stopped in front of my favourite jeweller in Plettenberg Bay, my eye was immediately caught by that exact necklace, made from unpolished stones! What amazed me was that it was the same green-gold of the energy centers I had worked with in France, and the Crystal Pyramids in the Pyrenees. I was told to wear it the entire time I was in France! It not only energized me, but worked powerfully with me.

The more I tuned into the Monségur area, the more I became aware of the incredibly powerful underground energies and forces there. The word Pyrenees is similar to the word Pyramid, and is thus a reminder of what these mountains are really hiding.

I was being prepared for the greatest journey of rediscovery of my entire life, yet also a deep homecoming. It was as if all the events and experiences until that point, had been preparing me for this journey.

Additionally, it was the opportunity to finally lay the ghost of Cécile de Foix, "Sissi" to rest. She had been with me since I first recalled the burning at the stake, and slowly but surely, during all these years when I had these memories I wrote them down, adding my own research.

Why had she been burnt?

Why had she been burnt alongside the Knights Templar?

Why was she hunted down like an animal?

What had happened to all the manuscripts she had smuggled out with the help of the Knights Templar?

What secrets did she die with, which have never been divulged?

## JOURNAL ENTRY

**14 February 2016**

"Let me not speak of Love stringing mere platitudes –
So much of what is said of Love
is put out there
without the soul's deepest longing
expressed to the depth of Being
and ideal Grace
that Knowing
which goes beyond mere words ...
Let me not speak of Love
without my heart and soul engaging –
that Love held within
the deepest sanctuary
the Sacred Temples of my Soul
where purity reigns ...
No let me not speak of Love
With words which have no meaning

and are not infused with Soul ...
But let me speak with
Love, Grace, Gratitude
of moments when
I glimpsed the Glory,
the Sanctity,
the Bliss,
The Ecstasy
Expanded Consciousness
infused with that Being One
with you –
the Sacred Fires ignited,

and ALL in ALL in ALL
expanding into Omni-Verse and Omni-potence –
beyond ALL ...
With All-that-is
I lay
my utmost purity
the flawless beauty of my Soul
At the very feet of LOVE
May Love be in my every word
My Being
May Love be what I truly AM ...
So, the Blessings of this Love
touch the core heart, soul, Being,
the Infinity within yours,
and may the Rain of Blessings
pour forth in endless streams
the Rivers of Life itself ...
And may the Angels of Love
shower
the Infinite Grace of Being
upon you!
I love
for I can do, be, am, become
no other
than LOVE ...
Love loving.

**Judith Küsel**

\* \* \*

CHAPTER 2

# An Epic Journey Begins

An Epic Journey has magic woven into it, and I was never certain about where it could lead me, although I was equipped with a basic map. As the journey unfolds the soul is challenged to break free from all norms, all restrictions and allow the ego to dissolve, as one becomes an instrument played by Divine hands. So often during this journey, I had to allow myself to melt into energy fields in order to shift them. Somehow through it all I was downloading massive information contained in these fields, while simultaneously, having to free so many souls in these places, who were begging to be freed.

In reality, France proved to be such a multi-dimensional challenge for me, that it often had me reeling. I continually shifted both backwards and forwards in time, as lifetime after lifetime spent there previously, appeared to weave together and often overlap.

France is sensual, with its innate love of beauty and sumptuous expression of life itself. There are so many underlying energies – so much that has been buried deeply within the psyche and the subconscious that is voice-less, for it could not be expressed. There is so much which is still hidden and secret, and only those who can truly see will notice, while others will walk through it, over it, and be none the wiser.

I was reminded of Avalon, where the Magicians and Wizards ruled, and it was from them that the later Druidic High Orders of the Celtic People materialized. The Trickster, the Joker, the Fool is everywhere, but look deeper, and you will find that the soul of the people emerges, the soul of Humankind, and indeed, here in the womb of the Goddess, of Mother Earth, she is everywhere. She has not been forgotten, she is a living, breathing entity, and she shows her beautiful face far and wide.

In the distant past, where Paris now lies, there was a huge inland lake with multiple islands, as part of the Lion Kingdom. Later, this was incorporated into the Temples of the Sun, with the seven original islands. To the Ancient Ones these were sacred, and were thus slightly distanced from the mainland, and one could only gain access if it was granted, as High Priests and High Priestesses ruled here.

The Temples of the Sun, were built in concentric circles, some were in crystal pyramids forms, and some were reminiscent of the Buddhist Stupas The seven islands each anchored in a different aspect of

*Figure 1. Buddhist Stupas.*

the Sun Codes and Keys, which were directly linked to the 7th Sun of Illumination.

The Sun Temples were linked with the Sun Paths, and were, without a doubt methodically measured and laid out, so that long after the Lion Kingdom had disappeared, and parts of Avalon had sunk under the Atlantic Ocean, the Celtic people still followed them with precision, as they were their beacons. Later when some tribes moved west once again, they already had their paths mapped out, as the Sun Paths were ancient, and stemmed from way back in Elysium.

They were primarily linked to the 7th Central Sun of Illumination, rather than to our own sun. Furthermore, they connected all the sacred sites, and the 7 Ancient Mystery Schools, which had long survived even after the Fall of Atlantis, and in the times of the deepest darkness, they were symbols of light and hope, which kept the State of Illumination steady, and often saved Humankind from sinking even further into the abyss.

Not only were the Sun Paths in the highest alignment with the Crystalline Pyramid Grids and the Spinal Column of the Earth, but they connected directly with the mounds which had never been used for burial purposes, but were linked in a complex way to power energy centers. Similarly, these connected directly to the Sun Temples, the Standing Stone Circles, the Crystal Pyramids and the Crystal Pyramid Grids, as well as the Spinal Column of the Earth.

All of these worked with the same Spiraling or Vortex Energy, the Sun Discs, and also to the Vibrational Frequencies of Light and Sound, as these all vibrated to the same frequency bands. This made natural energy resources accessible to everyone.

The Sun Temples were places of immense illumination, where the Halls of Wisdom, blended with the Halls of Records, and the Halls of the All-Knowing, All-Seeing and All-Being. Science and Metaphysics were one and the same, indeed, what today would be termed as magic, was merely their profound knowledge of how to manipulate energy and energy fields, in shape-shifting, in teleportation, in telekinesis and in atomic and laser technology, which went way beyond anything we could even dream of. In addition to this, there was the power of sound …

Interestingly, when Julius Caesar invaded Gaul with the Roman armies, long after the highly sophisticated Lion Kingdom, Avalon and Atlantis had fallen into the Dark Ages, he found the following: *"For there were among them such innumerable horns and trumpets, which were being blown simultaneously in all parts of their army, and their cries were so loud and piercing, that the noise seemed to come not merely from trumpets and human voices, but from the whole countryside at once."* (Polybius)[1]

Subsequently those islands were submerged when Avalon fell, and Paris was a swamp-like area, with

---

1   Polybius was a Greek historian of the Hellenistic period noted for his work *The Histories*, which covered the period of 264–146 BC in detail.

only pockets of land remaining. This protected the ancient sites, but within the collective subconscious memory banks, the sacredness of some of the places lingered, despite attempts to annihilate all traces of the past.

It is not only Paris that holds these ancient clues, the Sun Paths, the Sun Temples, and Goddess sites, the Mystery itself, there are in fact other centers of interest.

Concerning France, and the subsequent unfolding of this Epic, it is essential to understand the deep inner psyche of the people, which culminated in the French Revolution – "*Liberté, Egalité, Fraternité*" (Liberty, Equality and Brotherhood). Deep down within the collective soul of France, the Ancient Ones and the Ancient Sun Codes are remembered. She might have wandered off course, had her soul squashed and trodden on, and often buried deeply, but it always rose again, and re-emerged – they could never silence her! Perhaps this is the lasting legacy which French people bring to Humankind – that of the freedom of the soul to express itself, in every way it can, regardless of race, gender or faith.

Yet, the shadow which tends to hang over the self-same glorious people, is the one I had to go and find and release.

Additionally, as this story unfolds, you will discover that it also embraces the story of the women of this land from days of yore. The most remembered ones, such as Mary Magdalene, Joan of Arc, Cécile de Foix, and her aunt, Esclaremonde de Foix, all who had to bear the unspeakable. They were so often forcibly silenced and brought to heel, yet they never wavered, and bravely stood their ground in times of immense darkness. We must remember the men, and how often they too had to hold the keys and codes of Illumination, alongside the women, as both paid the highest price for doing just that.

Their story will be told here, intricately woven into the landscape, as they are intrinsically linked in this Epic, and all it embraces.

In France, one has to see with the eyes of the soul.

Antoine de Saint-Exupéry in *The Little Prince* said: "*It is only with the heart (soul) one can see clearly, for what is essential, is invisible to the eye.*" That a Frenchman should have expressed such truth, is no accident, but by grand design, for in fact his writings epitomize the story of France, all its people, and indeed all of Humanity.

Here I was, for the first time in my entire life, winging my way to the Northern Hemisphere, and into France. Often, in the past I had closed photographic books of France in the Library, when I came across certain sections. I could not look at the pictures, because something deep inside of me did not wish to remember, and what I was supposed to recall at that stage was like a closed book. I just could not go there.

Yet, I was being called back to France, and had been preparing for so many months, downloading information, doing remote energy work, tapping into sacred centres from afar – and I was finally flying towards the very enigma of my own soul.

I was in for the greatest adventure of my life!

When I landed after a sixteen-hour flight in the early morning at Charles de Gaulle, I felt overwhelmed to say the least. I had never been in such an enormous airport and that in itself was quite a discovery! Help arrived in the form of beautiful South African angel, who assisted me through customs, saying that she had been to Paris three times, and just loved it here!

When searching for accommodation in Southern France, and for someone to organize my seminars, my higher guidance sent me help in the form of Kristina Kahnlund. This proved to be an old soul connection, and therefore a continuation of work we did before.

I recognized her immediately, such a loving and gentle soul who proved to be invaluable during my Epic Journey through France. Swedish born, she always felt she belonged to France, having spent much of her life here in the South, in St. Julia de Bec, where I spent the majority of my two-month visit. She was not only fluent in English, but also in French. Without her, it would have been very difficult to do

*Figure 2. Map Showing St Julia de Bec.*

the work I had been called to do and I am ever grateful to her for her invaluable help. She would often during the course of our journey, and all which happened around it, say: "I love being Sherlock Holmes!" meaning that she loved solving puzzles and helping me.

From the moment I actually stepped outside onto French soil I had a deep sense of homecoming. Although the language was foreign, it felt familiar. So often I had a sense of déjà vu as I drove through Paris, as I tuned into it as it had been before. I fell in love with Paris in ways I cannot explain, and I made it my business at the end of my trip, to spend more time there!

Knowing I was South African, as we drove through Paris, the taxi driver deliberately made a detour and my sense of homecoming intensified as I was shown the Eiffel Tower, the Arc de Triomphe, until we finally arrived at our hotel in a suburban area near the metro train services.

I had barely settled in, when I began tuning into the Energy fields in and around me. Indeed, this would culminate in me doing energy and releasing work, from the very moment I stepped out of that hotel, late afternoon, as Kristina wanted dinner at a Vegetarian Restaurant, opposite the Notre Dame. I later realized that this was by cosmic design and not due to her fondness for vegetarian food!

We decided to walk and I was in my element, for as we strolled down the street, I was even more intrigued by the varied architectural styles. Medieval houses were squashed between Gregorian and Greek styled homes, with beautiful wrought iron balconies and doors. Indeed, I sometimes just stood and stared at the doors and entrances, with original owners' sculptures flanking either side of these impressive doors, embellished with intricate designs and even symbolic patterns, which simply fascinated me.

*Figure 3. Notre Dame.*

*Figure 4. Medieval architecture.*

*Figure 5. Kristina and the waiter.*

*Figure 6. Me loving Paris.*

I was slowing down Kristina, as I was now in architectural wonderland – I have always loved architecture, and my career as a Librarian began in a Library for Architects, Engineers and Quantity Surveyors. More than this, the different styles triggered my soul memory banks and I was relieved when Kristina decided to rest at one of the Coffee shops next to the road.

It was now already nine o'clock and I was unaccustomed to such long hours of daylight. We had moved into a more open area, and again with that deep sense of déjà vu, I recognized a protruding cathedral tower and had cold shivers. I knew we were walking towards the Notre Dame, but as we stepped off a curve, I had such powerful energy coursing through me that it halted me in my tracks. I instinctively knew then that a powerful energy line passed through here, and pointed to the tower. "Oh, that is where the original island was in the Seine, and where the Palace of Justice now is. See, we are heading towards the Notre Dame!" I told Kristina, that we had to return the next day to explore. The reason was not really clear, but I knew that I did not need to visit the Notre Dame, but rather go to that building. Little did I know then what would happen to me there, albeit cold shivers should have warned me!

When I finally crossed the street, I was immediately drawn to a small enclosed circular garden right on the corner. I felt that this tiny garden with a fountain had been placed there deliberately, as a marker for the energy lines. There was a bower of red roses over the entrance with such good energy, that I felt inspired to take some pictures.

*Figure 7. The happy honeymoon couple inside the bower.*

*Figure 9. Sainte-Chappelle.*

Suddenly a delightful young Brazilian honeymoon couple appeared, and asked us to please photograph them right there! The bower of roses, the fountain and garden, plus energy lines, were somehow a sign! Kristina obliged by taking pictures, while I was busy tuning increasingly so into the energy fields.

We finally had a very delicious albeit very late dinner at the restaurant opposite the Notre Dame, while the sun shone until 10 pm. In due course we eventually returned to our hotel, and I was bone tired and fell into an exhausted sleep.

The next day, we returned to that spot, out in front of an open square with restaurants. The spire I had seen the evening before, turned out to be that of the chapel next to the Palace of Justice where Marie Antoinette was held prisoner before her execution.

Sinister energies were being emitted from within the complex and I was told to open up the energy lines to Versailles from this spot. I was stunned, but then I had tapped into the energy lines there, so this must be the link up.

*Figure 8. The Palace of Justice.*

"No, I don't want to go there, we need to go this way!" I exclaimed, as we stood in front of the gilded gates of the Palace of Justice. Deep and profound memory banks were being triggered within me. I had been present right here during the French Revolution!

Whenever I looked at the church, Sainte-Chapelle, my tummy churned, and I felt that something dreadful had taken place there! This whole place was so

*Figure 10. The Conciergerie. Intense energy work done here.*

familiar, it felt just like I was Marie Antoinette awaiting execution!

Suddenly she was there, next to me and so very real. Furthermore, as I read the huge sign in gold on the arch of the massive building: *Liberty, fraternity, equality*. A reflective sense of irony came over me, accompanying a deep sense of intense trauma.

I always knew that I was beheaded in the French Revolution, from the time I first learned of it, and I was now being confronted with something I had never expected on my second day in Paris!

We now passed part of the Conciergerie,[2] where all 4,000 prisoners had been housed, including Marie Antoinette during the Revolution. I refused to go inside – it was as if I was stepping back in time so I halted next to the great clock at the tower opposite the Seine.

---

2   The Conciergerie (French pronunciation: [kɔ̃sjɛʁʒəʁi]) is a building in Paris, France, located on the west of the Île de la Cité (literally "Island of the City"), formerly a prison but presently used mostly for law courts. It was part of the former royal palace, the Palais de la Cité, which consisted of the Conciergerie, Palais de Justice and the Sainte-Chapelle. Hundreds of prisoners during the French Revolution were taken from the Conciergerie to be executed by guillotine at a number of locations around Paris.

I was now progressively tuning into Marie Antoinette, hearing her story.

She was brought to this prison in a barge, along with her attendants and ladies-in-waiting and what followed here was pure torture for this soul, in more ways than one. She was in fact not beheaded publicly as later stated, but sacrificed in the lower part of the church whose spire I had spotted on that first day, after being brutally and repeatedly raped by men releasing their pent-up hatred and anger on her, as a symbol of their woes.

They sacrificed her where once a Goddess site had stood, and consequently the church was deliberately built on top of it, with the energy lines running through. She was by no means the only one sacrificed in the lower storey of the church, out of sight, and unnoticed. That this was in fact a Goddess site, would be revealed, a little later in amazing ways.

She emerges as a tragic figure, forced into an unhappy marriage with a brutal man incapable of intimacy. She had never known a day of freedom ever, and the greatest of all irony is that she would be sacrificed in the very palace that declares and proclaims: Liberty, Fraternity, Equality!

I stood shuddering! They beheaded her after her sacrificial death and then guillotined a look-alike. The populace of Paris had no idea what she really looked like, so the switch was easily done, but the head, which was waved around, was that of Marie Antoinette, albeit three days old!

I emerged from my reverie, called now to free these poor trapped stuck souls from times even before the Revolution.

I was accustomed to doing energy work in open spaces within nature, and in Reunion, as mentioned in my first book, I even had to do this on a high mountain, mingling with hikers, but this was the first time ever, that I had to accomplish my work in the middle of a teeming city, filled with tourists. I called in my helpers to provide the ideal place, where we could have some measure of privacy, away from the shifting crowds.

*Figure 12. Site of more complex energy work.*

The Seine drew my attention, and I remembered being taken to this fortress in a barge. (It felt quite strange to me sometimes, as I sensed that I had been Marie Antoinette, and subsequent happenings in Versailles and the Louvre affirmed this. Maybe that is why I had always sensed that I had been beheaded during the Revolution, even if I immediately blocked out such thoughts!)

I turned round and to my astonishment saw that the building's façade had changed dramatically, since rounding the corner. I was facing two Renaissance towers, and knew that this was where the prisoners were bundled into, so it was exactly where I needed to do the energy and releasing work. I positioned myself in direct alignment to them, and felt the energy coursing through me. I beamed energy into the building and the whole complex, literally from deep down into the earth and upwards from the Seine.

Immensely powerful green and gold spiralling energy moved through me, sweeping everything clean as simultaneously stuck souls were released, but to my utter amazement, their heads appeared first! Then followed the bodies of those poor souls who had been guillotined, or sacrificed, or died here, especially women and children, including Marie Antoinette.

## JOURNAL ENTRY

**11 August 2016**

I saw them, Marie Antoinette and the women and children, surrounded by priests! Then the church, Sainte-Chapelle, from which I had such a foul feeling, indeed sinister, and I knew that sacrifices had taken place in the hidden and secret chambers of vaults inside! Such was the trauma I picked up on there, as Marie Antoinette was sacrificed and her soul severely traumatized and trapped right there! I am getting very clear confirmation that later a surrogate look-a-like was publicly executed.

Since the masses had no clue what she looked like and were baying for her blood, they had no idea that a switch was made! Indeed, so many were sacrificed here and in underground systems. Kristina said that she had been inside the church and that it had two levels (I pick up clearly that it has three, one level hidden and underground), with only the top level accessible to tourists. As all these souls were released, all the collective negative energy was transmuted into the purest God force energy!

Marie Antoinette then appeared, so happy to be finally freed and unrestricted! During her entire life she was imprisoned in a Golden Cage, from which there was no escape! She never knew nor understood why all of this had happened to her. She never knew why – a truly lost soul who never experienced happiness for an entire lifetime! A tragic figure indeed.

When this work was completed, I felt that we were being scrutinised from the Towers and I told Kristina that we needed to move.

*Figure 13. Lion Statues.*

We went around into the deserted street and rounded the corner to find Lion statues everywhere. The outer façade of the building was pure classic Gregorian Style with an abundance of sculptured reliefs. Indeed, I found steps flanked by two sphinxes, with three Goddess statues on either side!

The entire building was dedicated to the Goddess Aysis! In addition, there were lions. This, is where Napoleon's great legacy materialised, the French judicial system! Beautiful and with quite different energies on this side of the complex, yet, nobody bothered to go there, as there were no tourists in sight!

It was now lunchtime and we both needed some rest but I knew that there was still more energy work to be done. We opted for the Restaurant in the

*Figure 14. Sculptured reliefs.*

*Figure 15. Me standing on the bridge.*

*Figure 16. The Pont de Bir-Hakeim.*

*Figure 17. Detail on The Pont de Bir-Hakeim.*

square, where a surly waiter aggravated Kristina. She wanted to leave, but I knew we had to be there. I was instructed to go downstairs to the ladies, and to clear out the remaining unsavoury underground energies!

I did just that, now totally unobserved, and removed all remaining trauma from the secret atrocities that had occurred there, clearing the energy lines all the way up to Versailles. The first part of the work was done!

The waiter in the meantime was even more aggressive, especially now that any residual energy lines were clear! We were relieved to leave the square as Kristina now remembered that the Statue of Liberty, the Paris Replica of the one France gifted America with, was further down the Seine River.[3] This proved to be Divinely guided, in so many ways!

As we were following the River I immediately identified the Louvre, and felt a deep sense of homecoming once again. We drove over a double storey bridge and the buildings on the other side fascinated me! I felt I knew this place, but from another time, when there was no city here, only a chateau. I had no inkling how I knew this, but I discerned that somehow I had been previously involved here, or had lived here before when this area was not part of the city itself!

When the taxi halted we were both astounded: we had arrived up on the Island of the Swans, and there across the River two swans were gliding along! Another Sign! Those were the first swans appearing on my journey through France, where I was reminded of the Swan King and Queen, time and again!

The Pont de Bir-Hakeim Bridge (previously known as Pont Passy), was renamed after the second World

---

3   The most famous of the three, however, is the replica on the Île aux Cygnes. It was given to France by the United States in 1889, three years after the French presented the US with the original Statue of Liberty. The Statue of Liberty was a gift to the US in the 1870s from the French.

War. It was a revelation in itself, and incorporated immensely interestingly metaphysical symbols and was also in direct alignment with the Eiffel Tower, as was the Statue of Liberty. The Eiffel Tower cleaved the sky – symbolic of the male power and a penis, reflected in the modern skyscrapers flanking the river – all in the shape of a phallus, with pyramids on top and incorporated in the design, one even had three! An accident? No, by design!

It was the bridge which grabbed my attention, and I also observed that the Energy Lines moved through me where the great statue Wedekinsh stands, which reminded me of Hermes. Yet, what really caught my eye was the Central Arch of the viaduct, designed by Jean-Antoice Injalbert, and within this Central Arch, are two stone-statues in relief, figures of "Science and Labor" by Jules-Felix Louten and "Electricty and Commerce" by Jean Formige. The bridge itself was build circa 1905, but its very grandeur and style, with its incorporated symbols carefully hidden within these sculptures, spoke volumes. Most tourists were

*Figure 18. The world globe on top of the caduceus!*

*Figure 19. The Goddess Sophia.*

hanging around, taking photos of the Eiffel Tower and Hermes, and were not even interested in the Arch itself. Yet, there I stood, in awe and wonder.

To me this Arch was not built by accident, but by grand design, and it had a far greater esoteric meaning, than its descriptions imparted!

**JOURNAL ENTRY**

On one side a woman with her right foot on a scroll and in a Philosopher's pose – yet she is veiled and her breasts naked with a veiled lower half. Her right hand is outstretched and resting on geometrical and mathematical tools. She seems to be holding secrets, or hiding them, rather, or holding all knowledge hidden on earth. Her foot rests on open scrools and manuscripts. Thus she contains wisdom and knowledge – the Goddess Sophia!

In between her and her male counterpart, the serpent and staff appear with the world globe on top of the caduceus! Serpent energy = Goddess vortex energy!

There were spirals everywhere, depicting the self-same energy!

The male reclines, like Socrates did, and faces her. He is her Divine Counterpart. Yet he does not have the

*Figure 20. The male, like Socrates reclines, facing her. He is her Divine Counterpart.*

*Figure 21. Another view of the Goddess Sophia.*

tools she has. The composite whole points to the fact that he cannot access the hidden, the knowledge, the secrets without her!

On the other side of the arch, the same scene is repeated, but now he is an old man, aged – but she is eternally young! The serpents, caduceus, and spirals all repeat themselves. Masterpieces in sculpture, this was the one thing about Paris, I will never forget!

*Figure 22. The Seine.*

The way this bridge was placed, was of course by design, and not accidental. For once this part of Paris had been one of those original 7 islands surrounded by an inland lake, an ancient Goddess site, and all again linked directly to Versailles, where I had to open up the massive Sun gate. I had found my second energy beacon, and was about to find the third, just further down the Seine.

All were in direct alignment with the Eiffel Tower, flanked by huge skyscrapers with pyramids!

We then walked toward the Statue of Liberty on the Island of the Swans, a man-made island and there the swans appeared again. I was fascinated by the architectural designs of the skyscrapers. The nearer we came to the Statue, the more I could sense the energy lines growing more potent. There is another bridge crossing the Seine, just in front of the Statue, and this was transformed into a playground.

Standing before the statue, I felt intense energy surging through my entire body and knew I would have to stand somewhere in line as children were all over it. I then did massive energy line clearing, and linked the energy lines from there to Versailles, via the Ile de la Cite and Ile St. Louis.

I had just stepped onto French soil, and just completed my first day in France and already had released so many stuck souls and opened up intensely important energy fields.

Marie Antoinette, came as an unexpected twist in the story, and surprised me. Yet, through the holographic unfolding for my whole journey in France, this was but one of the incredible events, which would unfold.

Now Versailles was waiting, and I had no idea how I would do the work I had been asked to do there. All I could do was trust and release it all into much higher hands as I drifted off to sleep …

\* \* \*

Dearly Beloved
You are in my thoughts
in my heart
deep inside of me …
And I smile.
You bring me joy
such fun
such laughter –
it bubbles over,
it expands
into a million stars
and galaxies
and lights up Universes …
Yet there is a depth
within you
a breadth of knowledge
which I wish to delve into
never-ending
and it expands
my mind
my vision
and sometimes
overcharges
only to expand some more …
To have you inside me
to embrace
the length,
the breadth
and ALL of YOU
is the greatest gift
the Divine
ever bestowed upon me
Infinity
evolves
when we
become
AS ONE!
I thank you.
I so appreciate you.
I love you ad infinitum!

**Judith Küsel**

CHAPTER 3

# The Sun Gate and the Sun Discs of Versailles

It certainly stirred my soul, the Temple of the Sun God[1] when seen from afar, especially by spacecraft from that time. Those who visited her by amphibious means, often stood and gazed in awe and wonder, as she shimmered with pure white gold. Through the massive dome of the Sun Gate, a colossal vortex energy of pure gold poured out and moved up into the heavens, connecting the Sun Gate Portals of Sirius on through to the 7th Central Sun of Illumination.

This Centre directly linked the Crystal Pyramids in the Montségur Pyrenees area with landmasses that had sunk offshore from Brittany and Carnac, which now stands on its own as a reminder, then Stonehenge in England, Newgrange in Ireland, the Sun portals in Portugal where the Templar Holdings once stood on the conical hills, which in fact are still the buried Sun Centres, and then with Malta, Delphi, and Giza, as well as what once stood in the area that is now New York, and the land that has sunk under the sea in the Gulf of Mexico. It also linked up with Brazil, and further down to Zimbabwe, and the Spinal Column of the Earth.

This Sun Gate linked Lemuria and Mu to Avalon after the fall of the Lion Kingdom, where land mass had risen from the sea, from which the Lemurian Civilization began.

It also connected directly with seven other Earth centres located in Southern Africa, Ethiopia, the Himalayas, the Philippines, Hawaii, the Ural Mountains, and the landmass that tore off from what is now Easter Island and South America.

Yet their story is for another time, another space.

The entire Sun Gate Complex was one massive energy centre operating at a high frequency and vibration with such advanced technology that is no longer accessible and has long been forgotten.

---

1  Versailles was designed to be the personal temple of this god on earth, decorated with statues and symbols of Apollo, of the sun, and of Louis himself. The classical themes throughout the palace underlined the divine right of France's kings and queens to rule without limit. Wikipedia.

Additionally, it housed a massive centre of Learning, literally a place where the greatest minds from the Intergalactic Federation often gathered, as Earth was still very closely aligned with the other galaxies, and some Planetary Councils from other planets in this solar system had their own faculties here, namely: Jupiter, Venus, Saturn, Uranus, Neptune, Pluto, and Mercury. At that time Mars was still in immense transition, having suffered the most during the Wars of the Heavens.

The main galaxies involved in the Higher Teaching and Learning centres were from Orion, Sirius, Pleiades, the Bear Constellation, Lyra, Andromeda, The Milky Way Galaxy, Pegasus, and Cygnus.

A complex exchange of knowledge and energy interactions transpired here, as it was an extremely important centre of technology and knowledge, symbolized by the 7th Central Sun of Illumination. For when the heart and mind are fully illumined, the higher soul self has access to endless information held within the cosmic Mastermind pool. Thus the great Sun Temples were not only places of worship, but places of higher knowledge and technology, as the Sun itself illuminates the heart, soul and mind.

It was not accidental that one of the most important Mystery Schools was based here, the School of Metaphysics. It worked in tandem with its branches, the Alchemical School in what is now Southern France, Northern Spain, Portugal, and the High Magic or Wizard Schools, which were in the area that has now sunk offshore from Brittany, Ireland and Britain, and thus follows the deeply unconscious recall of Merlin and his ilk, by Humankind. We will come to this School in due course.

The schools here were divided like the later Druidic High Orders into three categories: The High Order of Wisdom inclusive of Metaphysics and Science, The High Order of Bards, and The High Order of Mystics. The latter were the High Priests and Priestesses who served as Transmitter Channels and were the link between the 7th Heaven and Earth.

One has to understand this in the context of higher Wisdom and Knowledge, there was no distinction between the core sciences and metaphysics, as they were understood to be one and the same. The fact that the Bardic Orders were independent, was mainly due to higher uses of sound and sound frequencies, the oratory sciences, the philosophical schools, and likewise the power of the human voice, as used in higher healing and other advanced metaphysical curative methods.

It was on an Epicentre that stood on a high mountain slope, almost like a huge constructed mound surrounded by valleys, filled with highly advanced technology, working with spiralling energy and energy fields, linked directly with the Spinal Column of the Earth, the Crystal Pyramids and Crystalline Pyramid Grids.

The Sun Temple in its prime was considered one of great wonders of architecture and engineering feats built it by the Lyrans, and attracted tourists from other galaxies and star systems by the droves.

Likewise large numbers of tourists and multiple buses blocked the entrance to modern day Versailles on our arrival. It felt surreal and somehow like moving backwards in time instead of forwards.

We had taken the Metro train and I thoroughly enjoyed the journey, as I had needed time to assimilate the energies, and to orientate myself and tune in. When we entered or passed forests or wooded areas near Versailles, I had a great sense of déjà vu, remembering that Marie Antoinette had preferred living in her hunting lodge, rather than in the palace itself. Being reunited now with this massive complex triggered many things inside of me, in addition to tuning into energy fields, and the massive sun gate I had been called upon to reopen here!

Before his birth, a French woman prophesized that Louis XIV would be born as the Sun King, to radiate and glitter and be just as illustrious as the Sun. He was the last born child of older parents, and was raised by his mother, while the country was being ruled by a Cardinal. He had a great love of the arts

*Figure 1. Louise XIV.*

and the finer things in life, yet the golden splendour of the Sun Palace, became a gilded cage for those living in it, especially Marie Antoinette. I would meet up with Louis himself much later, in the Louvre, yet that was closer to the end of my journey. So many twists and turns still had to be experienced on this quest, and Versailles served as the actual gateway within a massive portal.

Versailles in truth is the Sun Palace, built on the site where the Sun Temples had once stood. The site had changed dramatically, indeed the truth is deeply buried underground, but somehow the soul of Louis XIV, must have had an ancient link or soul tie with the Sun Temples, resulting in his innate longing to recreate what had been there before! Indeed, it became his lifetime obsession.

### JOURNAL ENTRY

**8 August 2016**

While at the restaurant I was being tuned in and prepared for the work ahead. When we arrived at the gate, it was to find the place milling with tourists. Indeed, the queues to enter the Palace and the Halls of Mirrors, which I would have so dearly loved to have seen, were incredibly long. Even the queue to the gardens was substantial!

After a long wait to enter, I was overwhelmed by the sheer majesty of the landscaped gardens and the extent of them. The only drawback was that the 15 fountains were not operational, which was a pity, for it would have been a spectacular sight.

The statues themselves, all over the gardens and buildings, celebrated art forms, especially the beauty of the feminine form! Versailles itself was a tribute to the Goddess herself, and incredibly sensuous and beautiful. My love for art and sculptures, architecture and landscaping, was stirring and expanded here for I was in my element!

At first we meandered towards the steps, which led to the Orangerie.[2]

The intricate use of sacred geometry, within the landscaping caught my eye, but my sensors were pointing me in a different direction and we thus returned to the main gardens, wandering toward the lake on the border further down.

There were an incredible number of white marble statues, 155 in total, exquisitely created and a celebration in themselves! Engrossed and admiring these statues, marvelling at the beauty and craftsmanship, I was inadvertently led to a place between huge

---

[2] An orangery or orangerie was a room or a dedicated building on the grounds of fashionable residences from the 17th to the 19th centuries where orange and other fruit trees were protected during the winter, as a very large form of greenhouse or conservatory. Wikipedia.

*Figure 2. The Sun Palace.*

*Figure 4. Celebrating the feminine form.*

*Figure 5. More beautiful gardens.*

*Figure 3. Versailles Gardens.*

*Figure 6. Well laid out gardens stretching in all directions.*

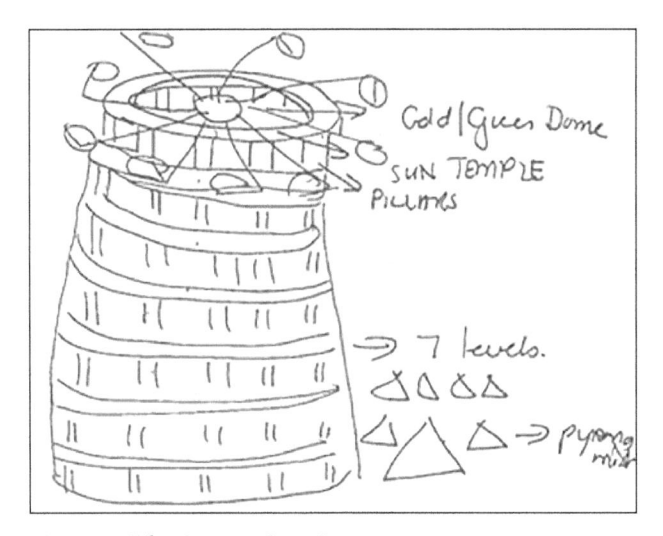

*Figure 7. The Octopus Sun Gate.*

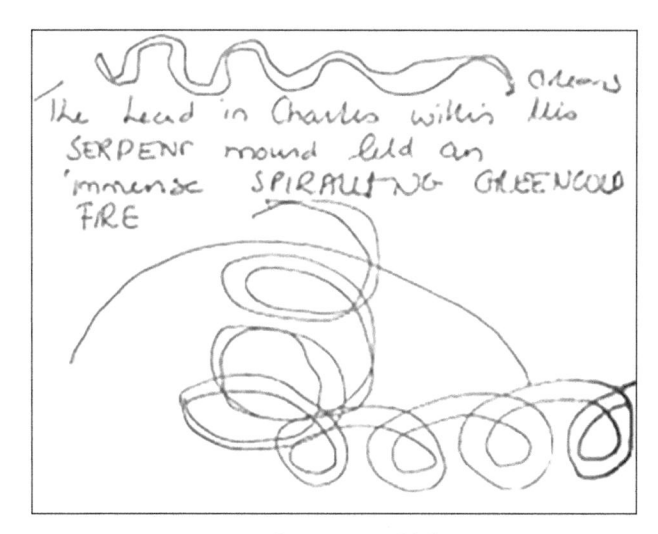

*Figure 8. Immense spiraling green gold fire.*

hedges, next to the main fountain. I was shown a bench there and told to sit down. I told Kristina that this was where I needed to do the energy work, for I was now in direct alignment with the Sun gates, which were underground, and thus concealed some distance away, under the impressive landscaped gardens. Little did I know who I would find behind my back, much later!

I closed my eyes and tuned into the huge Stonehenge, the Sun Gate, and Sun discs. Immediately I could see them in my mind's eye, as I entered a much higher and altered state.

The bench we sat on was secluded, as the main throng of tourists were in the region of the fountains. I also knew that they would place a veil of invisibility over us, and that no one would notice us.

A massive Sun Gate then appeared. It was like an octopus with arm-like swastika tentacles protruding, and resembling the number 7 at each end, with a twirling and swirling sun disc. The whole "Octopus" (Sun Gate) was rotating like a giant clockwork or spiralling energy. The Sun Temple now showed itself – like Stonehenge (see sketch) but with the gold and green dome, it had 7 tiers or levels, with 7 pyramids. It spiralled upwards, like the proverbial (and much later remembered) Tower of Babel.

It was completely covered with see-through green and gold crystal, inlaid in red-gold and white-gold with the swastika-like symbols having 7, 9, 11 and 12 arms respectively, depending on the size of the circle (and the size of each symbol). The latter were spike-like but dancing clock-wise, like the inner clockworks were hooking into a wheel.

Then 7 pyramids appeared – green-gold with golden swastikas like vibrating rivers, or like electronic signs, pulsating green and gold.

As I worked on these energies to activate them, the green-golden fiery flame ignited and everything began to rotate and spin.

The Sun Discs now detached themselves and hovered over the whole.

Just like in Antarctica, some hovered over me and began to activate the keys and codes within me! My whole body was shaking and my head buzzing!

There were so many tourists around but somehow with Kristina sitting next to me, helping to hold the energy, we remained invisible. This was intense work and was done with help from the Cosmic Hierarchy gathered around me.

While doing this massive energy work, many stuck souls who had been trapped in that area appeared. A significant number were slaves, the poor indentured souls had been forced to create all of this, and many had come from Africa. Yet, there were even more souls gathered there – from the time when the Gauls sacrificed people to the Sun Gods at certain festivals long after Atlantis had fallen, and thus at a time when Humanity had already slipped into forgetfulness.

All of these souls were set free and there was much celebration at their release.

## JOURNAL ENTRY

At last we could relax and be more tourist-like and found a food kiosk hidden in the mazes.

As we returned to go back to the main entrance, we meandered up a different route and to my utter amazement I found the Cave of Apollo, hidden behind the place where I had done the energy work! It was in direct alignment with the Sun Temples, as though it had been deliberately placed there!

I was fascinated by the statues inside this cave and wanted to see them close up, but soon the whistle of a security guard, had me back on the official paths. I was quite disappointed, for I felt that there were underground tunnels or chambers carefully hidden away. I picked up on secret fertility rites, and that the tunnel systems had somehow, in ancient times, linked up with the Sun Gate.

The entire Sun Gate was now pulsating and open, and vortex energy was pouring into it – liquid green-gold fiery energy!

Again, I was shown the following (Figure 10):

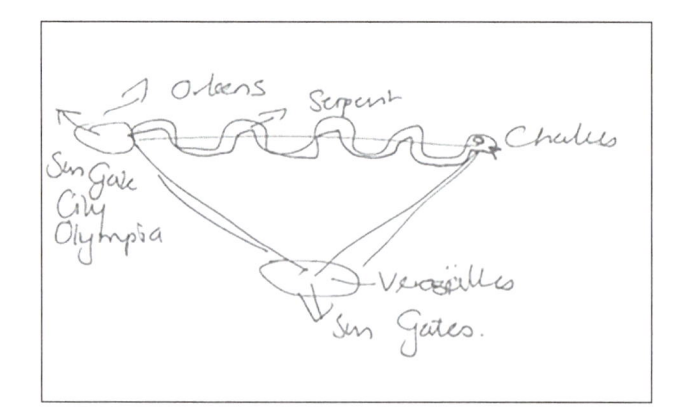

*Figure 10. The Sun Gate.*

The Sun Gate at the City of the Goddess Olympia near Malta, linked the serpent energy to Chartres (1) and to Versailles (2).

With the opening of the Sun Gate at Versailles, I now had to link it to Chartres, to complete the triangle or pyramid!

*Figure 9. The Cave of Apollo.*

*Figure 11. Standing in the Gardens.*

Returning slowly but surely to the entrance of the gardens, I once again admired the statues, the formal gardens, and the sheer magnificence and beauty of the place. I remembered the stuck souls I had freed here earlier, and reflected: *"Such splendour, but at what cost to human life, and also to those overburdened by taxes. No wonder the French Revolution exploded."*

Perhaps, true freedom is not to be found in impressive palaces etched in gold, but deep within the soul itself. When the soul is free to soar and fly and roam where it wills, it heeds no earthly impediments.

Yet a truly empowered soul, is one who is wise enough to stand on its own two feet, not allowing itself to be disempowered in any area of life at all.

Perhaps that was the original ideal which fired the Revolution, and which inspired the great French Philosophers, like Voltaire. Yet, ideals may turn into nightmares in the hands of people, trying to apply such principles. The truth is that whatever is inside a person, has ripple effects on the whole, and if the inner soul self, cannot walk in harmony with itself, it will not walk in harmony with the rest of humanity.

Such is the lesson of Versailles and the French Revolution.

Liberty, Equality and Fraternity, start within, before they can manifest in the outer world.

Little did I know, that what I would find in Chartres, which would affirm the self-same spiritual law.

* * *

CHAPTER 4

# Chartres

My first two days in Paris had already proved eventful as I had begun to understand why I had undergone so many activations and downloaded so much and received crystal clear guidance as to where I should go, tapping into the secret history, the hidden energy fields and energetic imprints of the landscape itself. I had no inkling of the enormity of what I would need to clear, to release, and indeed tap into once again. Certainly, this had become a multi-dimensional journey, being played out on many energy levels and energetic fields, simultaneously.

I was preparing the way for a total rebirth of humanity at large.

When one is led on such journeys, one becomes a mere instrument in much Higher Hands, realising that life itself is multi-dimensional and multi-faceted, with energy fields storing information continuously, and the more you tap into such fields, the greater is the need to become the field, in order to access its information. I often literally allowed myself to dissolve into the fields, to shift them. For the first time, I did this in crowded areas, while learning to assimilate the process.

Thus we continued to follow the instructions I had received long before I embarked on this journey, and from Paris, we then made our way to Chartres.[1] I immediately loved the village of Chartres. It had a lovely medieval feel about it, with charming buildings, lovely flower baskets, and friendly people. It also featured delightful coffee shops with quaint feudal architecture and cobbled streets.

The Cathedral is an architectural wonder, so layered and intricate that you can spend days just digesting its outer shell, never-mind the inner wonders. The artistry of the rose and stained glass windows speaks for itself, but to my disappointment the famous labyrinth was carefully obscured by chairs.

---

1   Chartres, a city in north-central France southwest of Paris, is famed for its massive Cathédrale Notre-Dame. The Gothic cathedral, completed in 1220, features two towering spires, flying buttresses, Romanesque sculptures, pavement labyrinth and elaborate rose windows. The interior's blue-tinted stained glass is distinctive, and the nearby Centre International du Vitrail has workshops and exhibits on stained-glass art. Wikipedia.

PART 1: CHAPTER 4: CHARTRES

*Figure 1. Chartres Cathedral.*

Chartres Cathedral is steeped in so much symbolism and multiple levels of energetic imprints, which at times overwhelmed me. The Knights Templar built a living monument here to their own innate belief systems, imprinted into the building itself. Yet much has been added over time, and interestingly the glass windows were built much later, continuing their work. The further I travelled in France the more I realized that you could not take any church or cathedral simply at face value. So much that had been suppressed, stands there in full view. For if you truly wish to hide something, put it right under people's noses. Most will walk over or past it, not noticing that they are standing or walking on sacred ground.

However, to have built this cathedral on this sacred site was sacrilegious. From the Site in Orleans/Blois a serpent mound once wove itself all the way to Chartres where the main Goddess Temple Site

59

stood – the head of the serpent was there and the tail in Orleans/Blois. The immensely powerful serpent energy (spiralling, coiled) held an incredibly potent green-golden fire energy pulsating up and down the mound. The mound is still there, as one goes up a rounded incline to enter the Cathedral. (Interestingly, what I downloaded was confirmed in later research about the site itself, and the subsequent history of how it fell into the wrong hands.)

The Goddess Temples as well as those in Paris and Versailles, were held by 12 High Priestess Druids and the Queen of the Serpent/Spiralling Energy herself, Aysis-Ra-A-Hu-A-Ra!

She rules over these lands – High Priestess and Queen of the Fires of Illumination during the Lion Kingdom and Avalon.

She contained the powers of the Lightning Rod, the Serpent Energy (Kundalini), and the Mystic Rose of Enlightenment and Illumination accompanied by Alchemy Powers symbolized by the Chalice and Grail, the sacred womb of the Goddess!

Her domains stretched into the Pyrenees, Northern Spain, Portugal, and what is now the Atlantic (Britain, Ireland, New York and parts of the East Coast of the Americas, Europe, the Mediterranean Sea (then still a landmass), Africa and parts of Asia and Australasia as one single continent.

She was the consort of her counterpart, Osiris Ra-A-Hu-A-Ra, and hailed from Sirius/Lyra/Andromeda.

Where Paris and the Seine are now, there were once islands held within a vast inland sea.

There were 7 Sacred Islands and the Goddess Aysis with 7 Sun-gates, each housing 7 pyramids (Green/gold, Light Blue and Emerald Green crystal).

Each one functioned on a different vibrational frequency band but all worked as a single entity. Aysis was like the Queen Bee (Fleur de Lys), and she held the hive of these sacred and powerful sites together. It held the Four/Five Powers within it:

Fire Water Air Earth Ethers = I AM THAT – I AM!

She was Aysis-Ra-A-Hu-A-Ra THE SUN GODDESS and Osiris-Ra-A-Hu-A-Ra, was the SUN GOD and they both held and anchored in the Fires of the Illumination from the 7th Central Sun, the Sun-gates, the Sun Discs, as well the High Orders of the Mystery Schools, and Alchemists, which they established.

The Queen and the High Priestess of these lands was a direct descendant of the Royal Lineages of the Lion Kingdom and the incarnation of Aysis-Ra-A-Hu-A-Ra herself, long before Ancient Egypt and Ancient Greece and she held the lands of Avalon, the third Civilization, after Elysium, the first, and the Lion Kingdom, the second.

Her male equivalent was carefully chosen. He had to prove his own ability to hold the sacred Fires of Illumination with her as an equal partner, as a Sun God in his own right, as King, as Consort, as High Priest, and as her Divine Masculine counterpart, to ensure they would be equally empowered and enabled to effect the massive energy work that served the greater whole.

In this period people lived much longer than in current times, utilizing the powers of Elixirs to prolong life/health/wellbeing and subsequently the Keys and Codes of longevity and the Tree and Flower of Life. This was the 7th Heaven on Earth. Male and Female were in harmony with one another.

Although Matriarchy held sway, her Male consort was her equal partner within the Beehive of societal structures. She spun the hive of his Domain and together they created the honey, the offspring, and the fruits of the Serpent Energy MAGIC as they worked together as Equal partners for the greater good of all.

For thousands of years they lived like this as all Avalon prospered. There was no strife, there were no wars, no victims, no victors, and no persecutors.

Unity reigned. Balance. Harmony.

The Male in his Masculine Divinity was Powerful.

The Female in her Feminine Divinity was Powerful.

They were ONE.

Therefore the land prospered.

They used the gold, and the precious metals of their domain as the conduit for the serpent energy, as a gift from Mother Earth, and although gold served as adornments in their temples and so forth, it was considered part of their energy systems, often like a conduit, energy enhancer, a way of prolonging life – it was never hoarded, or used to control, or hurt or harm. It was used for the highest good of all.

Then seemingly from nowhere, out of the Earth came the same Race who had destroyed Marduk and the Lion Kingdom. It was believed that they had been scorched from the Earth (thus annihilated), but they had merely withdrawn into the darkness, the Underworld of Hades, and now wanted to own the power of the Serpent Energies for themselves. However, they were a very primitive, warlike, brutal, small, dark-haired people who were so immersed in darkness, that they had no understanding of Truth, or of the true uses of the serpent energy, nor the elixir of life.

All they saw was the splendour, the gold, the riches, and powers of those they were attacking, and they wanted it all for themselves – with no understanding!

First of all they conquered and destroyed in sight. It was as if they were mad – drunk on the blood of their self-appointed enemies whom they hacked to pieces.

As the populace of Avalon had no army, never having been in need of war machines and weapons, the Priesthood (Druids) and those with the Powers, now had to channel them in self-defence, as they saw their people being sacrificed, even eaten alive, destroyed, and raped. Reeling with shock after shock, they were forced to fortify their abodes, to take up defensive positions and to come up with some way of protecting themselves with whatever they could conjure up.

Indeed, with the devastation caused by these little men's war machines, the Matriarchy along with the clansmen who had remained true, were now forced to withdraw into their temples, their sacred places, and to use their considerable magical powers. Though their male counterparts the High Priests and High Kings now stepped in as well, they were often still at a loss about how to deal with what to them seemed like insanity, as the their nation's very roots (their sacred haven, Utopia), was being bombarded, raped, bloodied, battered and traumatized, while they tried to safeguard as much as possible to keep their immense knowledge from being brutally taken by those with no concept or understanding of the enormous powers of the Serpent energy. Thus they were forced to shut down and seal off their own powerhouses, their energy sources, to prevent them from falling into the destructive, enemy hands.

Thus the reign of Peace, turned into a reign of Horror …

Chartres was built on the very sites where the invaders, the conquerors, had openly killed the Druid High Priests, first by cutting off their penises, then slicing out their beating hearts and forcing the Druid Priestesses to witness this while shackled and chained. They were then repeatedly raped as the remnants of their nation had to witness this brutal show of force. They then sacrificed the Priestesses after removing their breasts, opening their wombs and vaginas with their swords, leaving their corpses to rot.

It was an act of mercy when riots erupted and those traumatised witnesses, now retaliated in extreme anger and outrage at the desecration of the Holy of the Holies and set everything alight. Indeed they even voluntarily leapt into the flames themselves, dying, rather than submitting to becoming slaves of the insanely cruel conquerors. They martyred themselves for their Sun King and Queen – with immense superhuman courage and this very heroism also speaks of the tragic, the unspeakable trauma, that which cannot be voiced when a mind has been pushed beyond all limits, causing the willing fighters to now rather die, than to lose their freedom, dignity, and their very soul!

Long before these events, the Queen experienced visions, leading her to slowly but surely with the help of the Sun King, shut down all the centres, the powerhouses of the serpent energy forces and all its powers originating in the 7th Central Sun, via the Sun Gate to Sirius. Included here were the Crystal Pyramids, the Serpent mounds, The Sun Gates, the Sun Portals, the Lightning Rod of the Earth and Staff and Sacred Chalice – indeed all that were the Sacred Power Tools, the knowledge, the technology, and the wisdom of Avalon.

In vain the conquerors then sacrificed others on the exact site, in their attempts to assume these coveted powers, abusing sexual energy in their black magic rites, and further enslaving the people.

In fact they were never able to regain what had been lost, but they even though they put the symbols of those they had conquered everywhere. They could never gain access to the hidden, and now powerfully sealed-off hidden knowledge of the Druid High Priests and Priestesses, indeed that of all three High Druidic Orders.

For the conquerors had fallen lower than animals and the gates and the knowledge pertaining to the 7th Heaven were now completely inaccessible to them, as the sun-gate via Sirius to the 7th Central Sun of Illumination was closed, and the Goddess withdrew her powers.

As much as they cried out to her, all those who had raped and sacrificed her, she did not answer and could not be reached nor found. However haunt them, she did – day and night!

When we entered Chartres I was immediately and quietly led to a left side gallery where there were four statues of women hidden in the gloom, hardly visible, with a beautiful rose frescoes, almost like silent witnesses to what had TRULY happened here on this site.

Yet, there was still something serene about this side-room, with these frescoes and I felt a deep sense of peace as they contained and emanated a certain energy, which counteracted anything that was negative.

Notice how the women each hold their hands differently and each one is carrying or concealing something. The woman on the right is pointing upwards to the chalice behind her. What is it that she is trying to tell us?

To me it was clear that these women were at the entrance as a side-show, for hardly anyone saw or were interested in them, but they certainly held the Goddess energy steady and anchored it in. If ever a side chapel, for that is what it seemed to be, was dedicated to the Divine Feminine and the powers of wisdom that she holds, it was this chapel, and it pointed to the Sisterhood of the Rose. Thus pure love.

*Figure 2. Chartres Cathedral entrance.*

*Figure 3. Frescoes.*

PART 1: CHAPTER 4: CHARTRES

*Figure 4. A closer view.*

*Figure 5. Pointing to the chalice.*

*Figure 6. Rose Fresco.*

*Figure 7. The High Altar.*

The cathedral itself is beautiful and the rose window especially so. I went from window to window, working my way around doing energy and clearing work. Often Kristina and I sat quietly on a side bench overlooking these windows, or the knaves within the cathedral.

At the entrance to the labyrinth itself, there is a sense of calm and balance. However the more I progressed towards the high altar on the right side, the more I was made aware of an acrimonious energy. At first I could not identify it. Kristina found a statue with her namesake St. Kristina, and while I was looking at it, I tuned into very perturbing energies present to my right, in an

*Figure 8. The trapdoor.*

63

enclosed area. I searched for an entrance or door, to lead where I sensed their source point was, when a man walked past, opened a door, and left it ajar. He seemed to come from nowhere, and I followed him, and found myself standing in front of the high altar. Yet, why was my hair standing on end?

I looked down and I was just about standing on a trap door which I knew led into underground chambers and tunnels and vaults, some of which were used for human sacrifice.

A place of worship and a place of extreme torture – dark and light! I shivered! I fled – and found a bench around the corner, where I quietly proceeded to do massive energy clearing work with the help of all the Ascended Hosts, especially with Archangel Azrael coming in to collect all the stuck souls there. And I had to release so many – poor and miserable creatures!

Slowly but surely the feminine energy returned and balance was restored, as pure unconditional love and peace moved in and I felt a great burden lift off me.

I was taken to the left hand side of the cathedral and noticed many incredibly interesting things here:

On the right hand side of the high altar etched into the very ancient building stones. I found these details. Notice what appeared to be an altar, or a box with symbols on it and from this issued spiralling energy forming a type of sun disc above. The figure on the left hand side, holds a staff with a coiled serpent spiralling around it. Notice his interesting head gear. The figure on the right appears to be female with her hand resting on the box. Her other hand holds a rose. Next to her leg, is something that resembles a chalice. On both sides of the box, I noticed spiralling energy or serpents and the same spiralling energy coiling around the pillar, or tube connecting the box with the disc. Some kind of fire or energy is flowing from the top of the disc.

I was reminded that the Knight Templars had been the architects and builders of this church, and it could well be that they deliberately placed this stone next to the high altar, under everyone's noses, depicting a very ancient reason that this site was so sacred, because it stands on the Goddess Serpent Energy site, and what is depicted is the truth about this place, this site, although it is encrypted.

On the opposite side, the whole wall is dedicated to Mother Mary and the female Saints. A strange thing happened when I was trying to photograph this, as I experienced a deep connection with the Divine Feminine there. Indeed I felt myself surrounded by her energy!

I was photographing the wooden frame above, when suddenly I felt the Goddess energy entering, and look what transpired in this photo. I was astounded

*Figure 9. Altar with symbols.*

*Figure 10. High altar.*

when I downloaded the pictures – for I had no idea that this had happened! Yet, notice the pale blue light and pinks. I also smelt the distinct perfume of roses!

Interestingly, I had to heal two women afterwards with a gathering audience in the middle of the (hidden) labyrinth. A woman was standing there, as I was waiting for a chance to enter, when I moved into an altered state, and began to beam healing energy into her through my hands. I had never done this in my life before, in a public place no less, and with a rapidly growing audience, but I was so filled with deep, unconditional love and I was feeling the Divine Feminine working through me in a very potent manner. In fact she was crying as she entered the circle when her whole being changed and she completely lit up. Afterwards she thanked me profusely, explaining that she had just gone through a tough divorce, and had just received instant and total healing.

Another woman who had sat watching this all, approached me next, and asked me to work with her as well, so I did on more of an energetic level.

Afterwards the healed woman and a Korean music teacher and Doctor of Music, who heals with sound sought me out. He was very interested in my energy work, for his inner ears had tuned into heavenly music while I had been working on her. She was a colour healer from Brittany! When I stood in the middle of the labyrinth, she saw light blue Goddess Energy surrounding me! Indeed, the photos confirm this. She was really interested in my tour of France, and the energy healing.

Chartres will never be the same again, and I am sure that those who congregated around me at that time, sensed that at a soul level. I was in a truly altered state when healing, merely an instrument used by much higher hands.

It took massive energy work moving around the cathedral a few times for I had to dislodge darkness from deep underground, creatures and things that defy description.

*Figure 11. Illumined High altar.*

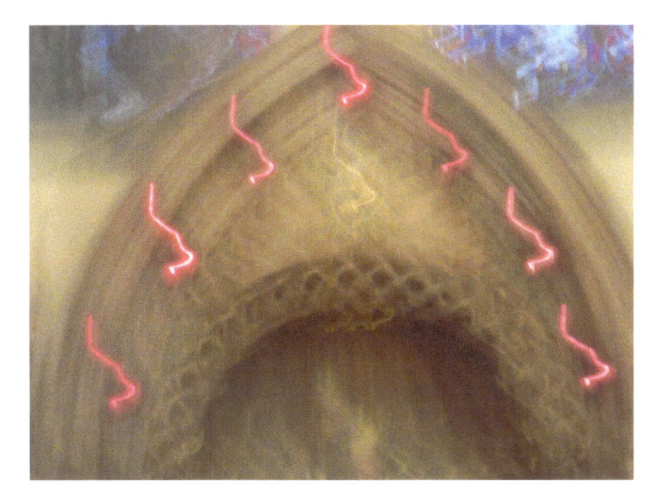

*Figure 12. Goddess energy entering.*

*Figure 13. Woman I gave healing to.*

*Figure 14. Me in the centre of the labyrinth.*

*Figure 15. Beautiful cathedral windows.*

Yet, miracles occurred there too, there was a beautiful balance, which led to a state of equilibrium which we both felt as we left the cathedral.

We found a most exquisitely decorated restaurant for lunch and to my amazement I noticed the following map on their wall, depicting the Knights Templar! Coincidence? No! All by grand design!

The next morning I slept in as I was exhausted from jet lag. I was told to rest and to stay in the hotel under the radar.

Then Mary Magdalene appeared to me just as Susan Kerr had foretold.

She will now be with me constantly, with so many others, to protect, guide me, and show me the way as the truth is revealed. She thanked me for doing the work and blessed me.

All is being prepared.

All is working.

Everything is coming together.

As it should.

Aysis-Ra-A-Hu-A-Ra.

*Figure 17. Entrance to one of the Doors.*

*Figure 16. Map showing Knights Templar.*

* * *

CHAPTER 5

# Jeanne d'Arc makes herself known

Following closely the route as demarcated by my higher guidance, long before I even set foot in France, the third leg of the journey now moved on to Orleans.

The vision of Chartres once having been linked with Orleans via a huge serpent-like mound or energy centre, fascinated me. If so, it must have been buried very deep underground, as this part of France was very flat with some rolling hills, but again I received confirmation that during the time of Avalon, this had not been the case.

The train journey to Orleans was pleasant, albeit a new experience for me, as I had two suitcases packed to the brim, and dragging them around onto and off trains proved to be challenging at times! I welcomed our hired car in Orleans, and so enjoyed watching the green and lush landscape flashing by, interspersed with train stations, towns and villages.

We arrived at the hotel and were having a lovely lunch outside when suddenly, out of the blue, Jeanne d'Arc appeared. She blessed and welcomed us to the town she had saved from the English. It came as quite a surprise to have this happen right there, but Kristina seemed to take it all in her stride, for which I was very grateful. She is very psychic herself and extremely sensitive to energies, hence they had brought us together for this trip.

Jeanne's message was crystal clear: "*Go to Blois Castle, and I will guide you to where you need to go, within the castle.*" Why Blois and not Orleans? Interesting!

*Figure 1. Orleans.*

*Figure 3. Some of the medieval and more modern structures we saw.*

In the late afternoon we took a stroll along the river, and I loved the medieval structures, mixed with the more modern ones. In addition, the ancient bridges were fascinating, with a unique charm. In my country we do not have any structures as old as this, and it creates a certain degree of timelessness and continuity, which I really appreciated.

I found the Blois connection very interesting, for obviously the energy work that needed to be done, would be done mainly there, and less in Orleans. Yet, I somehow had to be there in order to knit it all together. But why Blois castle?

On the 13 August 2016 Kristina and I drove from Orleans to Blois[1] – and I immediately recognized the Blois Castle.[2]

Jeanne, was then joined by Mary Magdalene, Sarah her daughter and Anne of Brittany. By the time we arrived, we had a whole entourage of these women, guiding us all the way. I was intrigued.

In fact we were urged to go to this castle, because it was directly linked with Jeanne's own story, and the

*Figure 2. Orleans riverside.*

family lineage she was born into, which had never been revealed. She told me that she was not a peasant as history had documented, but rather the illegitimate daughter of the Count of Blois, the King's Brother, and indeed she was older than has been recorded. She

---

1  Jeanne had promised to be with us, and indeed she was.
2  The medieval castle was purchased in 1391 by Louis I, Duke of Orléans, brother of Charles VI; after Louis' assassination, his widow, Valentina Visconti, retired to this castle at Blois. It was later inherited by their son, Charles d'Orléans the poet, who was captured at Agincourt and imprisoned in England. After twenty-five years as a hostage in England, Charles d'Orleans returned to his beloved Blois and partly helped rebuild the chateau as a more commodious dwelling. It became the favourite royal residence and the political capital of the kingdom under Charles' son, King Louis XII. Wikipedia.

*Figure 4. Orleans.*

*Figure 5. Jeanne d'Arc.*

*Figure 6. Blois Castle.*

*Figure 7. Inside the castle museum.*

was the Dowager Queen's daughter, and thus sister to Charles (who was the "Dauphin", meaning heir), who was soon to be crowned King and she supported him. Her mother, the Queen, secretly made sure that she was educated, even though she was given away at birth into foster care. Due to potentially dangerous circumstances, her true royal birth was carefully hidden, and actually her father was assassinated because of her parent's ongoing love affair. The Count never openly acknowledged her, although many people knew about her. Thus, she rallied to aid her Dauphin brother, as there was an unholy dispute over the French crown. She attended the Mystery Schools, and experienced multiple visions, which legend has recorded, as she was an open transmitter channel.

The first displays in the Museum at the castle captivated me as well as the spirals all over, swans, Sun Discs, and intriguing etchings in stone. Much of it must have been very ancient, probably dating back to the Celtic Gauls. I was fascinated to find that what I had discovered in Chartres, was present here as well. In fact it made so much sense, for by

PART 1: CHAPTER 5: JEANNE D'ARC MAKES HERSELF KNOWN

*Figure 8. Etchings in stone.*

*Figure 9. Museum exhibit.*

then what had once been known and understood as the serpent (spiralling) energy, with its uses by the Ancient Druids, was now totally lost and absent and only used for decorative purposes understood as the serpent (spiralling) energy with its uses by the Ancient Druids, was now totally lost and absent, only used for decorative purposes. Or maybe, not? I had a deep sense that this family held bloodline secrets, and was most enthralled by what I later discovered! I was enjoying myself, the Super Sleuth in me now fully awakened, and I had found an ally in Kristina!

The design had more curves and other elements to it, but it most certainly reflected essentially the same message I had found in Chartres. A coincidence? No! To me this irrevocably linked Chartres and Blois Castle together, and thus I knew that I would be called upon to do energy work here.

In what was said to be the King's room, I found quite a few ghosts like these ones which appeared when I took this photo. It was here that I found a painting called Adonis which fascinated me, as it seemed so symbolic. In the far right corner the castle of Foix appears, and note the two swans! I was travelling along multiple timeline strands here, and to me this painting was knitting the timelines together:

*Figure 10. Ghost like figures appeared.*

*Figure 11. Painting with ghosts and swans.*

*Figure 12. Equisite stained glass windows.*

*Figure 13. Burgundy dress.*

Jeanne d'Arc, Mary Magdalene, and Cécile de Foix! Marie of Orleans, born 19 December 1457, indeed married Jean of Foix, in 1476. Anne of Britany, was the child of Margaret of Foix, born in 1488. So here again, the Foix family was making itself known, as they indeed became the French monarchs. This is an important link in the story that is about to unfold, as this connects them directly to the Cathars, to the family of Foix, and the hidden secrets of the noble families of the Pyrenees.

To me this painting was not only a confirmation that I was indeed being led to the right places on my French journey, but what they were showing me energetically was one and the same, but with multiple strands. A holographic, compound, tiered picture was slowly but surely emerging, and I had to trust the process.

It was then that the exhibit led us into the Queen's Chambers, where I was riveted by my discovery, finding the self-same symbols carved into the furniture everywhere! I was reeling! Someone had done their utmost to preserve the hidden history of the family in the intricate designs!

Jeanne d'Arc now made her presence felt, and guided me into the Queen's small adjacent prayer

*Figure 14. Beautiful furniture with the Caduceus.*

room, and told me that this is where she had met her (real) mother, and where she had secretly been anointed by her, and by the secret inner members of the hidden Orders! Indeed, Jeanne had stayed here in the castle, prior to leaving for the Battle of Orleans.

The prayer room had a wonderful energy about it, and the stained glass windows were exquisite. Each window depicted the Goddess in her many forms and expressions, again laden with symbols:

> Notice the red dress. The ancient High Priestess wore burgundy red dresses, which depicted their rank, especially if they belonged to the Sisterhood of the Rose. Note also the Roses held in the apron!

I received an intense anointing there in that room, from Jeanne, Mary Magdalene, Anne of Brittany, and others.

According to history, Jeanne was born on the 6th January 1412 and burnt at the stake by the English (who wanted the French Crown for themselves) on 30th May 1431. However Jeanne told me that she was about 21 years old then, which brings into question her true date of birth. The noble families often gave children

*Figure 15. Our tour in the horse drawn carriage.*

born out of wedlock away, so she being entrusted to others at birth was not unusual.

The noble women never nursed their babies, but employed wet nurses from the very outset. When one reads the history of the happenings around the Count of Blois and his mistress the Queen of France, then understanding dawns. Indeed, their affair caused the Count to be assassinated, as his brother the King, was indeed insane and had been so for years. There were further bizarre events exacerbating these strange circumstances, such as the 100-year war between France and England over the same throne, and the ensuing political intrigue, which must have been quite something! It also made sense to me why the English were so keen to get rid of Joan – for a peasant would be no threat to them, however the Queen's daughter would!

This is the oldest part of the Castle, where I picked up the energy lines and knitted those of Blois and Chartres, with those of Foix and Monségur, plus Versailles and Paris. The first triangle was now complete!

I was most intrigued to discover the following beautifully decorated piece of furniture in that room: Note the Caduceus, the serpent and spiralling energy, and the lute. All pointed directly to the Secret lineage of women, who held the secrets within themselves, and served the Goddess.

Cecile (as me) had come full circle. Through losing her third child Roger, to her own brother, who had forcefully adopted him (according to tradition held in the Pyrenees, the ancestral lines went through the women), her own lineage and descendants, from more than 200 years later, would anoint her in the prayer room at Blois Castle. Astounding!

My soul's gratitude knew no bounds. We will come to Cecile's story a little later …

A beautiful golden energy now prevailed, as we proceeded to wander through the rest of the castle, but found that only one section housed the Museum. On approaching the official castle chapel, I felt a distinct sense of unease. I sensed some very strange, dark energy emanating from within, and refused to enter, but rather sought out the open spaces with a wonderful view over the city.

We later went for a charming tour of the city in a horse-drawn carriage, and that just ended a very blessed and amazing day!

As we returned to our hotel in Orleans, we went for another stroll and a late dinner. I loved the ambiance there, and my passion for architecture was stimulated by the contrast of old and new, with medieval houses and buildings often adjoining modern shopping centres.

The encounter with Joan of Arc was certainly one I will never forget, especially the anointing in the crown room. To me that room had such beautiful and peaceful energy, which I had not felt anywhere else in the castle, and it had come as a complete surprise.

Without a doubt, I found Joan of Arc in the most unexpected places in the rest of France, and in churches, where she would always be depicted with one knee bare, which confirmed that she was a high initiate. France holds many mysteries and frequently, what they wished to hide, was placed right under people's noses – hidden in plain sight!

*\*\**

CHAPTER 6

# The High Order of the Bards

I began to connect more and more easily to the French countryside, as we drove west from Orleans to Carnac. It was just as well that I was a passenger, as my entire body periodically shook from head to toe, when I was tuning into the energy lines and fields of the areas we were travelling through. I read the landscape in multi-dimensional forms, thus tapping into what had existed before. One could say, I was remote-viewing the land in its previous state, tuning into the different vibrational frequency bands. I was multi-viewing in other words, as I always did when travelling into new areas. When we arrived in Brittany this perception expanded, as I was now truly entering the 7th dimensional state, and what had once been Avalon.

The traces of the Celtic races are more noticeable here, for the land itself links to the sacred centres, which have now sunk into the Atlantic Ocean. Additionally, I started to feel the presence of the Druids in a very potent way!

It was here that they had used their voices (singing, instruments, chanting, etc.) and sound technology to perform higher healing through music and the oratory

*Figure 1. Map of the area.*

arts, like poetry, in conjunction with the spiraling energy and the elixir of life itself! They knew how to engage the human voice in rounds, using vowels accompanied by string and percussion instruments, with the Uilleann pipes and Bagpipes which they invented, and additionally the harp, which was sacred to them. This city housed one of the greatest High Druidic Schools for Druid Training, on a very high spiraling energy spot.

Today this city is hidden and forgotten.

It was this immense energy which I had picked up from afar, before I tuned into it.

We turned off to a place where there were buildings between vineyards and a sign pointing to a golf course and restaurant. Who would put a golf course in the middle of a forested area and vineyards and why?

We found an ancient forlorn, dilapidated building, next to the restaurant, and parked alongside some oaks. I immediately tuned into what seemed to be a ruined chapel across the road on the far side of the restaurant, and told Kristina that was where we needed to do the energy work.

In as much as I was tuning into the City of the Bards, the surrounds had a neglected and abandoned feeling, despite the presence of a restaurant and golf course. I immediately sensed that the buildings were not supposed to be there, for the Ancient Ones would want to prevent anyone from building on their sacred sites!

We decided to have lunch first, as we had come a long way and still had some distance to travel before we reached Carnac.

When we sat down, I had to smile when I saw the young waiter as he looked like a Bard! Indeed, it was as if he had stepped out of the City of the Bards, but in modern day clothing!

We asked him for the name of this place and nearly fell off our chairs when he said: "The Place of the Bards!", as he translated the Breton name into English. Wow! This was the most powerful confirmation of what I had been tuning into. The next question was why a golf course had been built there.

We asked him what had happened and were told that the residence had originally belonged to an estate with a Château, which had burnt down time and again, and the ruins we first saw were all that remained of the original stables, and across the road was the empty shell of the chapel. Eventually the penny dropped that this was sacred ground, as the ancient groves were guarded by the Druids and Ancient Ones (of course they did not know that), and so it was decided to rather turn the place into a golf course. The fires then ceased, as people finally got the message, and were wise enough to build the golf course, AROUND these most sacred sites and not to invade them. The Guardians and Keepers of the Druids allowed only the restaurant and golf course to continue to remain – anything else would just either burn down or residents would get spooked out!

Ahh, you do not mess with the Druidic High Orders and the sacred City of Gold! I thought it was very funny!

*Figure 2. Dilapidated building.*

*Figure 3. The waiter.*

PART 1: CHAPTER 6: THE HIGH ORDER OF THE BARDS

*Figure 4. Neglected building on sacred ground.*

We had a delicious lunch before walking towards the chapel and the forested area behind, where I was being called upon to go and do the energy work. I was surrounded by the Druids in their droves from the moment we stepped out of the car, and then they flocked around us. Kristina loved the chapel ruins and went inside, but I was being escorted further along and shown exactly where the energy fields were and where to stand.

I was now tuning into the Golden City and was shown that this site linked up with the energy lines from Orleans/Blois/Chartres to Carnac and the Pyrenees. It was a major centre for it was right on the golden energy Sun Path Lines and therefore through music, song, and sound frequency technology, along with the spiralling energy, this had been a place of immense power and importance. It had been a vibrant Golden/Green City and a happy place. The Guardian and Keepers wore golden breastplates with the spiral emblem pinned to the cloak over their shoulders, both men and women. They wore huge golden torques and a golden circlet on their heads, with the same spiral etched into the gold, with spiralling earrings. They were very tall, with blond to auburn hair with a reddish tint, and blue, green, and hazel/brown eyes.

The High Priestess wore a golden Torque with the same spiral and serpent upper arm bracelets which

*Figure 5. Kristina in the chapel ruins.*

77

*Figure 6. Beautiful surrounds.*

depicted her rank. She wore a circlet around her head, which was inscribed with the Caduceus sign, as she held the serpent energy.

I was then told to proceed with the energy work which they would amplify by adding their collective energy. I stood there behind the chapel and faced the forested area, as I now had to totally dissolve into the spiralling energy fields in order to direct this energy to Carnac to open up the energy lines from here. The Druids encircled me, and brilliant orb-like light danced in the trees, green-golden. Thousands gathered around me, dressed in white robes. We were reactivating what had been sealed off millions of years ago when Avalon fell, and after we had completed the work, there was much dancing, singing, and rejoicing.

I wanted to linger at this very special place, but Carnac was calling and we had to continue with our journey.

*Figure 7. Golden energy.*

To my amusement when we drove off, we now had passengers in the backseat, as three of the High Druids had joined us for the remaining trip to Carnac!

My head was spinning as I was trying to integrate everything that happened, while Kristina was driving.

The Standing Stones were waiting for us …

\* \* \*

CHAPTER 7

# Opening of the Star Gate at Carnac

Before we embark on the next phase of this journey, we need to pause for one moment and go back in time to what was once Avalon.

Avalon arose from the remnants of the Lion Kingdom, where Carnac now stands, offshore from the coast of Brittany, where there once was a massive pyramid and mound, a standing circle complex which was without a doubt the powerhouse, the energetic capital of Avalon.

It housed one of the Druidic Headquarters, linked directly to branches in Versailles, and other Headquarters in the Pyrenees, in Delphi and also in what is now Vancouver and New York. The Atlantic Ocean was not as extensive as it currently is, indeed, there were inland lakes and seas, but no oceans. The entirety of this area included parts of Britain, Scotland and Ireland.

Its sister colony of Avalon, and one of the Seven Headquarters lay further up in what is now the North Sea, adjacent to Norway and Sweden. This formed what in my Soul Readings, is often referred to as

*Figure 1. Churchill Hotel, Carnac.*

the Nordic Kingdom, and a part of the 7 Kingdoms which incorporated Avalon.

We will pause at the Command centre for one moment. It has sunk offshore from Carnac and Brittany, which once assimilated the Alchemy Mystery School Branch of the High Druidic Orders, the 7 Crystal Pyramids of Sound Alchemy, and the huge serpent mounds, one of which we have already

79

encountered between Chartres and Orleans. These reflect those found in the USA, as said – that part was a section of the main continent which had not as yet separated.

The standing stones at Carnac are just the tips of a series of massive temple domes that protruded with the largest crystalline dome, long since destroyed and gone. They stretched far out – indeed most have either been buried under sand or sea. There were 7 domes, each equipped with liquid crystal tubes, or tube-like structures, which worked with the crystalline and sound energy technology. Each cylindrical feature of these massive sound chambers, worked together with the 33 sound octaves, as held in the Spinal Column of the Earth. So, these 7 domes worked in unity, to reflect the sections of the 33 sound octaves, utilizing the principles of sacred geometry, with the sanctified number sequences and mathematics.

As each octave of sound was held within a Tetragrammaton of sound, it worked much as the one (from a total of 33) that people remember: Yod Hay, Vod Hay, the Sacred Name of the Divine.

When the enormous catastrophe of an invasion befell Avalon, which will be expanded upon in detail in later chapters, huge destructive explosions totally remodelled the entire landscape. The Pyramid Temples and most of the serpent mounds disappeared under the sea, as land masses were ripped off, forming the new Continent of North America, while the visible remaining standing stones at Carnac, were covered with granite layers, created from molten earth. The original liquid crystal is still within them, but crystallized underground. So, each of these standing stones visible above the ground, still vibrate to sound, and the sacred geometrical original layout is still in place in the etheric.

I literally had to reactivate an ancient holographic energy field, which the ancients were able to tap into, step into, and actually command to manifest whatever they set their intentions on, in the physical reality. Likewise, they could teleport themselves, or shapeshift into any chosen form. It all worked with sacred geometrical principles, with the core sciences of Mathematics, Physics and most importantly Alchemy.

The standing stones themselves are but a remnant of something much vaster. Remember that the original Stonehenge-like stone circle stood at Versailles with the Sun Temples. Carnac links to that, and directly to the Pyrenees. They are 7th dimensional, and thus work on incredible high energy fields, using science which we do not have access to at this time, but will regain as we evolve.

Here then is the account of that journey:

Arriving in Carnac after some delay, as we had got lost, we finally found the Winston Churchill Hotel. When booking our accommodation online, the name of that hotel had attracted me most, as I had no idea that the Churchill family-owned property there. Subsequently my room was directly adjacent to their original house, and it somehow felt a little like home, since Churchill had been a war correspondent in South Africa, during the Anglo-Boer War.

JOURNAL ENTRY

**16 August 2016: Carnac**
We arrived in Carnac last night at the Hotel Churchill around 8 pm, and to my utter surprise I was told that my room had been upgraded – and I had a whole, huge apartment with a magnificent view over the ocean.

It felt like a miracle, indeed!

The next morning after a good night's rest, I was called into action immediately at the site where we had found the first of the Standing Stones in Carnac at the very beginning of our trip. First of all, in the parking lot, we found the familiar Sentinel Stone which is the Guardian and Keeper, and asked permission to open up the massive Star Gate and energy lines, in order to do the work.

I had to provide the keys and codes, which had been given to me back home in South Africa, and also used at Versailles, and I was then allowed to proceed. This stone was marked in ancient symbols, which will stay hidden to those not tuned in, who cannot "see" for they in truth, are blind. Adjacent to it stood the remains of a very ancient oak tree overgrown with ivy, which held sacred wisdom.

In Carnac these residual standing stones – dolmens – are right next to a busy road, fenced off with locked gates, so we were unable to enter. The very narrow pavements are situated between the fence and the extremely busy road, so I had to stand in the blazing sun, with continuous heavy traffic to do the energy work, in full view of everyone passing. In addition to this, it was a Public Holiday which increased traffic congestion and visitors to the site!

"If you want me to do the work here, then you'd better help me!" was my silent prayer.

I was shown that these Standing Stones work like the mechanisms of a clock, and when activated together, they open up the Star Gate Portal (Figure 3).

First of all, there are 3 Standing Stones standing next to the Sentinel Stone, and in alignment. One is the High Priestess and she works with the others. They all have markings on them (Figure 4).

1. The first had the same Central Sun marking etched into it, therefore was the key that unlocked all.
2. The second was the door which acted as a conduit to amplify the energy of 1.
3. The third was the mechanism which swung the wheels of the giant clockwork into action

Note: The Clockwork here is the holographic energy pattern, as described in detail above.

I had the feeling that the same alignment repeated itself in the forest – carefully hidden from sight and it could even have been underground.

I immediately identified the largest of the standing Stones as the Goddess Stone and therefore the chief wheel in the holographic energy field, which activated the others.

I was told to move the energies, after I had activated the field, from LEFT TO RIGHT, thus from standing stones 1 to 2 to 3.

Therefore, I then concentrated on first activating the spiralling energy to bring down the Green/Gold Fires from the 7th Central Sun to anchor them in.

*Figure 2. Note the massive face on the right-hand side.*

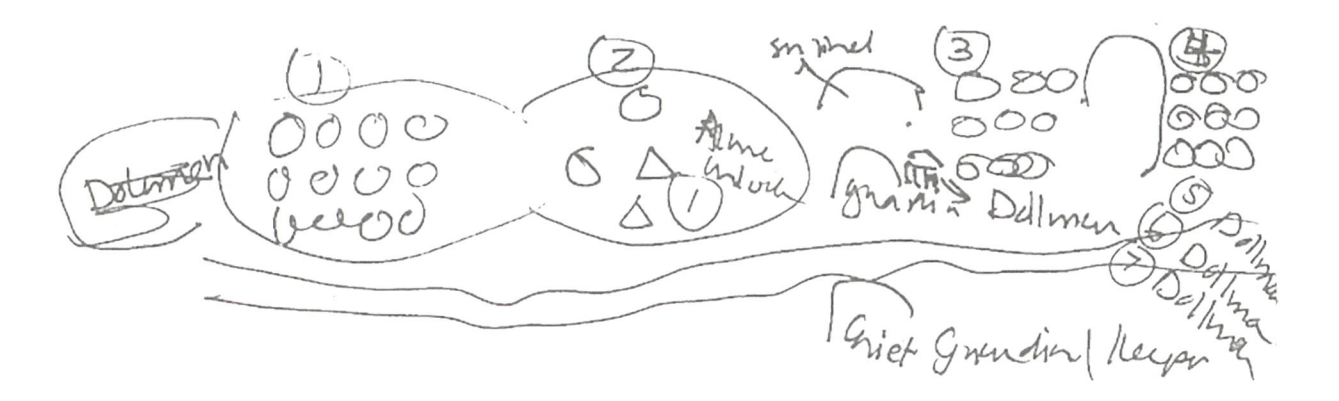

*Figure 3. The 3 Standing Stones next to the Sentinel Stone.*

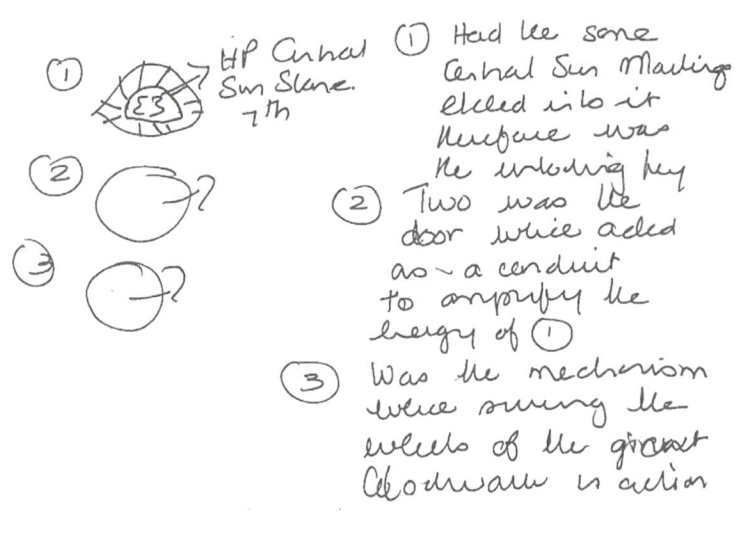

FRANCE: THE SECRET KNOWLEDGE OF MARY MAGDALENE, THE CATHARS, TEMPLARS AND AVALON

*Figure 4. Standing Stones standing next to the Sentinel Stone.*

*Figure 5. Standing Stone.*

*Figure 6. The Mother.*

*Figure 7. Druids around the Mother Stone.*

When they were anchored into the Goddess Stone, the whole entourage of the High Orders of the Bards, Druids, Archangels, Elohim, and Elohim Councils, and the Cosmic Hierarchy, moved in and surrounded and were interspersed among the stones, now adding their energies to that of Kristina's and mine.

Gradually all the Standing Stones became alive again with massive energy fields and slowly but surely the mechanisms of the clockwork started revving up causing the movement of the energies from left to right to begin. The energy moved into place slotting in as needed.

Then pure blinding green and gold fire poured down, and a huge celebration ensued, as the first mechanisms were freed and fully re-activated!!!!

The main stone was the Mother. The Druids gathered and encircled this massive stone, assisting me to move the energy. The area was filled with them, in long white robes. I literally felt myself being lifted into intensely high energy fields, as the energy started to move as directed, in powerful ways.

Look at the next photo, which shows how the camera picked up on some Druids, without my knowing. You can clearly see the white figures around the Mother Stone, filling the entire area. Note that the Ancient Druids were very tall, indeed they were giants.

Interestingly enough, this was not the only time that this happened on my journey. As I shifted into a much higher dimensional state to do the work, the camera followed suit!

I was working at a very busy intersection in the blazing hot sun. After the completion of the first section, we moved the car to the next section, and found some shade in an ancient walled grove, once again next to the busy road, separating us from the standing stones, as well as a fence. I immediately noticed two dolmens which were across the road from me, plus gigantic standing stones.

---

We moved the car to a side street next to an ancient grove. We were told to go into the shade and to do the work next to an old stone wall – the exact replica of those I had found in Mauritius!!!

I found the Sentinel Rock here – it was the only one of the Standing Stones which still had its original red-gold colour!!! It acted as a Marker between the Guardian Stone for the middle of the first section, and also the Dolmen guarding this. Again, I was given permission only after having given the keys and codes, and then I worked from left to right, as the energies of 1 now moved into 2.

Note the sentinel stone in the middle with distinct marking on it. It is the only stone that has retained its original golden colour!

In that regard, I asked for extra shielding and the cloak of invisibility and after massive energy work that was also cleared. Kristina and I were obscured from the public eyes, by the stone wall, and went more or less unnoticed. Every now and again a car would stop in the shade next to ours, to be moved again by the Cosmic Hierarchy.

Next there were two sphinxes guarding the portal above and I was given permission to proceed. The next instant immense lightning bolts of energy were coursing through me! By this time they had moved us deeper into the grove and we were protected by the walls and out of sight. The fires came down and now all the clockworks opened up with the assistance of our Helpers. Half the work had been accomplished and I was told that we needed to have lunch to replenish our energies as the 3rd part would be opened remotely from a different location!

---

*Figure 8. Standing Stones.*

*Figure 9. Sentinel Stone.*

*Figure 10. Another view of the stone.*

We were now sitting snuggly behind a stone wall in the grove, hidden from view. I took this photo from where I sat doing the energy work. Note the dolmen in direct alignment.

What fascinated me when doing this work, was the way the energy of all the standing stones, the dolmens and indeed the different sections of the massive Star Gate machine that encompasses Carnac, link up and work together, like cogs in an enormous wheel. As the energy activated and flowed through them, they came alive, filled with sound and light frequencies, which gave them the appearance of being see-through and dancing and swirling.

The whole energetic field transformed into a single spiral, connected directly with the Crystal Pyramid energy under the sea, which was still held by the Islands offshore from the Coast of Brittany.

Whoever first put these into place, knew exactly what they were doing, as this site undoubtedly links to megalithic sites all over world. They all work in unison, tuned into one another like a giant machine, into the Crystalline Energy Grids, and thus the Web of Life itself.

I sensed that one could indeed easily teleport oneself from here, travelling anywhere in the galaxies, and on planetary levels, as well as shapeshifting into any desired form. Assuredly, this was a most sacred and holy place!

*Figure 11. Horizontal view of a collection of Standing Stones.*

## JOURNAL ENTRY

It was lunch time, and we were both very tired, hot and hungry. Where could we find a restaurant here? We followed our noses down a trail, near where we were sitting and sure enough, we were led to a restaurant nearby. To our utter surprise we found a Buddhist-type Feng Shui Garden, and a restaurant with Goddess statues, and also those of Shiva and Shakti.

The lunch was outstanding gourmet food – such a treat after all that energy work in the burning hot sun.

We then passed the last standing stones intending to go to a sheltered spot in the forest, recommended by the receptionist, but it was overcrowded.

It was here that I found the most interesting stone situated in the garden of a home, next to the restaurant. It must have been moved there, away from the others and had immensely powerful energy emanating from it!

We tried to find the right spot to continue the work, as we had now discovered the giant stones, while walking along. I found the energy lines here to be very powerful, but there was nowhere suitable, as by now the place was flooded with tourists, and congested traffic.

We were led further away, to a dolmen hidden between houses, in what remained of the forest in a grove, and so we did the final work from there! I immediately tuned into all the holographic energy fields, and was able to do the work totally unobserved! Indeed, I was shaking from head to toe, and if I had not been sitting down, I would have keeled over!

The Star Gate now swung open!

However, we were exhausted – doing intensive energy work in the sweltering heat was no joke! After having a refreshing shower, I fell into bed and slept soundly.

We left quite late that morning, and were led to another dolmen (they all link up in a sacred geometrical pattern) on the left-hand side of the road, and there I found a whole collection of Menhirs and Dolmens and underground chambers!!

*Figure 12. Stone found next to the restaurant.*

*Figure 13. This stone caught my attention.*

*Figure 14. Stones all in alignment.*

*Figure 15. Dolmen.*

*Figure 16. Dolmens.*

When I was doing the energy work, standing on a massive rock facing the dolmen, a couple arrived, and nonchalantly sat themselves down on the sacred rocks. My helpers quickly moved them away, but the man kept barging in and I felt it was very deliberate! In fact, he was in real danger of disintegrating, as his body could not hold the high energy vibrations I was working with. Yet every time they moved him (the woman had gone away), he would just return. Eventually though the Cosmic Hierarchy removed him, and I was told that he had not asked for permission and had simply intruded.

During this time very powerful energy was coursing through me and being amplified, and it came in wave upon wave. I could barely stand upright. I was told that this opened up the entire clockwork system, with a holographic energy field under the sea, and with the ancient energy lines to the Pyrenees and Monségur, and then also to what is hidden in the 3 rd stone (diagram). This was massive work. I was totally exhausted.

The Star Gate has swung open thus now we are moving South with the energies.

---

We were now on our way to Vannes, where the next adventure awaited us, and where we would stay overnight, before we embarked on our journey to the South of France.

Carnac itself retains only a tiny fraction of what had once been there. It was here the initiates who worked with the high energy and holographic fields had trained to become Druids, undergoing initiations in the highest degrees of competence.

To even become a Druid of the first order took a full 21 years. One could not attain the higher-level ranks without stringent training and initiations, determined by the specific field of the Three High Orders one chose to serve in.

During the time of Avalon, there were the Magicians, the Wizards, the Bards and the High Priestesses and High Priests.

I was most amused to read the following information about another island, Île de Sein, offshore from Brittany, a bit further down the coast:

*"In the days of the Celts, it was the home of nine female Druids. The geographer Pomponius Mela described their peculiar convent in the mid-first century AD. Since they lived at the end of a solstice line, it was only fitting that they demanded of those who sought their wisdom a degree of navigational skill: "Sena, in the British sea, facing the coast of the Osisimi, is famous for a Gaulish oracle, tended by nine priestesses, who take a vow of perpetual virginity. They are called Gallizenas (Gaulish maidens) and are said to possess the singular power of unleashing the fury of the winds and the seas by incantations, of turning themselves into any animal they choose, of curing what is elsewhere considered incurable, and of knowing and predicting the future. But they reveal the future only to navigators, and only if they deliberately set out to consult them."* (Graham Robb, *The Ancient Paths*)

A remnant of those Priestess Druids who once were there? The island is a vestige of what has sunk under the sea. There is so much here that needs to be retrieved and remembered, but this would have to be for another time, another day. Indeed, I knew then that I would need to continue my work westwards, when the time came. For now, I was being called to the South of France.

\* \* \*

# PART 2

# THE LASTING LEGACY OF THE CATHARS AND THE TEMPLARS

CHAPTER 1

# The Journey to the South of France

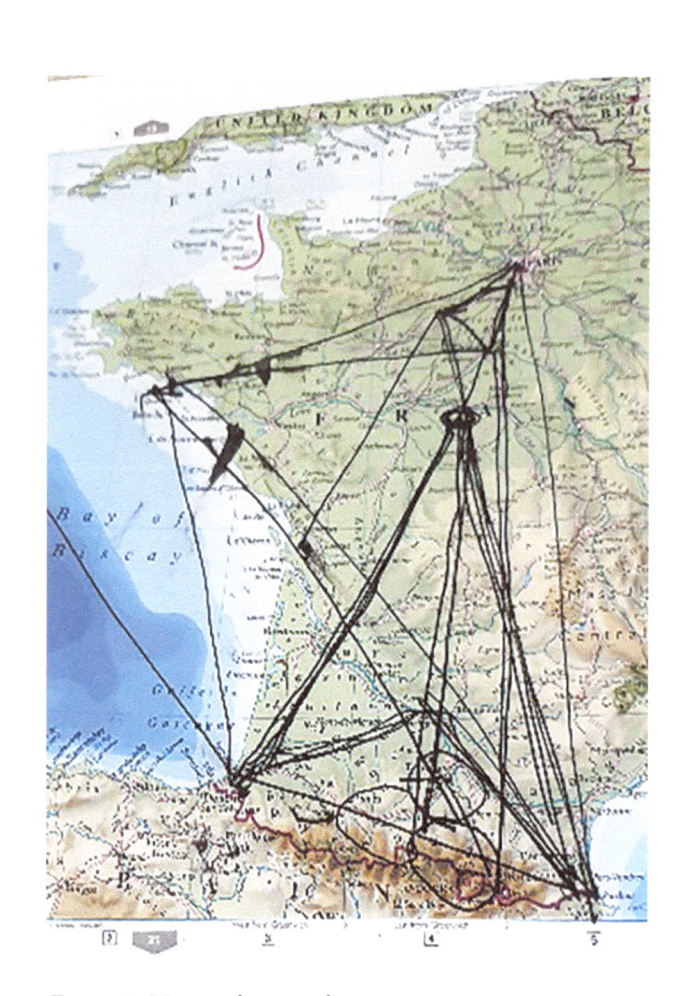

*Figure 1. Map with energy lines.*

I looked at the map of France, and the energy lines I had drawn. The first two triangles were complete now, with the energy work done. I'd had massive downloads of information in all the places I had visited, with the Golden City of the Bards, had come as a complete surprise.

Brittany itself had a certain and cast its spell upon me and I will surely return to these shores. I felt that this would be the starting point of other journeys to the west, for I had already been given a glimpse of the work to follow.

For now, the journey continued, first to Vannes and from there following the coast for a while before moving inland to cross the country to the South of France.

Carnac had been a journey in itself, a journey within a holographic journey, for it was directly linked to Avalon and all that had been lost, and with it the Three High Druidic Orders in their supreme purity. A whole chapter is later devoted to them and their ilk, in the history of Avalon. The Celtic people were a mixture of the two races – the remnant of those left in

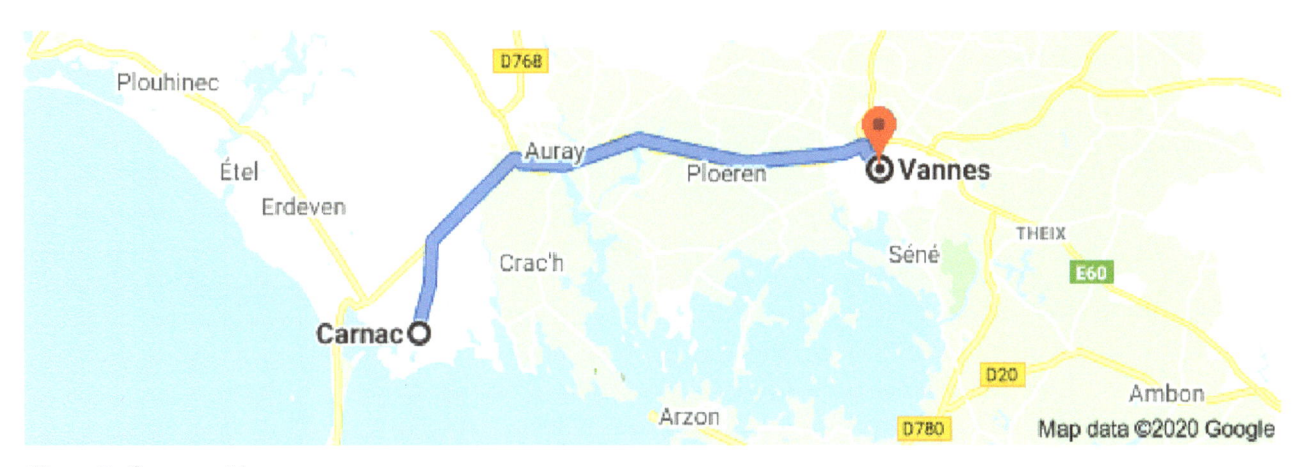

*Figure 2. Carnac to Vannes.*

Avalon, and the ruthless conquerors with whom they were forced to interbreed. The conquerors changed the Druidic Orders forever. They lost their innocence and their purity, and thereafter were known for their brilliance on one hand, but are also remembered for their willing participation in mass murder, and for the practice of human sacrifice.

No one records this better than Julius Caesar himself, when he invaded Gaul. The Romans shuddered at the multiple remnants of sacrifices discovered in villages and elsewhere. Yet the self-same Julius Caesar, discovered a society more advanced than his own, with sophisticated roads, bridges, and communication systems far exceeding that of the Roman army, along with their skills in utilizing sound technology in battle.

They were well versed in science, astronomy, sacred geometry, sound vibrations, and so forth. "The Celtic Druids investigated to the very highest point the Pythagorean philosophy", said Hippolytus of Rome; "they practice divination from 'calculations and numbers by the Pythagorean art'. Celtic art was a scientific attempt to decipher the secrets of creation, 'for offerings should be rendered to the gods by philosophers who are experienced in the nature of the divine and who speak, as it were, the same language as the gods' (Diodorus Siculus[1]). In order to learn that language, they 'conducted investigations and attempted to explain the system of interrelations (or variant text, 'the inner laws') and the highest secrets of nature' (Timagenes[2])." (Graham Robb, *The Ancient Paths*).

They knew of the Sun Paths of Avalon and followed them to the tee, and later migrations of the Celtic Tribes, held to these Sun Paths, and charted them even into the Black Sea areas, Hungary and the Balkans.

The enigma of the Druids with their high science versus their human sacrifices, has its roots in the demise of Avalon. One cannot understand the ultimate truth, if one does not grasp what occurred with the Three High Orders of the Druids, when the invasions began. At no time did Avalon ever have to defend itself, so they had no army, and when they

---

1   Diodorus Siculus or Diodorus of Sicily was an ancient Greek historian. He is known for writing the monumental universal history *Bibliotheca historica*, much of which survives, between 60 and 30 BCE During his life Timagenes wrote a Universal History (until the time of Caesar) and a History of the Gauls. These works did not survive but are known through quotations in other historians.

2   During his life Timagenes wrote a *Universal History* (until the time of Caesar) and a *History of the Gauls*. These works did not survive but are known through quotations in other historians. He was a Greek writer, historian and teacher of rhetoric. He came from Alexandria, was captured by Romans in 55 BC and taken to Rome ).

*Figure 3. Vannes with its beautiful Medievasl Buildings.*

were brutally attacked, they were ignorant of methods of defence (see next chapter on Avalon and the End of Matriarchy).

The history of Southern France is inextricably linked to the fundamental legacy of Avalon and the Lion Kingdom. The Pyrenees themselves bear witness to this, for they hold the most Ancient Source, the Grail, the innocence and purity itself, as carefully hidden …

So the journey South was knitting the two triangles together now – the north and the south. Additionally, it was uniting the ancient hidden secrets and knowledge, as held within the Pyrenees, for they are extremely old, more ancient than ancient, and within them great mysteries lie.

For me it was the journey now back to my own soul memory banks, that of Cecile de Foix and Mary Magdalene, the Cathars, Templars and the Ancient Mystery Schools.

It felt like I was travelling through multiple timeframes and even multiple dimensions, all at once. As the rolling countryside slowly but surely shifted into the more mountainous terrain, and as the Pyrenees drew near, it felt increasingly so as if I was living in different timeframes simultaneously. It was just as well that Kristina was driving, for when I pick up energy lines, I shake from head to toe, and that is when I know that I am on ancient ground, and I'm able to "read" them and transport myself back in time.

## JOURNAL ENTRIES

**Vannes**

We are now in Vannes and this is the beginning of our journey south.

I just had to lie down as soon as we reached the hotel, after doing energy work at the dolmen, before we left Carnac behind on our way here, as recorded in the earlier chapter. They were now working intensely on my energy fields – I had expended so much energy in the last two days that my own energy fields needed to be adjusted and reinforced.

I have been told we now need to travel to Angoulême, and thus will leave early tomorrow morning. We went exploring in this antiquated city, and I just loved this beautiful old fortified town, with its Celtic feel and even found a Celtic curio Shop. It houses Medieval Architecture, lovely castle ramparts and a Marina.[3] It had a charming energy about it and I was delighted with the village squares in between these ancient buildings. Some seemed to lean over, and one almost expected people to appear in medieval dress. I so enjoyed it!

As much as I was entranced by the architecture, Kristina was drawn to the Cathedral which was squashed between these buildings where someone was playing the organ as we entered, but with strange discordant notes which somehow did not fit the interior nor the ambiance of the church. Indeed, the music was extremely jarring.

The reason we were drawn there was soon revealed, as we discovered a statue of Jeanne d'Arc and I was immediately attracted to the energy there. As I stood there taking photos, I experienced immense energy coursing through me, and I received a crystal-clear message that I was now being anointed with the Pathway of Roses and subsequently the ancient Mystic Rose initiations and that roses would manifest everywhere for us, showering down upon us – meaning that wherever they appeared, the path had opened up and thus would lead deeper into the mysteries, the work I had to do and the intense downloads of information for this book.

Note how her right knee is exposed (Figure 4) – this is the sign of a high initiate and one who has been anointed. This was a profound confirmation of what I had been given in the chapel at the castle in Blois.

As I was tapping into the energy, there was an unusual turn of events. I was busy photographing the column in the middle, which had drawn my attention with its carved symbols – and when I downloaded the pictures much later, to my amazement, I saw that they had been altered by the energy I had felt so intensely!

*Figure 4. Jeanne D'Arc. Note the exposed right knee, which denotes her as a high initiate.*

---

3   A marina is a dock or basin with moorings and supplies for yachts and small boats.

**17 August 2016**

We left Vannes early this morning to go south to Angoulême. We first went down the west coast of Brittany to La Rochelle. Remarkably we found a mound at the place where we had breakfast, and at Kristina's seaside resort where we stopped over.

We noticed something really bizarre along a stretch of the road. We were passing through what looked like a mound cut in half, to make way for the road – but there were huge pillars cut into sheer golden rock, huge megalithic blocks! I was astounded, and begged Kristina to stop, but we were in a no stopping zone on the national highway. How could they carve a road through an historical site? Maybe that was why one was not allowed to stop here?

I felt that the mound had been cut in half. A bit further on, we discovered a little village where some of exactly the same golden blocks appeared to have been used as building material for the local buildings!

We stopped at La Rochelle, where Kristina wanted to swim in the sea. I was called to do some energy work there, in the place where we had just had breakfast. I sat down on a bench, and proceeded with it. I was teleported to Tenerife, the Canary Islands and then Madeira, taking the energy lines I had opened there from Cape Town, passing through Portugal, and then through the South of France (west coast and Atlantic) right up to Vannes and Carnac!

*Figure 5. Figures appeared.*

There were lions there, which had caught my attention in the first place, but then figures appeared as well, and it was downright surreal

We had supper on the square where we had seen the delightful medieval houses, returning to the hotel to prepare for the next stretch of our journey south.

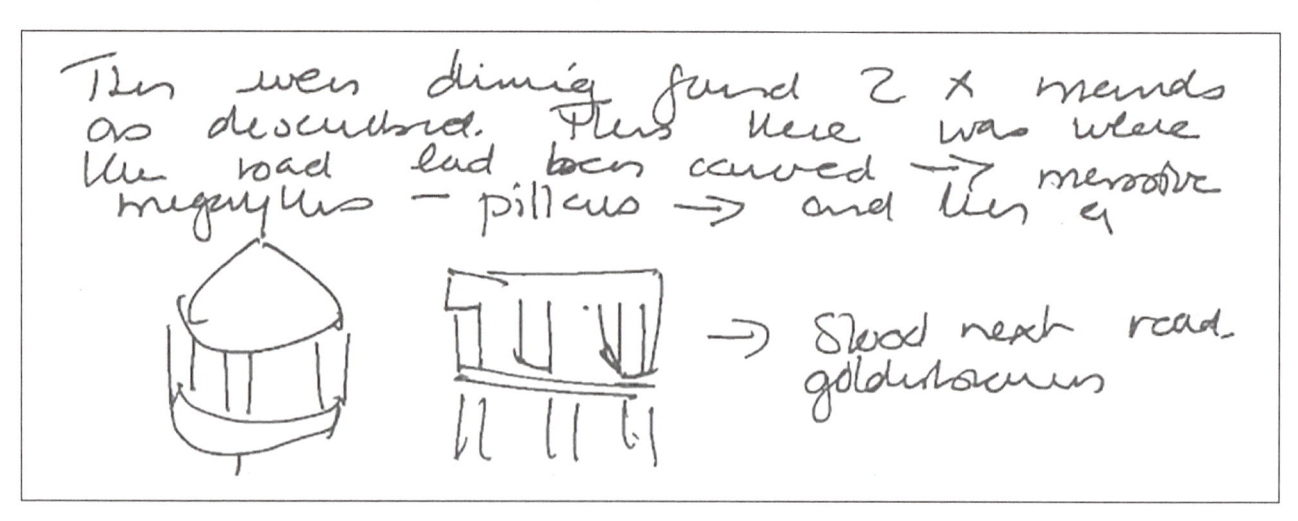

*Figure 6. The mounds cut in half.*

*Figure 7. The white swans on the River Aude.*

*Figure 8. The old manor house.*

All these lines were now being knitted together and reactivated by me! I was like a spider spinning a golden web of energy lines, weaving a sacred geometrical pattern.

A massive pyramid appeared, green-gold and this straddled the unified field, adding in energy lines from the Mediterranean (Malta) to Versailles, Chartres, Blois, Orleans, Carnac, Portugal, and the islands. It was huge!

I was again told everyone would come, like the 12 original Rainbow tribes, from the East, West, North, and South to be lifted now from the 5th to 7th dimension and that those who could not make the move would disintegrate.

From La Rochelle we moved inland driving to the west. Kristina had booked us into an old manor house in Angoulême, next to the River Aude, and to my amazement was filled with white swans. I have never seen so many swans in my life, and to me this was just another sign!

The old manor house, was charming enough and I had a huge four poster bed and en-suite bathroom to myself.

That night however I could not sleep as I became aware of the owner's ancestors, who had never left their home, hanging around the four-poster bed! I first had to release them before I could sleep.

Kristina, who was upstairs, had the same encounters, and slept fitfully too!

The owners were unaware that by inheriting the manor house, they were inheriting all the souls still attached to the place. Even furniture attracts energy, as do all items that one uses in one's personal life!

\*\*\*

CHAPTER 2

# The Fires of Illumination – Occitania

*"I had to span dimensions – I had to become all that
has been before, and is
still to come ...
My soul has come full circle ...
Rise up Illumined Ones!"*
(Judith Küsel – Saturday, 15 September 2018)

As we entered Southern France, following the path of the Aude river, I had a profound sense of homecoming. It felt like I knew every single mountain, hill, rock, tree, river, spring. I was spanning dimensions and timeframes, teleported back and forth, and often had great difficulty grounding myself in the here and now.

Simultaneously I was reading the landscape, picking up the energy lines, reading the trauma and pain so deeply etched in the countryside that in some places, I was often moved to tears.

I had no words to express this.

My soul knew!

For my soul had lived and suffered here. Also, my soul had served in profound ways in this region – where often the pain, the trauma, the suffering had been too great. Therefore I was unable to voice it, or express it in words – I just felt it to the depths of my being.

It was however not just the anguish I felt, but also the remembrance of what was hidden underground within the mountains, that permeated the landscape and energy lines.

It was still there in the rippling waters, in the majestic and sometimes almost surreal Pyrenees peaks. It was etched into the land, and into the very heart of what had once been Occitania, the light within one of the darkest ages of Humanity's history.

It was the land of enlightenment, where women held equal rights and hereditary lines supported identical opportunities for higher education. It was the land of the Troubadours who still belonged to the Ancient High Bardic Orders, and who sang their songs, which even now still haunt this region, resonating through the empty castle walls, rippling through the land.

It is the land of the Knights Templar and the Cathars, who paid the highest price for holding sacred and secret that which they had vowed to never reveal to the uninitiated, or to those who would exploit, or misuse what they held so near and dear. Those secrets

*Figure 1. Map showing Occitania.*

were never disclosed, and will not be, until the Fires of Illumination rise up to a peak once again, when the nucleus of Humanity is finally ready to receive their magnitude.

Moreover, in every single church I entered, I saw Mary Magdalene in the centre of the altar, rather than the usual crucifix. She has not been forgotten, neither has the Divine Feminine, the Goddess herself. Even the unspeakable brutality of the Inquisition, the mass genocide of Occitania, could not kill her, could not stamp her out of existence. Somehow, this region clung onto her, and nowhere is this more apparent than in their churches.

Occitania spanned Southern France and Northern Spain. They had a common language, the Langue D'Oc,[1] and the noble families intermarried, so consequently, the King of Aragon was cousin to the Count of Toulouse and the Count of Foix, as well as the Viscount of Béziers and Carcassonne.

In addition to a common language, they also shared a long history, which they could trace back to Roland, the great hero of the "Song of Roland".[2]

They were indeed the remnant of the Ancient Celtic People in this region, who had even survived the onslaught of the Roman Empire. Certainly, their roots were much older, and they undoubtedly could trace their history to the time before part of that ancient land sunk in the west, along with the setting sun. It has been recorded that the Ancient Celts stood on the west coast, and lamented over their ancient lands that had been lost to the sea.

---

1   Occitan, also known as lenga d'òc by its native speakers, is a Romance language. It is spoken in Southern France, Italy's Occitan Valleys, Monaco, as well as Spain's Val d'Aran; collectively, these regions are sometimes referred to as Occitania. Occitan is also spoken in the linguistic enclave of Guardia Piemontese. Wikipedia The langues d'oïl are a dialect continuum that includes standard French and its closest. Wikipedia

2   The "Song of Roland" is an epic poem based on the Battle of Roncevaux Pass in 778, during the reign of Charlemagne. It is the oldest surviving major work of French literature and exists in various manuscript versions, which testify to its enormous and enduring popularity in the 12th to 14th centuries. Wikipedia

Furthermore, it was from Spain and Gibraltar that the Ancient Sun Paths of the Celts stretched right through France, Britain and Ireland, into the Black Forest, and the Alps, and later the Celts followed them as their tribes grew in numbers, eventually finding their way to the Black Sea.

Yet, the Celtic People had their roots in Ancient Avalon, long before Atlantis, and undeniably in the Lion Kingdom, with the Lion People and their red-haired legacy. Thus the High Druidic Orders were already steeped in the long oral traditions and teachings of their people, for nothing was ever written down.

It is not, as some believed that they were illiterate (indeed, Julius Caesar recorded that they were well versed in Greek), but rather that knowledge was stored in energy fields, and in the standing stones and circles, in a way that is invisible to the naked eye. After all, they came from a long, ancient tradition of alchemists and of wizards, who could literally manifest and dismantle anything at will!

Occitania, in a higher sense was a remnant of ancient knowledge, as the Dark Ages dawned, and was in its own way, light years ahead of the rest of Europe. The people were cultured, and had gleaned their knowledge of sacred geometry, algebra, and maths through the Moorish rulers in Spain and further afield. Truly, some of this knowledge originated in the Ancient Mystery Schools of Egypt, Greece, Haran, in Delphi, Israel, and so on, and of course the most important wisdom of all, was held there in the heartland of Occitania, carefully hidden.

Previously they had already been forced to preserve this knowledge with the advent of the Roman onslaught. The conquerors discovered that a much higher form of civilization already existed within these lands, but they imposed their own ways, exactly as Napoleon later so eloquently stated: "History is always written by the Victor!" The Romans stamped out the higher knowledge, by enforcing their own much lower version of things, by brute force.

*Figure 2. Crusaders.*

Rome had already been superseded by the Greeks, who tended to bring culture and philosophy to the fore wherever they settled, and were much more refined. Then there were the world travellers, the Phoenicians, also a remnant of the Ancient Celtic Race and the Lion Kingdom. Actually, the Romans by this time had travelled down the east coast of Africa and into the Far East, using maps found in Egypt and elsewhere.

The Mediterranean Sea with all its ports, was rife with cross breeding, which actually had existed from ancient times, long before the Roman Empire and long before Ancient Egypt and Greece, which were essentially one and the same when recolonized by the Atlanteans, who established both colonies on the foundations of what had been left of the Lion Kingdom. When Atlantis fell, more of the land sunk under the sea, and thus the inland seas grew into what is now known as the Mediterranean Sea.

Occitania was the hub, the central place, where all these civilizations met and mingled and during the time of Mary Magdalene, Pontius Pilate had a home in that region, as well as none other than King Herod himself! This is very important to remember in the context of what will be revealed, for it shows that there already were Jewish settlements in Occitania, during the Roman occupation.

It was the very fact that Occitanians were so tolerant of both the Jews and the Moors (whom they often employed as scribes and librarians of their vast collections of manuscripts gathered from around the ancient worlds), as mathematicians, architects, engineers, etc. that brought the wrath of the church down on them during the Cathar times and resulted in the third Crusade, and the Albigensian Crusade.[3]

Yet, the Celtic links with Delphi are even more ancient than this, as the Occitanians led an army across Italy and the Alps to the Balkans, and into Delphi, where they laid siege. After a lengthy blockade, they looted the Treasure of Delphi, and returned it to the Pyrenees. It did not bring any glory to its people, however, as many subsequently began to die from strange inexplicable ailments.

The High Druidic Orders were summoned, and pronounced their verdict that the treasure had caused the deaths, and demanded that the entire loot be thrown into a massive lake in the Pyrenees. According to legend, the illness ceased, but all the fish and aquatic life died. The deadly contents within that treasure remain unknown, but it most certainly seemed to have been radioactive, extremely lethal, resulting in death.

The link to Delphi emerges time and again, as none other than Pythagoras himself was apparently at Monségur as a High Priest, and also in Delphi, as a High Druid, who established his very own Mystery School in Italy.

This confirmed that Delphi and the Oracle were linked to Occitania, and that the Celtic Race had already traversed the two regions. In addition, remember that, as stated elsewhere, there were 7 Mystery Schools in Ancient times and their students travelled among all of them. Mary Magdalene, notably was born in Occitania, and was an initiate in the Mystery Schools in the Monségur region, before she went to Egypt, and then onto the Essene Community in what is now Israel. She returned to Occitania, to establish her own ministry. Jesus later joined her, they had five children, their first born were twins, and their son remained in Egypt and never went to France. He later travelled to the Himalayas where he died.

Mary and Jesus taught in the Mystery Schools, and expanded their ministry across the region. He was in charge of the Alchemy School while her ministry with the other Marys (High Priestesses) was more general and was directed towards all people. It was indeed the "Gospel of Love" from the Cathars. The Gospel is one of more than ten thousand pages, an ancient manuscript, with parts of it contributed by none other than "The Teacher of Righteousness of the Essenes". Its roots though are far more ancient, stemming from the first of the Aysis-Ra-A-Ru-A-Ra Mystery schools in Occitania itself. (Note: "The Cathar Gospel of Love", which has been remembered, is but a tiny fraction of that which survived from the massive original manuscript.)

This extensive manuscript was so loved and embraced by the Cathars as a basis for teaching everywhere, that for safety reasons it was smuggled away, and will never be revealed, nor see the light of day, until such time as the Love Codes, with the Fires of Illumination are returned to those ready and able to receive them.

In fact, the Cathar Bishop, Esclaremonde de Foix, insisted that it be dismantled into smaller sections. Her brother, Ramon Roger, the Count of Foix, and his youngest daughter Cécile, smuggled them out of Occitania, and the manuscripts remain concealed to this day.

---

3   The Albigensian Crusade or the Cathar Crusade was a 20-year military campaign initiated by Pope Innocent III to eliminate Catharism in Languedoc, in southern France being launched against them,. Wikipedia

We will come back to this later. For now it is important to understand the link between Mary Magdalene, the Cathars and the Essenes. It is essential to expand this to include the remnant of the Mystery Schools elsewhere, in order to grasp the whole picture. By the time the third Crusade was launched against the Cathars, and correspondingly all of Southern France, these pockets of Enlightened Beings were like shining Beacons of Light, illuminating the whole region. They outshone the church by far. When the spotlight shines on those hiding in the dark, they hate it, for then they have to rush for cover, as their own hidden agendas are revealed. The darkness wanted to stamp out the light, and additionally, it desired to use their secrets against them.

Fifty years before the genocide of Occitania, a Cathar prophetess foresaw it all taking place, so at this crucial time the nobility, the Keepers and Guardians of the Grail Secrets met and decided on a plan of action. The Cathar Bishops were always represented by a High Priest and Priestess. The lower ranks of the Cathars, the simple people were never initiated into the highest hidden truths. Only a handful ever knew the truth, which they would never divulge, even unto death.

At this meeting, the Knights Templar came into being, and were in reality one and the same as the Cathars. Certainly they belonged to the same families. They decided to retrieve what they knew was waiting to be reclaimed in Israel, and would fall under the mantle of the Military Order, but would in fact be a Priestly Order, that concealed the same Mystery School. They knew that they would have to defend the precious manuscript with their lives.

The shadow indeed had fallen upon Occitania, and from then on it became a life or death battle, as whatever secret knowledge they had could not be divulged, and would be protected at all costs.

Such then was Occitania.

And I was there in the beginning, and I was there at the end …

My life indeed was now turning the full circle …

The Fires of Illumination were being returned through me – I was but an instrument and knew that I would have to release so much, in order to bring in the fires to anchor them once more in Occitania, and in those places I had clearly drawn on my map, long before I arrived there.

The green and gold fires would descend again, and the souls who had once paid the highest price would return, indeed they already have, as the Cathar Prophecy is being fulfilled. They did not die in vain – they have risen, and will rise again!

* * *

CHAPTER 3

# The Greatest Secret and Hidden Treasure

In the greatest of all Knowing, that which one truly seeks from the heart and soul, the depths of one's Being, becomes a Quest. One is a truthful seeker, and pursues the Ultimate Truth which is a Higher State of Being. One will not settle for the mediocre, and is willing to let others call you a Fool, transcending all challenges and obstacles to find your path, often leaving behind family and friends to find the ultimate Truth and all it contains.

The Quest is the ultimate One, where the anti-hero(ine) becomes the hero(ine) against all odds.

The Epic Poem of Parsifal[1] has within its core heart, this Quest. This poem in fact has its Ursprung, the urtext, in a much older manuscript which was held within the Love Courts, the Troubadour and the High Bardic Councils and in that of the inner teachings of the Cathars and Templars, never revealed to the Uninitiated. It found its way to Germany in a manuscript smuggled out when Occitania was reeling under the full force of the Inquisition and the third Crusade, as one of the worst genocides ever ensued.

This poem however was allowed to surface, as it wished to remind humanity of the core and hidden truths, which Occitania held in its custodianship.

One of the first recalls of my own past life, was linked to the utmost Truth and Treasure the Cathars and Templars held, often under dangerous circumstances which I helped smuggle out, loyal to my oath sworn to my father in that lifetime, Ramon Roger, the Count of Foix.

This recall became my own Quest for the truth, culminating in this book.

The deepest of meanings, the deepest of secrets are often kept right under peoples' noses, where they will literally fall over them but still not see. So much has been written about the Templar Treasure and

---

[1] *Parzival* is a medieval romance written by the knight-poet Wolfram von Eschenbach in Middle High German. The poem, commonly dated to the first quarter of the 13th century, centers on the Arthurian hero Parzival and his long quest for the Holy Grail following his initial failure to achieve it. Wikipedia

*Figure 1. Foix Castle, my home in my life as Cecile.*

hidden deposits of Gold, and additionally the Cathar Treasure, which, according to legend, was smuggled out of Monségur before the final burning at the stake of the 200 Cathars.

If you wish to keep your enemy off the trail, and to plant false clues, and spread false rumours, you aim to obscure the truth in any way possible. Particularly in this case as the Inquisition were not really in search of the truth, but fanatically intent on stamping it out, to allow their own lies and warped lies to rule.

I had one vivid past life recall of riding my white horse up into the wildest and most isolated peaks of the Pyrenees. I knew these as a child, for with my half-brother Lupo, we had roamed there, often practicing our falconry or accompanying my father when he visited relatives or his castles elsewhere. After all, we belonged to the Three Regions, where the greatest of all Secrets were kept within the three families who held custodianship over them which were: Foix,[2] Bearn and Comminges.

I was now high in the Pyrenees, on the top of a sheer cliff. I left my faithful horse, and dressed as a man, had to descend while carrying some of the most treasured and ancient manuscripts holding the secrets of the Cathars, strapped to my back. I do not know how I managed that, for I hung onto the vertical Cliffside by the tips of my fingers, my feet somehow finding a place to anchor. Desperation gives courage, so I persevered till I found the well concealed entrance to an ancient cave, to journey deep inside in search of somewhere safe to deposit my treasure, sealing it off, to ensure it would never be discovered. This place had a natural spring, so I survived on the clear water, along with my provisions. The climb down the cliff was one thing, but to ascend again, was an act of immense courage. I did however reach the top and my faithful horse came to greet me.

The soul memory bank haunted me when travelling in the Pyrenees, as I recalled vast underground tunnel systems, and of one such system linking my place

---

2   The Count of Foix ruled the independent County of Foix, in what is now southern France, during the Middle Ages. The House of Foix eventually extended its power across the Pyrenees mountain range, moving their court to Pau in Béarn. The last count unified with King Henry IV of France in 1607.

*Figure 2. Castle at Soula.*

of birth, Foix Castle, to all the other major centres, and additionally, there were immense tunnel systems under Monségur itself.

When I finally arrived at Foix and Monségur with Kristina, who insisted on going there prior to my seminars in Couiza, it certainly was a deep soul homecoming for me. The report of that trip is elsewhere, but when I stood gazing up at the castle and surrounding mountains, I knew exactly where the Crystal Pyramids were hidden, as all merged together as one. Over and above that, I knew where the ancient hidden pathways were as my memory banks were alive and active. It was not something I wished to share for with the recalls, so much past pain came to the fore, but it was also mixed with intense joy and deep love for this sacred place.

As I journeyed through this region, opening up energy centres and releasing so much of the distress and pain, my memories were steeped in the tireless assistance from the Knights Templar in smuggling out additional manuscripts, documents, items that looked like tablets, and gold scripts. The latter were sheer sheets of gold, filled with ancient symbols from the time of Avalon, spanning millions of years.

Many of these were kept in my father's, the Count of Foix's, vast library, one of the most extensive libraries in Occitania, inherited from his ancestors and added to, on his first Crusade, as the younger son. When his brother died, he returned and assumed his title. During the Crusade, he discovered many antique manuscripts in locations he intuitively knew of, for guidance came from ancient secret sources, held within the three families, mostly through word of mouth, and only relayed between trusted ones who belonged to the inner secret circles of the Cathars.

At that time, through her gift of prophesy (the Cathar High Priestess was a Prophetess), the three families realised that the timing of the first Crusade coincided with exactly this self-same ancient oracle which had also foreseen that around this time the Fires of Illumination would arise in Occitania. Through knowledge of this prophecy, contact was made with another branch of the same Ancient Mystery Schools, which later were referred to falsely as the Bogomils[3] when in truth they were merely branches of a much older Source. Through the meeting with the Bogomil Elders, they were able to pinpoint the exact location of the remaining hidden Manuscripts and the secret depository.

When he returned, Ramon Roger married Philippa de Moncada, from the House of Béarn. Subsequently through this marriage, and the deep alliance of the three families and holders of the Grail secrets, one of the de Moncada family, Hugo de Payen was ordained to go to Jerusalem, to find that collection. Once he was there, he established the Knights Templar Order, to guard the depository that had been found. This Order was in reality a branch of the same Mystery Schools and inner teachings as the Cathars, and it was created with two distinct orders within its ranks – the Priesthood, and the Military wing. The latter was created to defend the secrets within their own ranks, as well as those of the Cathars.

The Prophetess had predicted that the church would declare war on the Cathars, because Pope Gregory was power hungry and served the darkness, wanting desperately to get his hands on the manuscripts and inner secrets of the Cathars and Templars.

At that point, the third Crusade was launched and it soon became obvious that certain families were being specifically targeted and besieged by the Crusaders more so than others, and nowhere was this more apparent than in the manner in which the young Viscount of Bezier and Carcassonne who came to plea for his own people, was murdered in cold blood, even though he was flying the peace flag.

The Viscounts of Bezier and Carcassonne were indeed related to the same Secret Families and Pope Gregory knew this.

Enter another figure belonging to the very same family group, King Pedro of Aragon, cousin to both the Count of Foix, the Viscount of Béarn and the Count of Toulouse, and married to Marie, the Countess of Mirepoix. When the crusade was confirmed, King Pedro arrived to defend his own properties as he held the ancestral lands there. The manner in which he was killed has often been questioned, but it appears that he too was murdered.

With such happenings, the Count of Foix, with his cousin the Count of Toulouse, and the other families, knew that they now had to defend their lands and secrets.

Before the crusades, Ramon Roger of Foix and Ramon the Count of Toulouse went to Rome to meet with Pope Gregory. No matter how much they pleaded, it fell on deaf ears. Ramon Roger was an eloquent speaker and a Troubadour, and all who heard him speak reported that he spoke with authority, as a highly educated man, as his Library would attest to. He had in his employ many highly accomplished Moors, including a Prince from the House of Leon, all translating manuscripts from Arabic into Occitan, and he had a very keen interest in sacred geometry and maths. He was greatly loved by his people, especially as he was a poet and musician and was judged as being fair and just.

It was Ramon Roger, who now had to defend the high Pyrenees, as his cousin the Count of Toulouse tended to be rather fickle and more accustomed to Love courts and the finer things in life, and was definitely not a warrior. So Ramon assumed a leadership role, one which did not sit lightly upon his shoulders. He was a deep thinker and with his sister Esclaremonde, the Real Bishop of the Cathar church,

---

3   Bogomilism was a Christian neo-Gnostic or dualist sect founded in the First Bulgarian Empire by the priest Bogomil during the reign of Tsar Peter I in the 10th century. It most probably arose in what is today the region of Macedonia. Wikipedia,

*Figure 3. The Black Madonna.*

and his wife Philippa, another High Priestess, were now left with safeguarding what they could with the help of the other two families, who were the Secret Keepers.

It is there that the bond between the Knights Templar (Viscount of the Béarn) was now strongly forged to an even greater extent and depth. After all the Grand Master of the Templars was directly related to them all, as were the founder members, all now sharing a common secret that needed defending. That secret was not only valuable manuscripts and such-like, it was simultaneously the combined legacy of the Essenes, and more than this Mary Magdalene herself, whom the Templars had declared their official Saint, together with John the Baptist. Now, she is the key here to the Ancient Mystery Schools and the same hidden knowledge, held in the Pyrenees together with the other groups, of which the Essenes were one. It was connected however to the very secret and covert worship of the Goddess herself – often referred to the as Black Madonna, different from Mother Mary. She was symbolic of the Universal Feminine Divine, thus transcending all racial or cultural divides, and thus serving all of humanity as ONE.

Indeed the Templars and Cathars believed in Unity consciousness, knowing no division and accordingly were tolerant of the Spanish Moors and beyond that, the Arabs themselves. After all they came from the same roots, Avalon and the Lion Kingdom.

It was decided to protect as much of their inner teachings and knowledge as possible as with the continued utter ruthlessness of the Inquisition, with their barbaric torture and mass burnings at the stake, this was crucial and of the utmost urgency.

Ramon Roger then called in his youngest daughter, Cecile (Sissi), already an ordained Priestess, ear-marked to become High Priestess when her Aunt Esclaremonde died, and gave her the task of ensuring the manuscripts were safe. Simultaneously under oath, the Templar Grand Master, pledged to assist her secretly, even though the Templars were supposed to be neutral, they simply could not maintain neutrality in such circumstances, with their interconnectedness to the Cathars, and their combined secrets. After all, the Templars came from the same origin.

Many manuscripts were smuggled to Ireland, to Italy, to Germany, and even later to the far Baltic where the Teutonic Knights under oath, gave safe haven to many fleeing Cathars.

According to their own Grand Master's Prophesy, the Templars realized that they would also be persecuted in the future, so made doubly sure to safeguard precious documents. They created the nation of Portugal, master planned by St. Bernard of Clairvaux, even before they officially created their own order, creating a Templar State, keeping their most treasured knowledge safely there.

As much as most manuscripts were smuggled out, many never were. They were deposited and sealed off, and the Cathar Prophets stated that their content would only be revealed when humanity was ready for the next phase of Illumination, when most Cathar and Templars souls would reincarnate again.

More than this, some souls vowed to absorb the knowledge into their own souls, and vowed to return at the time when humanity would witness the rise of the New Jerusalem, and thus the New Golden Age, when this knowledge would be relevant and would assist the process in higher Illumined ways.

## The Gospels of Love also called the Books of the All-Knowing, All-Seeing, All-Being

The most important of all the Cathar Treasures was indeed, none other than the Gospel of Love. It was not a gospel per se, but rather a collection of 144 scrolls, each of which was a complete book on its own. It can be likened to the Bible, and indeed it was. Its Ancient Roots could be traced all the way back to Aysis and her first Mystery Schools, through the Druidic Traditions, the Crystal Pyramids within the Pyrenees and those sunk offshore, and in the Mediterranean Sea, as mentioned in my chapter about Carnac.

It held every core lesson of the Highest and Most Sacred Secret Teachings, shared only with those initiated in the required levels within the ranks of the Mystery Schools. Those with full access were the High Priest and Priestess, for the Cathars had Two Bishops, a woman and a man. The materials recorded within these scrolls, were in the form of symbols, and not in any written language. Likewise, knowledge in deciphering these symbols was handed down orally, with access to the hidden secret meaning, only made possible through particular keys and codes.

This entire massive Book (144 scrolls forming an encyclopaedia of knowledge) was the most treasured possession of both Cathars and Templars, who were the Keepers and Guardians of the Grail itself. They were sworn to secrecy, and never dared speak about it, and often resorted to giving false leads, to keep it hidden and sealed off until such time as when the humanity's mass consciousness would have risen adequately, so those accessing them, would neither abuse its contents, nor use it for power games, but only for the supreme good in the highest possible way.

Indeed, the content was such that only the High Priest and High Priestess and some of the inner ranks, consisting of the Council of 12, had the necessary understanding of it, knowing how to apply it wisely with unconditional love and pure intent.

It was no accident that the Cathars were known as the Purest of Pure. Indeed, their teachings were so unadulterated, with the intent of walking only the highest paths, that very few ever gained access to the higher knowledge and then only after years of initiations.

Another interesting fact about this Sacred Book, was that as part of the Essene community in Israel, before returning to France, Mary Magdalene was given three books, to be held in custody for humankind. In fact there were seven in total. She brought three scrolls with her under cover, and the Templars later discovered the other four in their secret hiding place. Just as recorded in the scrolls she went to France and retrieved them, along with several other very sacred items, which the Teacher of Righteousness had buried there. This was their own most sacred possession, and the most significant reason why she was chosen as their Patron Saint. John the Baptist, shared a matching Rank with her, but in fact the true Saint they revered was the Teacher of Righteousness, another John, and his wife, equal in rank as the High Priestess, Judith.

What has been remembered is but a tiny fraction of a vast book, which contained 144 Scrolls. It was considered to be a sacred direct legacy and gift to humankind from the Divine Mother, as the Feminine Side of the Godhead

This complete book was but one celebration, one single code of the Highest Order of Unconditional Love, and a full way of life, thus to live one's truth with integrity, while simultaneously expressing a deep honouring of all life itself.

This Gospel was considered so sacred, that it was totally sealed off as a comprehensive body of work, long before the Fall of Monségur. Indeed, many lost their lives attempting to keep it hidden and secret, often suffering severe torture from the Inquisition.

It was in truth not a Gospel, but is more like a Bible. It was one massive Ode to the highest keys and codes of Love, Power and Wisdom. It was a celebration of the Power of Love, with guidance on how to harness this Power, in co-creatorship, the transcendental, and the highest forms of alchemy and sacred alchemical union, for all those called to follow such a path.

It contained some of the following:

- The Divine Love Codes and Keys. Thus enclosed the ancient knowledge of the Tree of Life, lost to humankind. This was not a Tree in the actual sense of the word, but rather the stages of the higher Paths of an Initiate, into the Higher Understanding and application of such, in order to master self and co-creatorship by application of such Laws.
- Unconditional love spans all – the divinity within men and women. The deepest of self-love and then the culmination in True love between them, as well as those keys and codes of sacred union.
- Love codes as applied in daily interaction with other souls: namely between man/woman, children, family, the greater human family and groups. It had within its core the self-same community principles, the brother and sisterhood of humanity, as found in the Essene community.
- The Love codes applicable to Sacred Sexual Union and the Sacred Secret Rites. (Many of them came to them through Mary Magdalene and Yeshua as their Mystery Schools contained within them the more ancient roots.)
- The Love Courts in Occitania and the Troubadour celebration of Love, originated from this same essence.
- The Higher knowledge of Alchemy, and transcendental methods of enlightenment. The Practice of yoga or similar techniques, meditation, and the secret knowledge of death and resurrection – the rebirth into the New Adam and the New Eve.
- The Higher Knowledge of the uses of sound to open the heart centre to allow ever more advanced and the greatest levels of love – the love tones. Chants and vowels for opening the higher transmitter channels. Prayers at sunrise, sunset, noon and midnight, and seasonal prayers. Rituals. Sacred Rites.
- Loving Grace, forgiveness, Being the Love which changest all and everything within and without.
- The Sacred and most Hidden Teachings of the Brother and Sisterhood of the Rose, the Serpent and the Sacred Chalice. The Serpent in this case referring to the spiralling Kundalini energy as a path of Illumination and Enlightenment.
- The Gift of Prophesy and its application and uses within the community.
- Love Songs and Chants inclusive of the Songs of Songs, which had deep hidden sacred geometrical structures and forms which are activated when chanted or sung.
- Sacred Geometry and Sacred Maths, Alchemy. This included architecture, engineering, etc.
- Power Words of Love.
- Certain practices pertaining to alchemy, as linked to Avalon and the Sacred Hidden Knowledge of the High Druidic Orders, as metaphysical sciences.
- The Sacred Energy Healing Practices using the Power of Love.
- The uses of the Fires of Illumination in transcendental practices.
- The ancient knowledge of bilocation and teleportation.
- The Secret Inner Teachings of the Ancient Aysis-Ra-A-Ru-A-Ra Mystery Schools.
- The Uses of certain instruments in higher healing.

- The study and uses of the sacred geometrical patterns in flowers, plants and trees and application of these, e.g. Flower Essences and healing.
- Working with the Earth energies and energy fields.
- Working with the forces of nature.
- The True history of the world.
- It had maps of the Crystalline Energy Grids, with the knowledge of how to tap into them, as well as the underground tunnel systems, and the massive chambers inside the Earth, and openings to Agartha the inner world.
- Maps of the world, as it first was.
- The Divine Universal Laws.
- The Ultimate Illumined State.

This list is by no means complete, but just an indication of some of the contents contained therein.

It was known that the Cathars sometimes evoked lightning when burnt at the stake, viewed as part of their supernatural powers.

One of the healing chants and chants to open the heart which survived is the so-called Cathar Hymn, disguised as a cattle herding song to fool the Inquisition, but in truth, puts one directly in touch with Arcturus and the Higher Healing Powers.

The mightily important scrolls have never been found, and will not see the light of day, until the core group of 12 who sealed them off, will gather once more at the ordained time in Occitania, and they will recognize each other, through the eyes of the Soul. For each one holds a certain key and only the Highest Ranking Men and Women can open up the whole.

* * *

CHAPTER 4

# Foix, Monségur

In order to understand the next part of this journey, it is necessary to understand that I was reliving the story of Sissi, Cécile de Foix, youngest daughter of Ramon Roger, the Count of Foix.

I was born in Foix Castle in May 1200, at a time when there was already a strained relationship between my parents, Ramon Roger and Philippa de Moncada. My mother was a daughter of the Count of Béarn (today's Bearn is in Northern Spain). When I was six months old, Philippa left to join her sister-in-law Esclaremonde in Dun, to serve at the Girls' School she had established, and at the shelter for homeless women.

The rift between the two was caused by my father's love affair with a woman Loba, the Wolf, with whom he had a son Lupo – who was sent to my father six months before I was born – so he was my half-brother. We grew up together and were inseparable.

## The Story of Sissi (Cécile de Foix)

Ramon Roger married Philippa de Moncada in 1189. The couple had two children:
- Roger-Bernard II († 1241), Count of Foix
- Cécile married to Bernard V, Count of Comminges, in 1224.

Raymond-Roger fathered two illegitimate children:
- Lupo de Foix, Lord of Saverdun, and ancestor of the Earls of Rabat.
- Esclarmonde de Foix, married to Bernard d'Alion, Lord Donnezan, burned in 1258 as Cathar.

Sissi was born in May 1200 in Foix, Languedoc, the third child and second daughter, of Count Ramon Roger of Foix and Philippa de Moncada. The eldest child was a daughter Aimery (Esther) and the only son, Roger-Bernard, later became Count of Foix, until they added the title "The Great".

Sissi was very close to her father, whom she adored. He married Philippa relatively late in life (he had been the second son, and only inherited the title, after his older brother died.) Philippa de

Moncada was much younger, and the marriage was very strained at the time of Sissi's birth, as Ramon had strayed ... a much-advertised affair, mentioned in songs. He had a liaison with Loba, the She-Wolf of Languedoc, the subject of many a Troubadour's song, and her liaison with Ramon Roger, who outclassed all his rivals for her favours, had resulted in a son, six months older than Sissi, who went under the name of Lupo. Ramon acknowledged his son, and brought him home. Philippa, very pregnant at the time, barely tolerated him, and sought solace with her Cathar Parfait sister-in-law, Esclarmonde of Foix, who had opened up schools and boarding houses for girls and women, in the neighbouring village of Dun.

When Sissi was born, the astrologers of the time, predicted that this child would be one of the shining lights of Languedoc, as she had been born with the Sign of the Goddess. Ramon subsequently dedicated this child to the Goddess – much to Philippa's chagrin, and this worsened their already strained relationship.

The first years of Sissi's life were spent between her father's castles in Languedoc, and her mother's family, the Counts of Béarn, in the southern-most parts of the Pyrenees, in what is now Northern Spain.

The Counts of Béarn and Foix were of Ancient Celtic and Visigoth Lineage, which had its roots in the High Priesthood of Avalon (the land which is as ancient as this planet itself and existed before Lemuria and Atlantis. It was the Celtic Paradise, called Elysium, that all Celts remember as being to the west, which had sunk under the sea).

They were the direct descendants of the High Priests of Ancient Avalon, who fled the flooding of Avalon, and had once reigned supreme in that region. The Pyrenees is filled with massive Crystal Pyramids, which are far more ancient than the Egyptian ones. At this moment in time, they are not visible, as they subsequently disappeared under the forest, ground and trees in the area.

The Pyrenees are connected by underground caverns and a vast tunnel system to the other great Mystery Centres of the world, and to the underground world of Agartha.

The Languedoc Royalty had great ties with "The Ancient Ones" as they called the highly evolved beings that live in the cities, acting as mentors and teachers to the Royal offspring born with the sign of the Goddess, in the form of a distinct birth mark, just underneath the left breast, thus linking it to the heart chakra.

The chosen ones were brought to these underground caverns for initiation into the Ancient Mystery Rites, and trained as High Priests and High Priestesses for the Divine Goddess.

The worship of the Divine Goddess stemmed from Avalon, where women ruled in those Ancient Days. The High Priestess and Priests were divided into 12 distinctive groups, each one attached to a certain crystal pyramid temple that anchored in a certain colour ray. There were 12 Pyramid Temples, and these held 12 Crystal Skulls and 12 Crystal Keys.

In those days, the Druids were the healers of the 12 Celtic tribes, and fell under the jurisdiction of the High Priestess under whose ray they worked. They were an order in themselves. The others were the Bardic Order – comprised of the praise singers, the Keepers of Tonal Scale vibrations and the Order of the Royal Knights and Ladies, who were the lesser Royalty – and thus the ones not involved in the High Priesthood.

Ramon Roger and his sister Esclarmonde were both born with the sign of the Goddess, and thus were dedicated to her from an early age. They both acted as High Priest and High Priestess, and were of the Ancient Royal lineage of the Keepers of Records and Wisdom. It was in this capacity that they served their people. Both had the distinctive red-blond hair of the Celtic Tribes.

In Languedoc women had equal rights with men, were educated, and owned property. The lineage was traced via the female line of the family. Thus, Languedoc was distinctly different from neighbouring regions in France, Spain and Italy, etc. The nobles here were educated by the advanced Spanish Moor Universities, and they possessed vast libraries. They were light-years ahead of their neighbours, who were still lost in the dark ages.

Philippa de Moncada stemmed from the same Celtic Royal branch, and her brothers were the founders of the Order of the Knights Templar. Hugo de Payen took his nickname as founder of the Order, and was a trained High Priest himself. Thus, the connection between the Houses of Foix, Béarn (de Moncada) and Comminges with the Knights Templar, as well as the House of Aragon, was indisputable. The Templars were given property on their lands, and they acted as guardians and keepers of the Ancient Secrets.

Ramon Roger of Foix was a renowned Troubadour and served in this capacity in the Courts of Love. He took part in the Second Crusade with King Louis of France, and Eleanor of Aquitaine. He was an eloquent speaker, and a soldier and leader of repute, who was held in high esteem. He was a cousin to both the King of France and King of Aragon, and Raymond, Count of Toulouse, made him one of the most highly ranked Royals in that area. Through his marriage to Philippa de Moncada, the Foix lands and holdings had increased. He held amongst others, the castle of Monségur.

At the time of Cécile de Foix's (Sissi's) birth, Languedoc was still at its height of glory. In a way her destiny had already been determined by her birthmark, and the fact that she had been chosen for initiation into the High Priesthood of her people.

Sissi inherited her mother's looks, she had long golden-blond hair, and grew into a beauty who was her father's pride and joy. In many ways, she was spoilt, being much younger than her oldest sister Aimery and her brother, so she grew up wild and free, mostly because by this time, her mother had chosen to separate from her father, and was in training to become a parfait, like her aunt Esclaremonde.

She grew up wild, with Lupo as her constant companion. Her father tried to keep her in line as much as possible, and she learnt falconry and horsemanship from him. She could outride any man, and rode bareback. Throughout her life her horses, greyhounds and spaniels were her greatest companions and they accompanied her wherever she went. She also learnt to use a dagger and short sword, at her father's insistence.

At the age of six/seven she was taken to the Ancient Ones for her first tuition in the rites of the High Priesthood. She learnt about the power of the mind, meditation and the use of medicinal herbs. At the age of six/seven she was taken to the Ancient Ones for her first tuition in the rites of the High Priesthood. She learnt about the power of the mind, meditation, the use of medicinal herbs, etc.

When she was 10, the war in Languedoc broke out in earnest – her beloved father was involved in campaigns most of the time, as was her brother. Her married sister Aimery was often called upon to look after her, as were her mother's family. She also spent time at Dun, in the schools for girls.

She was however also entrusted with the ruling of her father's estates, while he was away, and more and more the responsibility for the land and people became hers. She was wilful and a real tomboy, truly her father's daughter, and she tended to do very much as she liked.

Her sister died in 1214 in childbirth, which further increased Sissi's autonomy. When the war settled into a kind of truce, after Foix castle was taken by Simon de Montford, her father took her to Aragon, where he recruited mercenaries, and employed Sancho Fernando Jaime de Leon, a Prince of the Royal House of de Leon, as her tutor. He was also a fine engineer and alchemist, and was hired to build siege engines and trajectories for the Foix family.

His main task was to teach Sissi the fine-arts of lute playing and Arabic, as he had spent many years as a student at the Moorish Universities and had also been to Istanbul, India, Egypt, and to all the places of learning. Sissi did not want to be educated, and she gave him a hard time. When the war resumed, they were left more or less to their own devices.

At the age of 17, he had to assist her father elsewhere, and wrote her a love letter in Arabic. She went after him, meeting him in the Pyrenees in a cave, where he became her lover.

Subsequently they lived together openly. Her father had no time for the conventions of that time, and he turned a blind eye to it. The war kept him very much on the frontline as the leader of his people, as it did for Roger Bernard her brother, and Lupo.

In the meantime, she had helped her aunt to rebuild Monségur Castle, and to fortify and strengthen it. She had two children; a boy named Fernando and a daughter called Philippa

While she was pregnant with her third child, her father died, and her son Roger was born, prematurely. To her utter shock her brother Bernard Roger, now Count of Foix, took the infant away from her, and adopted him. He was gay, and married to a much older woman, so they were unable to produce offspring.

He moreover promptly married her off to her cousin, Bernard of Comminges, who had been lined up to marry her, for her dowry. He was a huge and uncouth soldier – the exact opposite of her lover, and physically abused her, forcing her into 12 chastity belts as he was insanely jealous of her lover. She made no effort to hide her contempt for him, and her love for Sancho.

In a moment of rage, he nearly beat her to death but the servants managed to get her to safety at Monségur, where she recovered with the assistance of her aunt Esclarmonde. She sunk into a deep depression and was then reunited with Sancho, who had taken their other two children into safety, her half-sister Esclarmonde helped her daughter to escape to Ireland, where she married an Irish Prince.

She then went onto assist her people to safeguard their hidden heritage, and to smuggle the valuable manuscripts from her father's vast Library and the one in Toulouse, away to Italy and elsewhere. The Templars (her uncles were founder members – her mother's twin brothers were also part of the order), came to her aid, and together with Sancho, managed to get all the valuable documents to safety in Italy, Ireland, Germany and elsewhere.

The most valuable information that the church was looking for concerned her people, however she kept this inside her. She went alone to hide some of the secret codes, which had been recorded in writing, in caves and caverns very high in the Sabarthes Mountains, just as she had promised her father she would do.

In the process she was hunted like an animal, often having to hide in the caves and caverns but with the aid of the Templars and her brother Lupo, many people who were fleeing from the Inquisition, were brought to safety .

Sancho in the meantime went to Italy, and she did not hear from him for a long time.

The Templars were her allies. Yet, betrayed by a jealous sister-in-law, wife of another bastard brother, who acted as her body guard, she was arrested with five Knights Templar, and brought to the Bishop's Palace at Urgell.

The bishop had a long-standing vendetta against her father and family, and coveted her people's secrets.

He told the Templars that they could go free, yet they refused.

Subsequently they were all burnt at the stake when Sissi took poison, which had been given to her by her people, to use in the event that she was ever caught.

She died with the secrets of her people and the secret codes within her.

Her son Fernando, later became the King of Aragon.

Through Sissi's third child Roger of Foix, the French Royal Family, the Bourbon lineage was born.

Thus, wherever I travelled Sissi was with me, within me, and in a higher sense the journey was a deep remembering, while at the same time, bringing about profound healing. That healing would continue as I pursued the work in France, Greece and Egypt, and eventually came full circle in September 2021.

The day before we left to visit Foix and Monségur, I was inspired to walk through the Village of St. Julia de Bec, Katrina's home, in the heart of the Pyrenees. It is a lovely quaint village, with its own sphinx in the form of the Lion Mountain, which I loved, and which always seemed to shift and change for me. I paused at an old mill where I saw the remains of old terraces, and then Mary Magdalene suddenly appeared right alongside me and said she had lived there for a while during her ministry, when it had been a much larger village.

I climbed the steep hill, and on the summit, reconnected the pyramid energies of the Pyrenees, with Foix and Monségur. This was in St. Julia le Bec, where I was staying with Kristina. All those I had connected with in that Cathar lifetime appeared, alongside the Bards who were still accompanying us, and the Knights Templar.

First, I first felt the energies coursing through me, then I had an anointing on that mountain top in the highest alignment with the pyramid in front of me, and those of Monségur and Foix. It was quite beautiful reconnecting to these mountains – all alone, with no one else in sight.

Then I was shown the ancient white-gold Lion Kingdom Complex remains which had once stood here. These were the schools and abodes of

*Figure 1. The Lion Mountain.*

*Figure 2. Beautiful mountain sides.*

inhabitants of the Temples of the Moon: however, Isis later became Artemis.

It was a beautiful composite of pyramids and terraces, hanging gardens, glittering white/gold in the sun, and held the high leadership of Isis and the Sisterhood of the Rose, the Serpent and Chalice (Holy Grail).

The remains of the terraces and the pyramids are all around, with massive megaliths on the mountain peak, which had previously been a sphinx (see sketch).

Indeed, Monségur and Foix were now calling. I had come to revisit, to see them again, and I had no idea what I would find. They had haunted my memories, and my dreams, as I had experienced vivid recalls of my life as Sissi – Cécile. Additionally, I had carried out extensive research, and read so much about the Cathars and Templars during that time. Now at last I could go there in person!

As we drove towards Foix, the closer we came, the more the remembrances of my soul stirred. After all, I had ridden my white horse here day and night, and it had been my home and neighbourhood. Yet, through it all, there was still deep pain in the process of remembering.

Foix proved to be a bit of an enigma, a place I entered with high expectations, which were soon dampened by the very feel of it. The spirit of a place defines it, attracting or repelling one. In Foix I was finally reunited with the Castle which had haunted me for so long, yet it still felt like a closed book, even though many memory banks were now accessible.

The restaurant we lunched at, had a rather strange energy. Kristina refused to stay, and we decided to explore the narrow streets instead, moving towards the castle. She was in a patisserie, when I felt the urge to walk further up the street, only to be stopped in my tracks, as the scene suddenly altered: I saw men and women stripped naked, chained, whipped and driven like cattle, with huge, clanging iron ankle chains. They were Cathars, and then the scene changed again, and I saw them being burnt alive on the stake in front of the castle. I now felt a distinct sense of doom, which settled like a cloud over the whole town.

Yet the castle itself triggered my memory banks, and as I approached it, the more I appreciated just how archaic it was. It was built on the remains of the megalithic sites, which were there ages before it had become a medieval stronghold. In fact, I had been prompted to remember with great clarity, underground tunnel systems from this castle that linked directly to Monségur and other castles, accessible only to the initiated, and those who knew the secret of negotiating them.

Foix Castle. There is an interesting rock formation, on which the Foix castle foundations rest.

If you look carefully, one can see a giant face appearing inside the span of the bridge.

I was quite relieved to leave Foix behind, the doom and gloom, knowing that one day I would return to enter the castle, when the timing was right. Monségur now beckoned. As we journeyed on, I picked up on the energy lines and followed them, and then we were led to Soula, the place of the Sun.

## JOURNAL ENTRY

Today I had to go back to Foix and Monségur, as my soul was calling me there, and Kristina agreed to take me. I was also reconnecting with the energy fields, after having released so much yesterday.

Foix itself proved to be a challenge. Although I had wanted to explore the castle where I grew up in 1200 as Cécile de Foix, the youngest daughter of Ramon Roger the Count of Foix, in the end we resorted to viewing it from a roadside café, with bad food and angry people. Indeed, the energy in the centre of Foix was dark and negative. At one stage, we veered off into a side street, still searching for the way to the castle, or an open restaurant.

We found a patisserie instead. Kristina went in, while I ventured further, as I was drawn to a narrow cobbled medieval street and I was pulled up short, as I began shivering. The scene changed and then I saw men, women and children, being rounded up with chains on their hands and feet, being flogged, as they were driven like cattle by the priests of the Inquisition and some crusaders. It was downright horrible! I could

PART 2: CHAPTER 4: FOIX, MONSÉGUR

*Figure 4. Another view of the castle.*

not get away from there fast enough, and did not even want to go into the castle anymore.

I then knew that I would have to clear the energy lines in Foix from another location, and I was told it was Soula, Place of the Sun. Interestingly though, as I stood and viewed the castle from below, I saw clearly how it had been built with megalithic blocks on the foundation of a much older building. I remembered the tunnel systems, which I had often escaped into, which led elsewhere in the Pyrenees. There were many sentinel rocks here, and also what looked like the remains of something far more ancient.

We discovered an old road, and alongside it were mountains of massive megalithic structures, which certainly look surreal. Some resembled mushrooms with windows. There were also caves, massive dolmens and remnants of a gigantic Sun City.

There we found a place in the shade of old trees, next to the road, and I began my energy work, calling in all my helpers to release the stuck souls, and all the trauma and pain of one of the greatest genocides Humanity had ever witnessed!

*Figure 3. Massive portals and pyramids.*

115

Immense power surged through me – the souls were released, and the negative energies transmuted and transcended into the purest God force Light.

The spiraling energies moved in and cleansed and cleared, as I provided the keys and codes.

Afterwards we travelled along a spectacularly beautiful road to Monségur, which ties up with Foix, Soula, and massive portals and pyramids nearby, as well as underground cave systems, underground rivers and huge crystal chambers.

I immediately connected to the golden green pyramids underground at Monségur, and reactivated them. Instantly the spiraling energy pulsated through, and then pounded along, after being reactivated. Afterwards I was so grateful that this work had been done before the seminars started, and that the souls were laid to rest, as well clearing my last karmic residue with this region.

I was told that a totally new life would emerge from all of this.

I am freed!

Interestingly we did not climb up to the castle, but I was drawn to the mountains next to Monségur, more than Monségur itself. I immediately saw the caves, and I knew that within this mountain, which linked up with Monségur and those surrounding it, were mammoth tunnel systems and underground chambers. I also knew that many had been sealed off, energetically, so that no one could enter there, as they led to the Ancient Ones' abodes. There were so many sentinels, dolmens and megaliths on this mountain, where I had to continue the energy work. I felt an immense sense of homecoming to my true self, not only in Cathar times, but also before that. To me this was a sacred place, as all the mountains surrounding Monségur are sacred, and thus very very special. They still held their secrets, which I was called to retrieve and share with the world.

Three mystery schools had once stood here, one in Monségur, another further up in the mountains, connecting to Urgell, and also to the St. Bernard of Comminges lands, and those of the Viscounts of Moncada family, as well as the Foix. These three families were the custodians and guardians of the ancient secrets.

Monségur certainly stands like a massive invincible fortress on top of a huge pyramid. However, it was never a fortress, but rather a sacred temple. I could feel that sacredness, and something else I could not yet define. These memory banks would remain closed until May 2021, when they finally resurfaced. I still had to go through so much cleansing, clearing, releasing and inner work, before I could access that soul memory bank, in order to forgive and release it forever.

It was indeed here that I defended the scrolls that I was smuggling from my lover, who was also my teacher (and indeed my Twin Flame in this lifetime), who had turned against the Cathars. He definitely wanted the scrolls for his own sake. A scuffle ensued, he struck me with his lance in my right leg just below the knee, and as I collapsed, still managing to cling onto the scrolls for dear life, he threw me off the cliff!

I somehow survived, and was later rescued by a Knight Templar friend who took me to safety with the Templars, who nursed me back to health, and we shared a growing, deep and abiding love.

So, I had both in that lifetime. Betrayal in love, and a deep and lasting love, which goes with you through hell fire and beyond.

I could finally understand why I had never been able to reach the castle and summit when I visited Monségur. I first needed to forgive and release this memory bank, and thus be freed forever, as I freed this soul.

Monségur – the Beacon of Love and Light!

\* \* \*

CHAPTER 5

# The 7 Seminars, Group Tour to Monségur: the reopening of Mary Magdalene's Mystery School

I was wandering through many timelines here in South France, timelines of my own soul, and so often when the landscape shifted, as I was transported back into previous lifetimes, and was in a higher sense spanning dimensions and knitting timelines together, in ways I could not voice, nor fully understand. It was a deep remembering, yet at the same time, a reopening, reconnecting, and reactivating.

Long before setting foot here, I was told that I needed to teach seven seminars in France and by now the number seven was so ingrained in the energy work I was being called to do, that I simply followed instructions. I had never in my entire life, delivered seven seminars, yet I was willing to take another leap of faith. I was told that all those souls who needed to be there, would be there. Sure enough, 29 beautiful

*Figure 1. The Old Castle Hotel.*

*Figure 2. The Duc de Joyeuse Hotel, at Cuiza.*

*Figure 3. A Dolmen.*

*Figure 5. My view from the slope.*

*Figure 4. The group at the monument dedicated to the Cathars.*

*Figure 6. Seminar students on the slope.*

souls, from 11 different countries, gathered at old castle hotel in Cuiza, to participate.

Interestingly Kristina first suggested an ancient Abbey in Rennes les Bains, but the minute I saw pictures of it, I had the shivers and knew that something very bad had happened there and indeed it was the place where Mary Magdalene was murdered (this information was relayed to me by one of her direct descendants). Much later many Cathars were burnt there as well. It was definitely not the correct site for my unique seminars.

When she sent me photos of the alternative site, The Duc de Joyeuse Hotel, at Cuiza, I immediately felt the most beautiful energy there in this old castle built by the Duc de Joyeuse, in the seventeen hundreds.

A vision came into view of the area before it was built, as I was shown the old Alchemical School from the Mystery Schools that once had stood there where Jesus had taught. I saw Jesus and Mary Magdalene strolling along the Aude river with their children. It was a happy place and had never seen conflict and I knew right away then that this was exactly where we needed to hold the seminars.

The seven day seminars started with the first three days exploring in depth the Rose, the Serpent, the Grail, Sacred Union, Twin Flame Love, and the Brother and Sisterhood of the Rose.

The castle proved to be a perfect setting, with lunch in the Castle Courtyard with truly, a close-knit group of beautiful souls.

We decided on a one-day break and organized for ta group tour and visit Monségur.

This time we took a different route and as the road was winding itself up the mountains, closer to Monségur, the Pyrenees were spectacular in their beauty. It was the first time I travelled with so many people in a bus, and I had to reassure them that when I started shaking from head to toe, that I was not ill, but rather that I was tuning into energy and energy fields.

This became a mystical tour: When we arrived, I was immediately drawn to a dolmen.[1] I did not even know that they existed in Monségur, however I knew instantly that I must first do energy work before the group climbed the steep slope to the castle. There was more than one dolmen here, which clearly identified this as a very ancient and sacred site, and indeed these dolmens linked directly to Carnac.

It was here that I found the link to the Lion Kingdom and Avalon in the deepest sense and connected with the extremely ancient past of this site. Monségur was never a fortress – it was an old Goddess site. Actually, in ancient times it was called the Moon temple, and was accompanied by the Sun Temple. Their remnants are buried in what are now the ruins of Monségur, and extended over three mountains.

We climbed the steep slope and stopped at the monument dedicated to the Cathars. Interestingly, just as before, I knew that I was not meant to climb up to the castle. We had a short break on the slope and a meditation. "Every one of you is connected to this ancient site in some way. Your soul knows. Your soul remembers. Everyone needs today to go where your soul leads you on this site. You will know exactly where to go and what to do. You will have moments of deep revelation."

It was in silence that everyone dispersed – in all wind directions as if invisible hands were guiding each soul to where they were destined to be. I was nudged to move to my left around a corner, with the castle looming over me. I could feel the energy changing as intuitively I moved to stand in a certain spot with the very steep slope culminating in a stream running deep down below. On the opposite slope white cows grazed and I could see hay bales, created from the freshly cut grass.

From this point there was an ancient path leading around the mountain, and I sensed it had once led to the secret cave entrances. Indeed, Monségur itself was built on top of a massive underground cave and tunnel system which linked up directly with all the rest connecting the planet together. Even beyond that, it directly links together the abodes of the Ancient Ones, who live in the Inner World, Agartha to form a network.

I was guided to stand between two small rocks as energy coursed through me and intense energy work commenced, as I shifted into a very much altered and higher state. I was connecting to the Green and Gold Crystal Pyramids, deeply buried underneath this very mountain, and literally was weaving the energy lines from here to the Sun Temple in Versailles, to Chartres and to Carnac. It was concentrated work.

The next minute I was singing, indeed chanting. Previously, I had lost my beautiful soprano voice while working in the Middle East, and could no longer sing, so to be standing there and chanting for 20 minutes was indeed a miracle. Yet what was being transmitted through me was a very ancient chant, sung here by High Initiates for millions of years.

It consisted of the vowels, A E I O U, and was hauntingly beautiful. Soon cows started ringing their

---

1. A dolmen (/ˈdɒlmɛn/) is a type of single-chamber megalithic tomb, usually consisting of two or more vertical megaliths supporting a large flat horizontal capstone or "table". Most date from the early Neolithic (4000–3000 BCE) and were sometimes covered with earth or smaller stones to form a tumulus. Small pad-stones may be wedged between the cap and supporting stones to achieve a level appearance (https://en.wikipedia.org/wiki/Dolmen#cite_note-m43-1). In many instances, the covering has weathered away, leaving only the stone "skeleton" of the mound intact. Wikipedia.

*Figure 7. The Memorial Stone altar.*

bells as my song echoed over the valley with the birds singing joyfully in tune. (I was told later by my students that they heard my chant and the cowbells ringing in unison and were touched to their very souls.)

I was then told to return to the monument altar. On my way down, a student Carol told me of her amazing experience as she had in fact been led to descend the steep slope to follow a path around some trees at the base only to find two more dolmens, which she, too, was asked to sing open. Once done, she was instructed to return to the Altar.

I told her about the gift of my chant. "We need to make a prayer offering, and to gather three little stones, and with each stone, to say a heart-felt prayer and dedicate it on the altar." We found stones higher up, and then I began by saying my heart-soul-felt prayer over the three stones and placing them one by one on the altar, while chanting. Carol now joined in and then she too placed her prayer stones on the altar. We continued the chanting, as one by one my students came, some from the bottom, some from the sides, and some returning from the castle above. Each one now dedicated their prayer stones and joined in the chant until we circled the altar.

What unfolded was one of the most amazing and heart touching moment of my entire life. Silence reigned, as the ancient chant now was amplified, as even the tourists all stood in silence. The children even sat down and listened.

We were AT-ONE, one heart, one mind, one spirit, one soul …

While all of this was happening, I saw the 200 Cathars, all being burnt at the stake, going to their death, chanting and joyfully singing. Even the most hardened crusaders had tears running down their cheeks, while the priests and Inquisition stood silent.

The last remnant of the Cathars were persecuted until they all died out, going to their death purposefully to end the killing and burning of innocent souls. They were so filled with the Holy Spirit that later it was said white doves rose in a clear sky, and a bolt of lightning came down.

On that day, with our chanting around the altar, we freed the ancient Temples as in truth all Cathars have incarnated again, carrying within them the remembrance of the Gospel of Love.

My heart-soul-felt prayer that day was that the Gospel of Love would be returned to Humankind.

*Figure 8. Gathering around the altar.*

## JOURNAL ENTRY

**12 September 2016**

I can't believe that I am half way through my trip to France.

The seminars were a huge success with 29 people attending from 11 countries.

We went to Monségur and I sang for 20 minutes – me who has not sung for so long!

The white cows in the meadow on the mountain slope on the other side of the River, started swinging their bells and I sang for 20 minutes to the mountains and the grass, flowers and trees started to dance. What is more – I then felt that we needed to do a ceremony around the memorial altar of the Cathars (200) who had been burnt there voluntarily. I found Carol and we went to search for stones. She had just sung to the Dolmen elsewhere – I had just activated the one at the entrance. We did a prayer with Tonne who had been called in assist.

We began this offering of prayers and soon were joined by another member of the group and the four of were singing the song I had transmitted earlier.

We all then one by one joined in the circle, as each person came down from where they had been on the mountain, and learnt the song and joined in. Other tourists stood in total silence and listened in a respectful way, even the children.

It was a very sacred and amazing miracle.

We literally had to SING Monségur into BEING again.

I felt that the Ancient Song was given to me in vowels, so that our heart centres could open up more and more, and that whatever else needed to be released and opened up was unlocked within Monségur, Mother Earth and us. It was as if the huge shadow of Monségur had been released.

I saw at one stage that the Cathars who were burnt there, went into the fires singing, happily, for they had volunteered to sacrifice their lives, so that the massacre, the genocide of them and the people of Languedoc would stop.

Afterwards every single one of us had a different story to tell – a different version of what happened, as each one had a diverse task to do, or something to release, a miracle moment and intense inner healing of some kind!

Inger had a miracle in that Jesus and the Magdalene appeared to him and he experienced a merging of the masculine and feminine within him, with a violet flame.

Tonne experienced intense inner healing and so the list goes on and on.

---

Monségur, you will forever stay in my heart and soul. You called me here. It was here that in total desperation, after being hunted down like an animal by the Inquisition, I once stood and sobbed. I was despairing over the slaughter of my people, as with extreme anxiety along with the Knights Templar, with my brothers and sister, we tried to safeguard our secrets, our sacred knowledge and manuscripts! This happened a few years before the final round up of these 200 Cathars. Indeed I, too was secretly burnt at the stake, together with five Knight Templars, at the Bishop's Palace in Urgell.

In a higher sense that day with the students at Monségur, healed my soul – and so many others.

The Gospel of Love rose again! There was not a single soul present that day, who did not feel the sacredness of the moment. Everyone's soul was touched as something sacred and eternal had changed and shifted within them

We visited the village of Monségur briefly. The castle was towering above the village, like a huge beacon of Light and when the Sun and Moon Temples still stood there, it must have been an imposing sight.

Then we went onto Soula and the students were amazed at the incredible rock formations and the information I shared with them regarding this astonishing sight, where I had done such important energy work a few days earlier.

*Figure 9. Soula and the rock formations.*

*Figure 10. Beautiful and significant sunset.*

*Figure 11. Rock figure loooking like an ancient Druid.*

From there we went to Foix before returning to Cuiza. A Mystical and magical day!

It was late afternoon when Kristina and I made our way back to St. Julia de Bec, along a different route. As we were travelling, I felt intense energy running through me, and knew that this energy line linked to Monségur and that I was called upon to do some energy work there. A most stunning sunset drew our attention – which seemed to be like another indication that something massive had shifted for all of us at Monségur.

I had just finished this work, when further along an incredible form suddenly manifested out of nowhere: It looked like an ancient Druidic Figure to me, looking up to the heavens, as if praying. Notice its hands. Somehow it also depicted the plight of the

Cathars. It felt ancient and to be the Guardian or Keeper of this place. He appeared as poignant, sad, yet also inspired. A giant of man.

The next two days we were steeped in our return to the untold and never recorded true history of Elysium, and Lion Kingdom, blending into that of Avalon, and weaving in the Celts, the Druidic history. We moved into Southern France, and ancient forgotten history, touched on Mary Magdalene and then came to the poignant legacy of the Cathars and Templars. The long-forgotten Mystery Schools, the secret and sacred knowledge that Monségur and the ancient Crystal Pyramid Temples, buried deep underground still held. For indeed, the Pyrenees hold the ancient Crystal Pyramids which once stood here and which are now being reactivated.

Following in the footsteps of Mary Magdalene we now moved to Rennes le Chateau and the retreat centre at Les Labadous, for the last day of the seminars.

When still in South Africa, when musing on my 7 seminars, I was given a clear vision that the last day had to be held on a plateau as we gathered to reopen the ancient Mystery School of Mary Magdalene once more. I had no idea where this place was, until I told Kristina, and she immediately perked up! Indeed, she knew exactly where it was as her soul had taken over custodianship, or guardianship of the site. She had been a Priestess who had served alongside Mary Magdalene. On this plateau once stood a building, reminiscent of the Alhambra in Spain, with a lion court in the middle with roses. It had been Mary Magdalene's Mystery School for women and girls.

When the patriarchy took over, they hated Mary Magdalene and the priestesses, for they feared their powers, so they attacked this school at night. Something exploded, setting the school almost instantly alight as the earth opened up and it was literally buried overnight.

Mary Magdalene was present, and escaped the catastrophe, yet paid dearly with her own life a few months later, when she was murdered in Alet-les-Bains.

Kristina was one who died in that fire and thus her deep connection to the site and she was called there as Guardian and Keeper.

This plateau, interestingly, is just outside of Rennes le Chateau. The previous owner had built a Lion Fountain on top of the plateau and I wondered if she, too, had had a vision of the school as it had once stood with the lion fountain in the courtyard? Kristina mentioned that the only other building left on the plateau was the remains of a tower.

I felt in my heart and soul that on the last day, we should have a ceremony there to reactivate the Ancient Mystery School. We decided to invite the group for lunch at the Labadous Retreat Centre, in the valley below, so we all met there.

A week before the seminars Kristina took me to see Labadous and I fell in love with the place. It had such wonderful energy and just felt right. We also visited Rennes le Chateau, but I must admit that I did not even want to leave the car as something did not feel right to me.

Rennes le Chateau has become famous because of the so-called Treasure, which the local parish priest, Bérenger Saunière,[2] was supposed to have found there. So many books have been written, linking the treasure with Mary Magdalene and the fact that she indeed was married to Jesus, and they produced five children, and this formed the secret lineage.

Bérenger Saunière decorated the church with some very strange statues, which I will come to later.

---

[2] The controversy around Saunière originally centered on parchments that he is said to have found hidden in the old altar of his church, that related to the treasure of Blanche of Castile, and that this was the theoretical source of his income.

*Figure 12. The Seminar participants.*

Suffice to say, it was a place I was not interested in exploring further, even though everyone else seemed to be fascinated by it. The energies there gave me the creeps!

The group met at Labadous Retreat Centre in the early morning as we decided to walk from the Retreat centre up to the plateau, where we would hold the seminars.

As we walked along the path, I immediately started calling in the Guardians and Keepers of the place. I never go anywhere to do energy work, without calling them in. They will not allow you access to the information, or the sites, or allow you to truly see, if you do not ask for permission first. They then read your intent, and will only allow you to see, with true vision, if your intent is clear.

I have never been stopped so many times in my life by these Guardians and Keepers, as that day going uphill to the Plateau. I had to give the keys and codes every time, before we could proceed. I was showing my students this, and how the whole face of the mountain in front of us, changed as I did this! They were astounded! Everything started to shift! The cliffs moved – it was like stepping into a totally different world!

As we arrived on the plateau I was shown exactly where we needed to sit in a circle.

Some locals joined us, as I had asked Kristina to invite them. I began the activation and ceremony. As I began activating the energy fields, a flock of herons appeared again in the sky – to me that was a sign that I could proceed and that we were surrounded by Beings of Light, all of whom we gathered here to help reactivate the Old Mystery School which once stood there.

The ceremony itself shifted time and space. We were spanning dimensions. We now chanted the very same chant which had been given to me at Monségur.

PART 2: CHAPTER 5: THE 7 SEMINARS, GROUP TOUR TO MONSÉGUR: THE REOPENING OF MARY MAGDALENE'S MYSTERY SCHOOL

*Figure 13. The plateau with the Lion Fountain.*

*Figure 13. The plateau with the Lion Fountain.*

*Figure 15. The activation and ceremony.*

*Figure 16. Surrounded by so many Beings of Light and Mary Magdalene.*

*Figure 17. Relaxing in the shade.*

125

*Figure 18. Ancient stone building.*

Exactly at that moment, a white eagle appeared in the sky – my totem! It was a sign that the work being done had Divine Blessing, and was sanctified!

If you ask me to describe what happened on that plateau, words fail me. I just know that I went into an extremely altered state. I straddled dimensions, as I wove strands of ancient energies together.

Simultaneously, all the souls present in that school when it burnt down were freed from the trauma they had experienced. The place was re-sanctified.

We were surrounded by so many Beings of Light and Mary Magdalene was there, and a hosts of others. All were pouring in their collective energy.

A miracle happened that day which is difficult to express in words. Some things are best felt and experienced in the depths of one's heart, soul and being, even if the mind boggles and cannot stretch so far!

It was releasing the Divine Feminine powers and setting humanity free. No longer could their voices be silent. Those voices will rise and they will be heard again. No more suffering.

Love poured in from above. Such Pure Divine Love. I felt my heart centre expanding and I felt how the Power of Love descended into the hearts and souls of all present, and into the land itself.

It was the Power of Love which would heal in the deepest sense, for the Power of Love is the greatest of all Divine Powers. The whole Omni Verse rests and functions and breathes Love.

* * *

All the time, while this was happening, I had the distinct intuitive feeling that we were being watched from Rennes Le Chateau. It did not bother me, for I made it my business, while in France, to go my own way quietly, and not to become involved in the intrigues and disputes which went on in some quarters, especially here in Rennes le Chateau. There were so many climbing on the bandwagon, as they continued to seek the so-called treasure, digging everywhere! What exactly they hoped to find, nobody knows.

After the ceremony I was prompted to take a walk further up to the edge of a cliff where I found an ancient wall, with signs of someone having dug there. The priest? Again, I felt that he had never found what he was truly looking for, and that his soul was still around – a tortured soul.

There was the remains of an ancient square stone building there, with a door. I immediately felt that this led to underground tunnels, and that somehow Saunière had entered them. There was the remains of an ancient stone wall as well.

### JOURNAL ENTRY

I felt that the Priest digging at Rennes le Chateau had disrupted the energies there and we thus repaired the energy lines. Indeed, later I saw this self-same priest, stuck in the church he had created. So he still walks, and digs there, and has not found rest, even though his secrets

*Figure 19. Saunière.*

went to the grave with him. Whatever he was looking for, or found, has not brought this soul peace, indeed, I felt that he sold his own soul.

I tuned into him, still digging there, digging, digging, and yet never finding what he was truly looking for. He never did, he never would, for in truth it has been sealed off. It is not accessible and only will become so, when humanity finally embraces the higher dimensional state of the 7th dimension, returning to Unity consciousness, and pure, unconditional love.

As I came nearer to the edge of cliff the scene changed. I had a clear vision of Jesus and Mary Magdalene sitting there, under the shade of an ancient tree with people gathered around them. They were teaching. As this vision came, I was struck by such harmony and beauty. A sense of peace and joy.

I was drawn to immense energy coming from higher up, along the river gorge. The landscape shifted, where the red earth now shows itself. Indeed this site, linked up directly with Monségur and the Crystal Pyramids.

Ancient, more ancient than ancient, all pertaining to the Lion Kingdom and Isis, for she started the Mystery Schools here in what is now the Pyrenees. One of seven.

I returned as the others were waiting for me – my brothers and sisters from other lifetimes, there with me, all contributing towards the completion of the work. I felt immense gratitude, awe and wonder!

## JOURNAL ENTRY

The group also opened up a massive energy centre on the plateau outside Rennes le Chateau, on the site of the ancient Mystery School of Mary Magdalene there, on the last day of our seminars. On this site she had a school for women and girls, with a massive courtyard of lions in the centre, reminding me of Alhambra, with rose gardens as they made rose oils and other elixirs. The men wanted to destroy the Priestesses, and therefore attacked by night, blowing the place up. The earth opened, and the school sunk into the ground burying alive the women and girls.

When we began the ceremony, a flock of birds flew over us, which was again a clear sign that spirit was with us.

I did the meditation.

As soon as I started that A WHITE EAGLE APPEARED!!! MY TOTEM ANIMAL!!! A sign that all my cosmic helpers were present.

I felt that the Priest digging at Rennes le Chateau had disrupted the energies there so we repaired the energy lines. Indeed, later I saw this self-same priest, stuck in the church he had created. So he still walks, and digs there, and has not found rest, even though his secrets went to the grave with him. Whatever he was

*Figure 20. Red earth site linked to Monségur and the Crystal Pyramids.*

looking for, or found, has not brought this soul peace, indeed, I felt that he had sold out his own soul.

All he did was disrupt the energy lines there and I had to now repair them.

It was a great gift to be able to teach again after so many years. 7 seminars and 29 beautiful souls. We bonded on all levels with just so much love!

I had to open up so many energy centres here in France and never had a days' rest! It started from the moment I landed at Charles de Gaulle Airport and never stopped, indeed on the day I left, I was still doing energy work in the Louvre and the Tuileries gardens! We had our farewell lunch there at Les Labadous. Love in the truest sense. Later there was drumming under ancient trees next to the river.

We all had experienced something amazing and unique in the last 7 days. It had bonded us together, as souls we all had done this work before!

It was hard saying farewell to these beautiful souls. They had become a part of my own being, and a part of my own soul.

It was with a sense of wonder that I went to bed that night – I had been told that all the souls who needed to be at my seminars, would be there. Indeed, it happened! They came from 11 different countries, yet it always felt as if we had known each before as indeed, we had!

Miracles happened at Monségur, and here at Les Labadous and during the seminars.

There was so much love and shared laughter, yet we also shared moments of intense inspiration, Aha moments, when all became crystal clear.

To me the greatest of all miracles was that we, as souls, found each other again in this lifetime – all divinely orchestrated!

Is that not a miracle in itself?

When I stood on the plateau, I was shown a mountain in the distance. I turned to Kristina and said: "That Mountain connects directly to the plateau and to the Mystery School which once stood here. We need to go to it!"

*Figure 21. Me feeling immense appreciation and joy with my group.*

*Figure 23. Farewell gifts for me.*

I did not know then that my life would change there, in ways I would only be able to fully understand a few years later, although I, and all those present were transformed on top of that plateau when we reopened Mary Magdalene's Mystery School.

That night she appeared to me, and thanked me.

I had tears running down my cheeks.

Words fail me.

Little did I know, what would be waiting for me, as a result of the massive energy work we had done here today.

\* \* \*

*Figure 22. Farewells.*

*Figure 24. My soul family.*

CHAPTER 6

# The Anointing at Bugarach

When I stood on the plateau after the reopening of Mary Magdalene's Mystery School, I was shown a mountain in the distance. It linked directly to the plateau and her School and I was told that this was where I needed to go to next.

After two days of much deserved rest, Kristina wanted to attend a music concert in a little village church. The church was packed, and three young musicians, two harpists and a contrabass player, teamed up to play the most unusual but beautiful music. It reminded me of the Troubadours. These music concerts are held all over France during the summer months, and are very well supported.

Afterwards we went on the most beautiful scenic drive, following the river, first through Rennes-les-Bains, with its natural hot springs. The remains of the Roman baths are still there, and it is a stunning place, filled with so much energy. As we rounded a bend there, hovering and brooding over everything was an ancient Templar Castle, in direct alignment with Bugarach,[1] where we were heading, and the plateau on the mountain I had been shown.

As soon as we approached a bridge over the river and narrow gorge below the castle, I felt intense energy surging through me. Indeed, this was a Templar Castle and was in direct alignment with an immense energy vortex energy center, which I was tapping into, coming out the mountain the Castle was situated on and the gorge next to it. It also aligned with the River and the Spa Village we had just passed through, where according to legend Mary Magdalene and Yeshua had once lived.

We stopped next to the road, as I had been called upon to do some huge energy work, and I literally became at-one with the energy and energy fields. I was shown immensely important vortex energy, which linked directly to the Crystal Pyramids at Monségur and further up in the Pyrenees. I now understood why the Templars had chosen to build their castle there. Such powerful energy poured through the river

---

1   Bugarach (French pronunciation: [bygaʁaʃ]; Burgarag in Occitan[2]) is a commune in the Aude department in southern France, around 35 km south of Carcassonne.

*Figure 1. Beautiful scenic drive.*

*Figure 2. The Roman Baths at a Spa Village we drove through.*

*Figure 3. Templar Castle.*

*Figure 4. Huge energies emanating from the mountains.*

and gorge and the vortex energy centre was hidden from sight, on the other side of the mountain.

The closer we approached Bugarach, the more I felt the extraordinary energy of this place. As I tuned into the underground tunnel systems, I sensed that there must be many, many caves here, as well as deep underground caverns.

I asked Kristina to stop near the village. The mountain itself was somewhat surreal. It was covered with the most dramatic forms, like something out of a science fiction movie. The energy emanating from it was brooding and intense, and linked directly to the vortex and the Templar Castle, as well as to Monségur and other sites.

*Figure 5. Brooding mountains with intense energies emanating.*

FRANCE: THE SECRET KNOWLEDGE OF MARY MAGDALENE, THE CATHARS, TEMPLARS AND AVALON

*Figure 6. Giant Guardian and Keeper.*

*Figure 7. The village.*

*Figure 8. Symbols dominating the altar.*

*Figure 9. Note the Templar and Cathar Cross! Note the heart with roses on it.*

I was literally shaking from head to toe. This place was far more powerful than anything Rennes Le Chateau could conjure up, and the energies were ancient. I felt the presence of the Druids here, even more so than at Carnac. The Guardians and Keepers showed themselves to me, after I had asked their permission, like the giant one shown in the above photo.

The sun was setting when we eventually meandered into the Village. Kristina wanted to replenish her water bottles from the village well, directly in front of the village church. My soul memories were being triggered. Kristina found the church door open and a light switch. We entered the silent and deserted church.

The first thing which caught my eye was the altar and symbolism on it. I was drawn there, as if by a magnet, and was fascinated by the sign which dominated the altar. There was no crucifix – only this symbol.

My attention was captured by the next item on the wall to the right of me (Figure 9). Note the Templar and Cathar Cross! Note the heart with roses on it!

I was standing by the altar rail when I felt such incredibly powerful energy surging through me and the next moment I was told to kneel down and then Mary Magdalene, Jesus and 12 High Priests and High Priestesses, Joan of Arc and the whole cosmic hierarchy surrounded me. I had an extremely powerful

PART 2: CHAPTER 6: THE ANOINTING AT BUGARACH

*Figure 10. Statue in the church. ISIS?*

*Figure 11. Woman carrying keys.*

*Figure 12. The Holy Grail?*

anointing there, and then the Fires of Illumination went through me and I anchored them in!

Some were Cathars, some were Templars, and some were Druids. Some were even more ancient than these.

I received an anointing there, which I cannot fully explain.

I then understood that this church had been built on top of the most ancient Goddess site and vortex energy centre, and in addition, it was definitely an ancient place where the High Initiates of the Ancient Mystery Schools of France, had held their anointing ceremonies.

I came out of an almost trance-like state, feeling dazed. Kristina was walking around the church, and in light of what had just happened, I also wanted to have a good look around.

I found the most interesting statues in this church which I had not seen anywhere else in France.

A woman with insignia, decorated with roses and seemingly carrying keys and codes? The Sisterhood of the Rose – ISIS?

The Holy Grail?

A pyramid in the middle of what looked like a Spiral?

Mary Magdalene. Notice what she is standing on? A serpent! This symbolized her having conquered her lower self, thus being in the ascended state. Furthermore, the serpent signifies that she had gained Gnosis, she had opened all her Sun energy centres, and thus was fully present in her higher body, her ascended and resurrected state, and the truth of her soul.

The Divine Feminine holds the serpent power, the spiralling energy, and in reality the highest of all Divine Energies.

The greatest of all surprises was still to come though!

Kristina was calling me to the far side of the church. "Look what I have found!" There was a niche in the wall, which had an altar with three candelabras. Kristina intuitively turned them around, and there, to our utter amazement, we found three faces: those of Jesus and Mary Magdalene, and we concluded that the third belonged to Joseph of Arimathea.

*Figure 13. A pyramid in the center of what looked like a spiral.*

*Figure 16. Jesus.*

*Figure 17. Mary Magdalena.*

*Figure 14. Mary Magdalene standing on a serpent.*

*Figure 15. Closer view of serpent.*

I was now shaking from head to toe! These were real images, this is what they had looked like in that lifetime. The fact that I was shaking meant that these were true images. (A few years later I was sent a photo taken in the cave in Egypt, and was astounded that the same faces were depicted. Coincidence? No – it was confirmation! Indeed, when I went to Egypt to continue this journey in 2019, I insisted that we visit the Gnostic Monastery in which the stellar shown on the pictures sent to me, was kept in a grotto (Figure 18).

Something had happened in that church, which had me reeling. I then understood that this was an ancient site. It had probably been a Cathar Church, for why else would a Cathar and Templar cross still be there? Additionally, I felt that this had been a temple dedicated to the Goddess, and thus her statue stood there, with the serpent at her feet.

Indeed, I had lectured in my seminars about the Sacred and most Secret Order of the Rose, the Serpent and the Grail, and all three were present in this church! It was a place where the highest initiates of the Ancient Mystery Schools had received their anointing! I sensed that his church held really ancient energies, symbolism, and sacred knowledge, to a much higher degree than the Church at Rennes-le-Château, which many rave about. In truth, that church is nothing compared to the one in Bugarach!

Maybe it was by grand design that this strange photo appeared on my camera. I don't know how it arrived there, but considering what had already happened there on that day, nothing surprised me anymore!

## JOURNAL ENTRY

I was drawn to the altar where a statue of Mary Magdalene dominated and the sun discs of 7th Central Sun were behind her. The whole church was filled with amazing symbols and I was told this was where the High Priestesses were anointed.

I was standing by the altar rail when I felt such immensely powerful energy soaring through me and the next moment I was told to kneel down and then Mary Magdalene, Jesus and 12 High Priests and High Priestesses, Joan of Arc and the whole cosmic hierarchy were surrounding me. I had an incredibly powerful

*Figure 18. Figures in grotto in monastery.*

*Figure 19. Fascinating photo I took with mysterious effects.*

anointing there and then the Fires of Illumination went through me and I anchored them in!

To our utter surprise we found candelabras with three faces on them, on one of the side altars – we only noticed these faces when Kristina turned them around – Joseph, Yeshua and Mary Magdalene! They looked ancient and I am sure that the faces etched on them were a true representation and likeness of them in real life.

The entire church was interesting. There was a huge statue of the Goddess on the side, stamping her foot on a massive serpent with interesting symbols which I photographed. Most significantly the Queen of Heavens was matched by the King!

I am still reeling from the anointing which was extremely powerful!

To me this church was the real link to Mary Magdalene and the Ancient Goddess sites, in spite of being tucked away. When I later visited Rennes le Chateau church I was greatly disappointed for in fact its energies were distorted.

Bugarach was one of the most important centres and therefore the Knights Templar build their castle overlooking this site, for they knew.

It took me a few days to try and assimilate the anointing. The journey itself had taken on a new meaning and form.

Something deep within me had shifted.

It was as if all the lifetimes before had led me to this moment. Yet, in truth it was but the start, a beginning, a rebirth, an awakening.

What was coming next?

\* \* \*

CHAPTER 7

# The Templar

Even before I set foot in France, a certain Templar was haunting me, indeed several of them. When I arrived in Southern France, this was intensified. I will never forget when we were travelling for the first time to Couiza, following the course of the Aude river, and we arrived at a certain spot.

"I know this place," I said to Kristina, "I have been here before! There is a Templar Holding next to the river here!"

"Yes!" she said, "But how did you know?"

I just knew! Indeed, when we rounded a bend, I saw the old Stone Bridge crossing the Aude, and I clearly saw myself riding across this bridge on my white horse with a company of Knight Templars!

The old Templar buildings and church are still there. I definitely had a distinct sense of déjà vu, but we had no time to linger as we needed to keep an appointment. I noticed the stable entrance, and cold shivers ran through me! I clearly saw how a Templar who I had known, had ridden his horse into the stables, and been ambushed and killed!

I was in a daze when we drove off, and Kristina promised to bring me back there later on, after the seminars.

That night when I downloaded the photos on my camera, I was astounded to see how the camera had picked up – both a horse and a man. If you look carefully, you can see these images on the photos below and on the following page!

*Figure 1. The Ancient Templar holdings, now apartment blocks.*

*Figure 2. The first photo of the stable entrance, orbs and strange figures start appearing.*

*Figure 3. You can now start making out ghostly shapes of a man and a horse.*

*Figure 4. The round Templar church we later visited at night, to listen to a music concert.*

The round Templar church, where we went later that evening to listen to a music concert, had acoustics which were otherworldly. That night I was so moved by the interior of the church, although it had been greatly altered, and eventually I went to sit outside on an ancient bench, where the Templars themselves must have sat many times. The stars were twinkling above me, and I once again had a clear vision of the Templar, and the awareness that he was riding to his death. I realized that I needed to return to this place in daylight, to help his soul find rest … And also mine …

Meanwhile I was receiving vivid impressions of exactly what had occurred here. At that time, when the Cathars were suffering so greatly, the Knights

Templar often participated in clandestine operations, to assist in safeguarding their secret knowledge. In order to do this, they worked with me and others in amazing ways.

This particular Templar had haunted me for so long. I clearly saw us meeting in the high Pyrenees, and it was a desperate liaison. I was reaching the end of my endurance and tether, hunted down like an animal, most often sleeping in caves, and scavenging for scraps of food. I had always been armed with a type of dagger or short sword, which I had learnt to operate from my brothers, thus I was well able to defend myself, if necessary.

Certain routes had been closed off due to the presence of the Crusaders, and we were now meeting to find a way around them. The only way to what is now Northern Spain, was through Andorra, where a Bishop resided who had a long-standing vendetta against my family, especially my father, who he had kept prisoner for some years, due to a land dispute. Therefore, I knew I was putting my life on the line by travelling through his territory, even dressed as a man.

We spent desperate hours together, for he had definitely disobeyed Templar Orders in order to meet me, and even more so through assigning five of his most trusted men to assist me on this journey, which proved to be my saving grace in so many ways.

He was aware however that his Templar Order ranks had been infiltrated, by those now leaning towards the Roman Church, who had hijacked the Templar holdings there. In this regard, he had already defied orders, and was loyal to secret information he had sworn to safeguard (concerning the Cathars and the pure and uncontaminated High Templar Orders, which was top secret, because of the defection of certain in the Templar ranks). I begged him to come with me, but he refused, knowing full well that he was riding to his death.

Indeed, I met my death before him. For when we parted, our company crossed the borders into Andorra, almost to the other side, on the way to

*Figure 5. The Templar Well he was thrown into.*

*Figure 6. Note the spiraling serpent energy on the wall, where the mechanism fits into. This is a sure sign that the Templars built this Well, at the back of their church on a high energy spot, thus indicating that the serpent earth energy is present, amplified by the waters below.*

Barcelona, when we were caught and dragged to the Bishop's Palace as prisoners. It was here we were held, and the Knights Templar categorically refused to leave me, even for a moment, which saved me from being raped.

Due to their refusal to cooperate, we were all burnt at the stake in the Bishops Palace courtyard, to the sound of the Priests singing the Psalter.

All I know is that I felt no pain. There was a sense of enormous release from my physical form, as I was surrounded by angels and archangels and so many Light beings. Literally I was being lifted into the Light …

He was put to death a few days later. When he crossed the bridge and entered the stable alleyway, he was pulled off his horse and asked to divulge his secrets. He refused. They cut his throat and threw him into the well.

Just before I finally left for Paris, Kristina and I finally found a moment to return to the Templar Holdings.

As I entered the stable alleyway and went around the corner, I found this well and was in tears. This is where he met his end.

I did my final rites of love for him, setting him free, and in a sense myself too, from all the old vows and oaths of secrecy and silence we had once taken. I cannot even try to put what I felt into words, for words fail me.

"No greater love has a man, than to lay down his life for his brothers."

Indeed!

This place, and this Well, will be forever etched in my soul memory banks …

\* \* \*

CHAPTER 8

# The Tragedy and the Triumph

My two months in France were now coming to an end. From the very moment I stepped onto French soil, I had been called upon to do massive energy cleansing, clearing and releasing work, as well as downloading so much of what had been lost in the mists of time, and either written out of history books, or never recorded at all.

It was in fact a traumatic journey of my own soul, as I recalled all my past lives there, the persecution, and the mass genocide of my own people.

Paris, Versailles and Chartres all have their roots in the time-zone of the Lion Kingdom, and it is from its ruins that Avalon subsequently arose. The ancient megalithic sites were from the Lion Kingdom, and later the Druidic High Orders used the same massive Stonehenge-type stone circles, and the Crystal Pyramids, to create their magic. They were High Scientists who knew how to manipulate energy and energy fields, and work with this power in order to co-create. Yet at the same time the Matriarchy was in her prime, and the Goddess reigned supreme.

The serpent mounds and energy centres in and around Chartres were concealed. The Crystal Pyramids were buried under the sea, just offshore from Brittany and southwards to the West Coast of Spain. Indeed, Britain belonged to the same vast continent, as did Ireland, and thus the Celts rose from the ashes of what had once been Avalon.

Many believe that the Celts had no written language. They had no need for one, for they still knew how to communicate telepathically and through their spiraling symbols. They spoke a long forgotten sacred geometric Light Language, which had been lost to Humanity when Avalon fell. The High Druidic Council kept this Light Language, and the Sacred Maths, Geometry and Astronomy, concealed and hidden, so only the highest of initiates could access such knowledge.

Why? At the time of Avalon's decline, Mu and later Lemuria had risen, and their inhabitants were androgynous beings, who took part in one of the most significant experiments on Earth. As Mu fell, Atlantis arose, although on a much lower frequency band – that of the 5th dimensional state, and not the 7th. The story of Mu, Lemuria and Atlantis will be told in other books.

The Celtic Races in fact spanned all of the *Ancient Supercontinent*. Originally there were 12

Tribes, and each tribe had their own High King and Queen, who ruled in tandem with the three High Druidic Councils. Yet, the Queen actually had more power than her male counterpart, and lineages passed through the female line. Indeed, she could choose her own consort, and he had to prove himself worthy of her.

My journey thus started at the height of the 7th Dimensional Lion Kingdom, followed by Avalon. Avalon had never known trauma and wars, until she was brutally and abruptly destroyed by invaders, so she collapsed in immense suffering, pain and bewilderment. Suddenly the same Druidic High Orders, who had never abused their own powers, had to use them against the invaders, and then were hacked to pieces when captured. The Druidic Priests defected to the enemy, leaving the women to defend the lands. It is perhaps here that the seeds of the Patriarchy and those who later infiltrated Atlantis and caused its demise, were sown.

Much later, when the Celtic tribes reunited, after surviving Atlantis, the Druidic High Orders were cleansed and cleared to the highest degree. Yet, as the tribes started bickering and fighting, even the Druids fell prey to corruption. Human sacrifices were an almost daily occurrence, and painstakingly recorded by the Roman invaders.

Every time there is any great trauma, it saturates the ground and clogs the Earth's energy centres. Sacrificial sites and battle grounds leave an imprint of suffering and pain, for thousands, even millions of years, and they need to be cleansed and cleared.

The Celts however (the Gauls were but one of the 12 tribes), were highly civilized, and they built sophisticated cities with roads and bridges. Later the Romans destroyed many of them, or simply built over the sites, and credited themselves with the achievements of others. Those who conquer love to wipe out their enemies, and then glorify themselves. Lest we forget.

However, most of the trauma which saturates many areas of France, can be attributed to the First and Second World Wars.

We drove along the west coast of France to La Rochelle, and as we entered the city, I felt as if I could not breathe. The agony which suffused the landscape was too much for me to handle. We passed a bunker and I felt quite nauseous. It was only when we finally drove over a massive bridge, and were amongst the salt pans, that I could breathe freely again. During my seminars a student from Brittany, told me that in World War I, the Americans had bombarded the city and killed many civilians, thus the ensuing intense trauma and pain. I am merely mentioning this, as a way of demonstrating how these events can block the energy, and leave their energetic imprint upon all those who live in such places.

As we drove through France, I was often called upon to cleanse and release just such trauma and suffering. Many stuck souls were liberated, as the Cosmic Hierarchy stepped in to assist them to finally make the transition, and leave planet Earth.

Entering Southern France, I felt like I was spanning many timelines, and moving through so much energetically. Not only did Mary Magdalene reveal herself, as I downloaded her unique story, but I was also asked to reopen the Ancient Mystery Schools of France (which in truth date back to Isis and the Lion Kingdom). She was but one of the High Priestesses who trained there, millions of years later.

It was however Sissi, Cécile de Foix, who came to the fore most prominently in my experience. While driving through the Pyrenees, I spotted caves everywhere, in which the Cathars had hidden. I knew where the underground tunnels were. Memory banks were triggered wherever I went. With it, I experienced the trauma and pain, not only of my life as Sissi, but also due to the genocide of an entire people.

The landscape speaks here. The souls speak.

PART 2: CHAPTER 8: THE TRAGEDY AND THE TRIUMPH

*Figure 1. The twisty road with cave entrances everywhere.*

*Figure 2. Faces appearing at the entrance.*

*Figure 3. Closer view of faces at entrance.*

*Figure 4. Continuous bends.*

Not only of the Cathars, the Mary Magdalene Priestesses, but also the Templars, who I will come to in due course.

A few days before leaving, after once again undergoing deep cleansing, clearing and releasing, we drove up a spectacularly narrow gorge, the Gorge de Galamus with sheer drops on either side. The road was so narrow that two vehicles could only pass each other on certain parts of the road, and we could not see oncoming traffic around the sharp bends. I tuned into the Templars and Cathars here with great intensity and accuracy. I felt their presence as I spotted cave entrances everywhere.

*Figure 5. Face in the entrance.*

143

Note the Faces which appeared when I was photographing the entrance to this massive cave. Immense energy was pouring from it, and I took many photos of this.

The landscape tells stories here to those who can tune in to it. Perhaps the fact that many of the small villages in Southern France are almost empty had a bearing on the general atmosphere of mystery and long forgotten stories. In certain places entire English communities had arrived, buying and occupying the forlorn empty villages and homes.

For many hundreds of years, as others came in to occupy the area, which had been stripped of its population by the mass genocide, and an overriding fear of the Inquisition, the Cathars and Templars were barely remembered.

Yet, now they have returned!

The Cathar Prophecy is being fulfilled. It prophesied that in circa 700 years, the laurel would rise again. Indeed, it has.

I can testify to this. So many of the souls who were involved here, who paid the highest price, have found their way to me for Soul Readings over the last few years. The Soul Readings tell of intense pain and trauma, detailing the atrocities committed on them by the Inquisition.

To me, this whole journey, has been both a releasing of souls, trauma and pain suffused in the landscape, as well as a journey of forgiveness and loving Grace. When a wound is infested, a surgeon uses a scalpel to open the wound, to clean and sanitize it, so that it can heal.

This is indeed what happened during this journey.

I had to dig very deeply into my own soul memory banks. I felt pain so intensely at times that it was beyond description. I did not even realize how deep those wounds were, until I returned home to South Africa. It has taken me almost four years just to heal from this trip, from all that I had been witness to, and everything that happened to me in those lifetimes.

A good friend offered to send healing, and she summed up the trauma and pain I was experiencing like this: "It is as if you were frozen in a time bubble and I had to unfreeze you, so that you could finally heal at the deepest levels."

Southern France was also frozen in the time bubble, and I had to liberate thousands of souls, and the collective trauma. As it healed, I too was healed.

Mountains are alive, as are the Guardians and Keepers, and the Ancient Ones. The Pyrenees are filled with them. As I called in the Ancient Ones, the entire energy of the places shifted, and the camera would pick up what the naked eye could not see.

Note the woman who suddenly appeared next to a cave I was photographing. Indeed, the cave wall seemed to have engravings on it.

*Figure 6. Woman next to the cave.*

While I was taking pictures of the hills near Gruissan, and feeling intense energy coursing through me, look at what suddenly emerged – a little gnome!

It was here on the south eastern coast of France that I spent my last two weeks. Gruissan itself became a journey into the megalithic sites, and that of the Lion Kingdom.

Interestingly, it was here where Mary Magdalene arose, in the most beautiful tribute to her I have ever come across (Figures 9 and 10). Note how Mary Magdalene is shown with her five children – confirming that indeed she was married to Jesus.

PART 2: CHAPTER 8: THE TRAGEDY AND THE TRIUMPH

*Figure 7. A little gnome.*

*Figure 8. Mary Magdalene and children.*

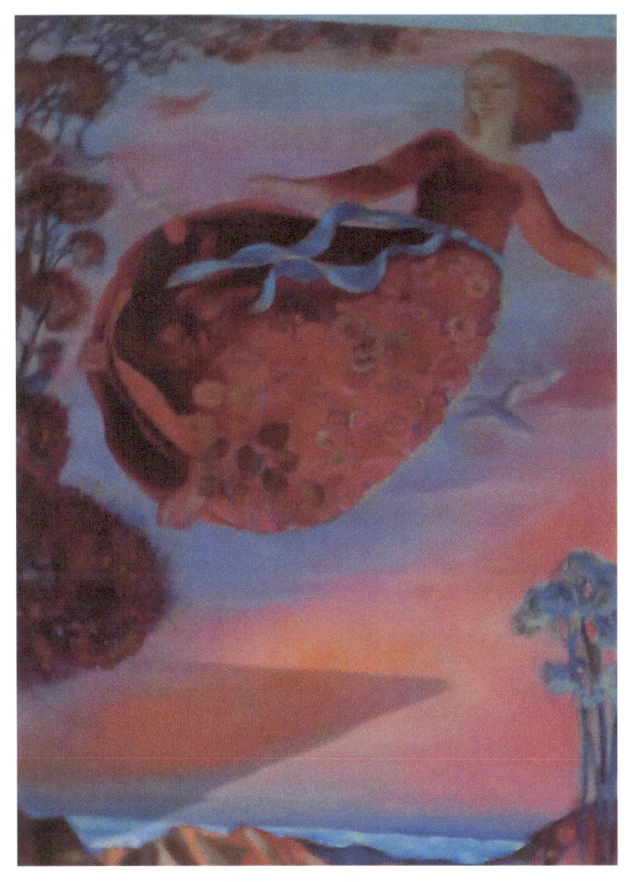

*Figure 9. Mary Magdalene ascending.*

In fact, I was tuning into her arrival, and her journey back home during this time.

The journey continued onto Collioure near the Spanish border. Time to just relax and be, here in Catalonia, which had once belonged to the King of Aragon, and was thus very Spanish in character. A lovely seaside resort, framed by the Pyrenees and vineyards.

This was taken on the Spanish side of the Pyrenees where I found a massive vortex energy source.

It was with a sense of a mission accomplished that I flew from Toulouse Airport to Paris. I had come to France to do intense energy work, to download the true history of the region and lay old past life ghosts, suffering and pain to rest. I had succeeded.

As I spent the last two days exploring the Tuileries Gardens and the Louvre, I felt a deep and abiding love for France. Around me, wishing me farewell, were Joan of Arc, Mary Magdalene, Sissi, and Marie Antoinette. The latter had a humorous twist, for it was in the King's Chamber in the Louvre, that I encountered the ghost of the Sun King, Louis the IV. "Hello!" He said, "I have not seen you for such a long time! Where have you been?" I laughed and told him that he had got stuck in a time-warp, while I had moved into a different century, the future. It reminded me, that past, present and future actually all exist simultaneously!

France is a true enigma – all time zones meet there, for it is the womb of the Earth.

*Figure 10. Spanish Pyrenees with massive vortex energy source.*

\* \* \*

## CHAPTER 9

# What did the Templars and Cathars hide?

One of the greatest genocides ever, took place in Southern France. What was it that the church had wanted to stamp out? The Catholic Inquisition ruthlessly tried to get their hands on the hidden knowledge and the secret teachings that the church felt it lacked, or more accurately, wanted to eradicate, since the Roman Church had been built upon untruths. There is much evidence of the latter, especially regarding the resurrection of Jesus, for indeed he never died on the cross.

It started with St. Dominic, who made it his business to emulate the Cathar faith, because he soon realized that they were dedicated, and pure – much purer and more devoted than any Catholic priest. Nevertheless he still wanted to annihilate them.

The Pope had no qualms when calling for a Crusade against the Cathars: "... *are called the Cathars or the Patarenes or the Publicani or by different names has grown so strong that they no longer practice their wickedness in secret ... But proclaim their error publicly and draw the simple and weak to join them, we declare that they and their defenders and those who receive them are an anathema and we forbid, under pain of anathema, that any should keep or support them in their houses or lands or should trade with them ... We enjoin all the faithful, for the remission of sins, that they oppose this scourge with all their might and by arms protect the Christian people against them. Their (Cathar) goods are to be confiscated and princes free to subject them to slavery ... Those who in true sorrow for their sins die in such a conflict should not doubt that they will receive forgiveness for their sins and the fruit of an eternal reward. We ... Grant to the faithful Christians who take up arms against them, and who on the advice of the bishops or prelates seek to drive them out, a remission of two years of penance imposed on them.*" (Source: "*The Knights Templar in the Golden Age of Spain*" by Juan García.)

This allowed bandits and outlaws to join in the Crusade, such as the utterly ruthless Simon de Montfort, who was given full command of the crusade, after assassinating the Viscount of Beziers and Carcassonne, who had come to negotiate on behalf of his people, in an extremely cruel manner.

To declare war, and to promise that killing and looting would remove all sins, is not only insane, but goes against the very concept of the Divine and Divinity itself! It was this type of insanity that Southern France and Northern Spain were confronted with. This included the ruling parties, as much as it included the Cathars and the Templars.

This book in essence wrote itself, from the very moment when I was transported back through time within my own soul memory bank, to the time when I viewed myself being burnt at the stake with five Knight Templars in the Bishop's Palace in Urgell, Andorra.

In the ensuing years, since that first vivid recall in 2004, I have had a passionate desire to explore why I was burnt, as the only woman among five Templar Knights. As slowly but surely the memory banks stirred and opened, I knew for sure that these men could have gone free, but refused to do so, because they would not desert me in my greatest hour of need. Their Presence prevented the Inquisition from raping me, as they had done to so many of the Cathar women, as my Soul Readings attest. Brave hearts, indeed.

This compelling memory came in 2004, and as I was still a Librarian then, I started to delve into any relevant book I could find, – often finding references in books I had no idea contained such information.

The Grand Master of the first 9 Templars, Hugo de Payens, was in fact a member of the De Moncada family, the Viscounts of Béarn – the same family my mother Philippa de Foix belonged to in that lifetime. I was her youngest daughter Cécile (Sissi) born in 1200, and my father, was Raymond (Ramon) Roger, the Count of Foix.

According to the Spanish historical chronicles, as recorded by Juan Garcia Atienza in his book *The Knights Templar in the Golden Age of Spain*, Hugo and Galceran de Pinos, the sons of the Admiral of Catalonia, the Lord of Baga and his wife, Berenguela de Montcada, answered the call of Pope Urban to join the first Crusade. Note that their mother belonged to the de Moncada family (some spell it Montcada), the Viscounts of Béarn, one of the three families who were the Guardians and Keepers of the secret teachings. However, since then I have found other evidence in Freddy Silva's book on the Templars, showing that they may have come from families in the Champagne Valley, although they were cousins.

Note that Northern Spain, and what is now Southern France, were once called Occitania, and had their own language, Langue d'Oc (or Occitan, a language connected to Catalan, still spoken by some today). As previously mentioned, all these families intermarried.

The Occitania nobility were actually light years ahead of the rest of Europe. I remembered that my father had owned a vast library of manuscripts and scrolls, and the Spanish Prince, trained in the Moorish Universities and in the Middle East, was in charge of it. Women were literate, and lineages followed female lines. Moors were imported as scribes and teachers, and thus geometry, maths, astronomy, and all the other sciences, namely knowledge held by the Arab world and beyond, was gathered within these libraries. In addition, the remnants of the Celtic and Druidic libraries were already there.

Long before the Cathars even made their appearance, there was cross-cultural pollination: the Ancient Celtics, the Gauls, the Greeks, the Romans, and the subsequent empires of Charlemagne and the Fisher Kings had all already been there. The libraries of Occitania, held all of these manuscripts, and codices.

The legend of Roland, as well as those of Apollo and Hercules, ruled over Occitania. Roland was an actual Frankish military leader under Charlemagne, commander of the Breton border, who died in battle in 778 in the Pyrenees. The Troubadours incorporated Roland's bravery and lasting legacy into their songs.

---

During my own research, I often found myself being drawn to mythology. One of the mythical stories that truly fascinated me was related to the Languedoc region of southern France (my past-life recall from there will be the content of my next book). In my search for the meaning of sound vibrations, I found that the whole of the Languedoc region (there are many pyramids there originating from the time of Elysium) was associated with the Greek God Apollo).

*Figure 1. The Cross*

"According to legend, Hercules gave the Pyrenees, and especially Monségur, to Apollo. Accompanying these was another gift – the lyre. There is also a fascinating link here to Pythagoras, who came from this area of the Pyrenees. Many of his own teachings, came from a source even earlier than this." (Judith Küsel, *Why I was born in Africa*).

---

If one looks closely at ancient maps of Occitania, the three family holdings of the Counts of Foix, Comminges and Béarn stretched over the middle and western parts of the Pyrenees. In addition, they were cousins of the Count of Toulouse, the Viscount of Beziers and Carcassonne, and the King of Aragon, not to mention the Count of Barcelona.

It is therefore no accident that Hugo de Payens, the founder of the Templars, came from the same region, and exactly the same families!

Hugo and his brother joined the first Crusade under the command of a cousin Raymond IV of Toulouse, in the Catalonian army led by the Counts of Roussillon and Cerdana. Areas of what is now Southern France, indeed formed a part of Catalonia, and fell under the jurisdiction of the Kings of Aragon and Barcelona.

It is noted that the Military Order was already in existence, long before Hugo arrived in Jerusalem. Interestingly, on his arrival he knew exactly where to go, and what to dig up once he was there!

What played out in Jerusalem, is that a fellowship of the knights was established, to protect the pilgrims. King Baldwin II presented this fellowship of knights with some buildings situated in the dependencies of the old Temple of Solomon, and this led to them taking on the name "Templars".

"It is here that their founder, Hugo de Pinos, "changed his surname to reflect his place of origin, and thus became Hugo de Bagá or, in Latin, Hugo de Baganis or Paganis. The French then came to call him Hughes de Payons or de Payns." (Juan Garcia Atienza) .

It is interesting to note, that Hugo De Payen went on a Crusade, and knew exactly where to go in Jerusalem. While there, he met with a Priest from an ancient temple quite near the site where the Templars had dug up something from the foundations of the remains of the Temple of Solomon. What did they find there, and how did Hugo know where to dig, and what to search for?

I believe that the ancient knowledge these families held within their ranks, including their connection with the Ancient Mystery Schools; (whose main seat was in Monségur) the immense libraries they collectively held; knowledge handed down orally and through the High Druidic Orders, collectively gave them access to the inner workings of the Temple of Solomon. Thus Hugo and his Templars knew exactly where to dig. Could they have even held the original architectural plans of the Temple Complex within their libraries? There may also have been collective knowledge of what had been purposefully hidden there.

Since all those who belonged to such secret societies and Mystery Schools were interlinked, even across the Arab and Christian divide, through those ties, the Templars had access to the ancient, hidden secrets through the ages.

The Templar holdings in Spain and Southern France, were intrinsically connected with the family holdings of those who were the true Guardians and Keepers of the Sacred Grail, so the secret knowledge these families held, was protected and kept within their own ranks. The King of Aragon, was cousin to the three families involved, and the lands they held were as much under his protection, as those of the

Count of Toulouse, and Viscount of Beziers and Carcassonne. Indeed, through intermarriage, they were cousins.

In addition, they were all in Occitania. They shared the same origins, the same language, and the same culture. This was long before Spain was unified, and at that time Northern Spain was composed of Leon, Navarre, Aragon, Asturias and Barcelona. The mainland, in what is now Spain, was occupied by the Moors.

These families were known to have a close interaction with the Moors. Occitania, was far more advanced at that stage than other parts of France, which were still in the Dark Ages. Occitania was highly civilized by European standards. They employed educated Moors, and their sons attended Moorish Universities. Manuscripts and documents were acquired through the Arabs. Maths, geometry and many of the ancient sciences came via the Arabs to Occitania.

The Troubadours were a vital component of this region, as they formed the remnant of the High Order of the Bards. They brought the ancient knowledge to those who listened, disguised in song and oration, and only the initiated truly understood the hidden order, the hidden meaning. Although their poems expressed the soul of the people, and celebrated the Courts of Love, underlying all of this was the Gospel of Love, and the ancient secrets this region held. Note that Count Ramon Roger de Foix and others of his ilk, were included within the ranks of these Troubadours. His Grandmother, the Viscountess of Beziers and Carcassonne, was the main Patroness, and to have her approval was in a sense, like being knighted into the High Order of the Bards.

The Templar Order was created, as deep down Occitania already felt an impending threat, the shadow of Rome looming over their heads. Although they practised tolerance and freedom of expression to a greater degree than any other medieval country of the time, there was nevertheless a stirring jealousy from the Church towards those who followed the ancient teachings of the Cathars, and the hidden teachings of that region. Indeed, the priests were known to openly have concubines, and were known for their hedonism and debauchery, while the Cathars stood out for their purity, integrity, devotion and quiet dedication to the Gospel of Love.

I have delved deeply into whatever records I could find about the Count of Foix, Ramon Roger, a Troubadour, and my father in that lifetime, taking part in the 2nd Crusade, and there was much to discover, as he was highly educated, and known for his articulate speech. Indeed, when asked by his cousin, the Count of Toulouse to speak on behalf of his people, he stunned those who were listening, with his eloquence and knowledge. His sister, Esclaremonde, notably shared the same ability, and she caused a stir at a meeting, when the priests told her to shut up and go back to her spinning! It was a direct affront to freedom of speech, and the unique status women held in Occitania, and most of all to Esclaremonde herself!

Please note that at this time, Catharism exploded, and the Pope and those of his persuasion, launched a campaign against the Counts of Toulouse, Beziers, Carcassonne, Foix, etc. asking them to eradicate Cathars. This proved to be an impossible request, for most of the nobles had Cathar family members, and if they were not Cathars, they belonged to the secret inner circles. They could not turn against their own kin and above all else, as Keepers and Guardians of the Grail itself, they could not turn against themselves.

The Templar Order officially now occupied the land and holdings given to them in Occitania, the various Spanish States (notably on and around the pilgrimage routes in the Pyrenees, towards Compostela), and Portugal, thus the sacred Grail, the sacred knowledge of Avalon, and all that was preserved by the Grail families, was guarded by the Templars and Cathars.

Although the Templars proclaimed themselves neutral, because of their own kinship to the Cathars, they were anything but neutral.

Remember the vast libraries, the collective wisdom held within this region. The Templars were known to have gathered manuscripts and knowledge themselves, when they still held properties in the Middle East. Reference is made to them even making contact with the Arab Assassins, for example. The Piri Reis Map which shows the world without ice, was first made known in Portugal, which later became the secret stronghold of the Templars, after their Grand Master, Jacques de Molay, one of the best-known Templars, was burnt at the stake. Yet, Portugal, had Templar holdings, long before that. Indeed, apparently when the Templar Order disappeared, the Portuguese seafarers used their own maps in order to circumnavigate Africa! Templar crosses and remnants have been found in Nova Scotia, Canada, therefore the Templars had access to secret maps and information, which no one else had.

When I visited the Templar holdings, I was struck by the precision of their work, yet also an atmosphere of serenity which surrounded it. Unlike the other places of slaughter, the energy in and around these places was tranquil. When I attended a music concert in the circular Templar Church where they were murdered, I sat on their ancient bench outside, and looked up at the stars above me. I felt a deep respect and love for these men (and women also, for they were indeed part of the order too.) I understood that although they were forced to take a neutral stance (as far as the church was concerned) they still put their own lives and holdings on the line, and safeguarded what they could, to assist the Cathars.

The Cathars and Templars tried their utmost to conserve, to defend and to secure for posterity the wisdom they held, fighting against all odds. The Cathar and Templar treasures were never material or physical, such as gold, and precious stones, but those of the mind, spirit and soul!

Much of the most valuable and secret knowledge, and their innermost mystical teachings were stored within their vast libraries. Many of the most secret insights, which detailed how to reach the transcendental state, often referred to as Gnosis, were never written down. Yet, this knowledge went further than just the state of Gnosis – it went deeply into the empowerment of the soul, and the deep inner reconnection with the Divine within.

The most valuable of all manuscripts the Cathars and Templars held, was the Gospel of Love, sacred volumes and a lasting legacy for Humankind. They adhered to its secret teachings, which essentially was a state of being – a transcendental state! A state of balance, unity and oneness. The highest state of Love is that of the synchronicity between comparative opposites. Polarity consciousness is breached. The Highest State of Equilibrium, is indeed Gnosis. There is only ONE.

Note that the Gospel of Love came through the Ancient Mystery Schools, the very same schools to which Mary Magdalene had belonged. She used these teachings in her ministry, and taught this truth to thousands, as she was a High Priestess in her own right. She brought these very important manuscripts and scrolls which belonged to the Essenes with her to France. Some were Egyptian, acquired during her sojourn there. She brought a few of the most valuable of scrolls back with her to France, and they contained the highest forms of Illumination, and uses of the Spiraling Energy, as held in Delphi, and thus the elevated states needed for transmitting the Oracle, or being an Oracle, a Prophetess or a Seer.

The Ancient Keys and Codes of Enlightenment, which they had inherited from the Ancient Mystery Schools in the region, were kept within their ranks, deeply secret and hidden, and they tried to conserve them in their own way. Note again, that the High Initiates were trained in the highest mysteries, and the most closely guarded secrets. The rank and file never had access to them. So it has been through all the ages and will continue to be – for only if one has attained a high degree of inner training and knowledge, can one handle the energy, and likewise the responsibility which goes with it all.

Mary Magdalene had immense support and assistance from Pontius Pilate's wife. It was through a circle of very high-ranking women and men that these scrolls and manuscripts found their way to Southern France, into the Library of the Count of Foix. Again, he was acting in his role of Guardian and Keeper of the Sacred Grail.

It was this very important knowledge that Mary Magdalene merged with the existing secret knowledge that was already held within the Mystery Schools.

It was this very important knowledge that Mary Magdalene merged with the existing sacred wisdom that was already held within the Mystery Schools.

When the soul is illumined from deep within, the soul's own memory banks trigger, and Cosmic, Universal and Omni-versal knowledge and wisdom is accessed. Such information is of greater value than any earthly treasures, the physical body is but an earthly vessel the soul assumes for a very short while, an eye-wink in eternity. The soul is eternal, and thus all knowledge from all the lifetimes on Earth, in parallel lives and universes, is recorded and preserved within it. Such knowledge can never be erased. The Templars and Cathars knew this: thus they knew that their enemies could burn their physical vessels, but never annihilate the soul and all its inner knowledge, indeed, enlightenment.

Within the Cathar and Templar Orders, connected to the Grand Masters, and the Cathar Hierophants, Unity consciousness reigned – and although they were only branches, they belonged to the self-same tree – the Tree of Life. The Eternal Tree of Life, that of the Divine Order.

The Cathars were the offspring, children, or branch, so to speak of the Mystery Schools. Many believe that the Cathars came from the Bogomils, from the Balkans, who were an extension or a branch of one of the most Ancient Mystery Schools and indeed, their origin does lie there, where during the Lion Kingdom, one of the 7 Mystery Schools flourished, hidden in the high mountains, and directly connected to Delphi and Egypt. Thus the Bogomils and Cathars had the same root – the secret Ancient Mystery Schools.

Remember that Pythagoras started off in the Druidic Orders, and then went on to study in Egypt and in Delphi, Greece. Indeed ,he was in Delphi for some time, before he finally opened up his own school in what is now Italy.

The Templars, always had a military wing, for outward appearances, yet hidden within the order were the priests, the scientists, the mathematicians, the architects, the engineers, and the seekers of truth and knowledge. Those who found shelter within their holdings, were treated with respect. They had a type of Kibbutz system going, just like the Essenes. Note that St. John the Baptist, their patron saint, was trained by the Essenes, together with Mary Magdalene, and this points directly to the ancient Mystery Schools, and the hidden knowledge and secrets held within the Order.

Just like the Cathars, the Templars never accepted the Christian cross. The Cathar and Templar crosses were nearly identical. Again, this points to a common root.

*"For the Templars, the cross was not a symbol of sacrifice, but of cosmic magnitude, which it had represented since the beginnings of Humanity's tradition, as in the red Greek cross ..."* (Juan Garzia Atienza).

The Greek Cross is a symbol for the Divine, thus Divinity, and is ancient with its roots in the Ancient Mystery School Traditions. Note that the equal arms, represent balance and harmony: "As above, so below. As within, so without!" It is steeped therefore in the Hermetic Teachings, and the inner secret teachings of the Mystery Schools.

This secret knowledge, the information, held by the Cathars and Templars, is truly worth more than any gold or silver or any earthly treasure that may exist.

They remembered deep down the lessons learnt from Avalon, which had no defence against invaders, and those who came after them – notably the High Druidic Orders. The lessons from the past, compelled them to create a Military Order, as the secret information gathered by them, had indicated that a conspiracy against the Grail Families, was brewing in Rome. It was the same secret knowledge and information, which had been held by Mary Magdalene, and for which she had paid the highest price.

Through their holdings, the Templars in the Middle East gathered manuscripts and more knowledge. Indeed, through the Ancient Mystery Schools, and the legacy of the Celtic Races and Tribes, which later moved into Turkey and the surrounds, they knew about things which the rest of Europe had no inkling of, as yet. In fact, often the quest for knowledge made them either friends across borders, or enemies for life. For the enemies only saw the gold they gathered, and how their coffers swelled, ignorant of the true treasures the Templars sought, which were more in the line of truth and knowledge, than material things.

Remember that vast libraries already existed within the three families, who were the Guardians and Keepers of the secrets. In that lifetime, before I was burnt at the stake, I had been busy smuggling out the manuscripts and scrolls, with the Knights Templar. We were literally dismantling the libraries, and exporting and hiding, safeguarding what we could. If de Montfort and the Inquisition had seized them, they would have either confiscated them and added them to the library in Rome, or burnt them, as they were known to do, wherever they conquered.

Indeed, de Montfort did capture Foix Castle at one stage. Before this however, the most important scrolls and manuscripts had found their way out of the country, or were purposefully hidden in places where no one could access them.

Of course, within the ranks of the Cathars and Templars, there were still those who could be bought by the glitter of gold and the false allure of fame and fortune. Again, the rank and file did not know what the Inner Ones knew.

The Inquisition records attest to flimsy reasons for the burnings, torture, rapes and judgments and of the thousands burnt, few even had the opportunity to defend themselves. They were merely rounded up like cattle, and burnt en masse. It did not matter if they may not have belonged to the Cathars. In times of great fear, even family members or close friends and confidants may turn against their own, to save their own skins.

Within the Templar ranks, unrest was stirring, and betrayal came from within their own ranks.

It does not mean that either the Cathars or the Templars were saints – in reality we are all both saints and sinners. When one reads about, or remembers on a soul level the atrocities and immense cruelties of the Albigensian Crusade and the wars, it is horrifying. The Cathar Lords, and those who were defenders of the Grail, were accused of terrible atrocities, in a similar way to what had taken place during the Crusades and the Inquisition. Wars bring out the best and worst in human beings. Undoubtedly family vows of secrecy and the desperation of seeing, all that had once been held dear, being burnt, looted and annihilated, would have tested even the most hardened of us.

It took me a long time to work through all of this – the purity, the shame, and the atrocities. Yet, in a moment of deep revelation, I realized that the same Inquisition, the Crusaders who were so intent on wiping out the Cathars and later the Templars, were but souls, who took on certain persona and roles for a lifetime, having soul lessons to master, and those lessons are not for anyone to judge. Rather, we must know that the Divine Laws are exact – one cannot evade the Divine Laws of Cause and Effect, nor the principle of soul responsibility. What you sow you reap, even if this process takes many lifetimes.

The Cathars were so committed to their path of purity and enlightenment, that they often distanced themselves from reality. Perhaps the greatest of all collective soul lessons to be mastered, is that one cannot divorce oneself from the darkness. The darkness serves as much as the light, they are inseparable, as both assist the greater whole.

Some souls may take it upon themselves to experience darkness in the deepest sense. In this process, they serve in their own way. We may not always understand why, yet in fact we are not here to judge.

Forgiveness is the true key to healing – not only individual healing, but also collective healing.

The collective trauma of genocide, as occurred in Occitania, had repercussions. A whole country was literally stripped bare of its inhabitants. As the people died, the once rich and prosperous country became poor and sparsely populated. The Cathar faith, or what remained of it, went deep underground. The trauma and pain was absorbed by Mother Earth, and the energy was stuck there for generations.

However, the churches of that region, in quite a public way, were keeping the memories alive – the Templar and Cathar crosses are still found everywhere, as are signs and images of Mary Magdalene.

So, what lasting legacy did they leave?

It may seem, to the uninitiated, that the church won. That the mass genocide silenced the masses, that nothing survived, and that darkness had extinguished that immense light the Cathars in particular, had shone on the whole region.

In truth – this is not so! One can kill the body, but the soul lives on.

Indeed, some manuscripts, and scrolls have found their way around Europe. I spent hours trying to trace these, slowly but surely. Some ended up in the Library of Cosimo de' Medici,[1] and in secret libraries of those who belonged to the Mystery Schools in other places. Some found their way to Teutonic Knights in East Prussia (Poland). Hildegard von Bingen[2] used the ancient Cathar healing methods to create flower essence remedies. Some manuscripts ended up in Austria and some in Ireland – bearing in mind that the same close family ties between the Celtic People, stretched across the Pyrenees, into Ireland. Again Avalon, and the Druidic tradition.

Some of the Manuscripts and scrolls, have not yet been found, like the many volumes of the Gospel of Love. These were purposefully hidden and sealed off, and it was prophesied at the time, that the souls who hid them would incarnate again to find them, when Humanity was ready to receive such information, and not misuse or abuse its content.

Yet, the ultimate knowledge, was never put in writing. It was stored in the deepest remembrance of the soul. It was through the oral tradition, the intense training the initiates endured to retain such teachings, and to master them, that the truth was stored, cosmically safeguarded. The soul can retrieve and access it. No information is ever lost. Cosmically, information is stored energetically. We have just forgotten this.

I stood in places in France, and was energetically downloading such information in the same way as I do soul records. For indeed, much of the information is stored in energetic pockets in the ground itself – yet, also imprinted in the Universal information systems. There are places which are programmed to store data in energy fields, and to synchronise them with the Solar, Galactic and Universal Energy Fields and Systems.

---

1. Cosimo di Giovanni de'Medici, called "the Elder" (Italian: *il Vecchio*) and posthumously "Father of the Fatherland" (Latin: *pater patriae*) (10 April 1389 – 1 August 1464), was an Italian banker and politician, the first member of the Medici family that de facto ruled Florence during much of the Italian Renaissance. Despite his influence, his power was not absolute; Florence's legislative councils at times resisted his proposals throughout his life, and he was always viewed as *primus inter pares* («first among equals») rather than an autocrat. His power derived from his wealth as a banker, and he was a great patron of learning, the arts and architecture. Wikipedia.
2. Hildegard of Bingen OSB, also known as Saint Hildegard and the Sibyl of the Rhine, was a German Benedictine abbess, writer, composer, and philosopher, Christian mystic, visionary, and polymath. She has been considered by many in Europe to be the founder of scientific natural history in Germany. Wikipedia.

Apart from the manuscripts and the scrolls, the lasting legacy is one of consciousness, and the highest state of being – Gnosis.

Note: Associated with the Mystery Cults!

Gnosis indicates the highest states of consciousness: The All-Seeing, the All-Knowing and the All-Being.

It indicates the full opening of the third eye, and thus the higher transmitter channels – the All-Seeing, All-Hearing, All-Knowing. Indeed, the transcendental state, where polarity and separation dissolve into One. Unity Consciousness is the much altered and much higher transcendental state that one enters when one has transcended polarity consciousness, and become As One with Divinity, and all it entails, indeed All-That-Is!

The inner circles, the most advanced initiates, strove for the highest transcendental state. Whether Cathar or Templar, whether Mary Magdalene and those of her ilk, or the Druids – it was this supreme state of Being, which was the ultimate highest state of existence. One often had to ensure years of initiations and training, test after test, before reaching such a state, and it was an ongoing process of mastery. Ultimately it indicated the mastery of self.

"To thine own self be true," stated the Oracle of Delphi, where Mary Magdalene went for her training and initiations into the Higher Transmitter States. The same oracle declared, "All things in moderation." In truth the state of balance, the middle point between the two extremes is the ideal. The middle point brings not only balance, but it is there that the higher states of being are found. Not in polarity, but in balance and perfect poise, equilibrium. This is the highest state of Being, where polarity merges into one and the seer and the seen become as One.

It is also the highest state of unconditional love. In such a balanced state the heart centre is wide open, and gratitude comes to the fore. One becomes grateful for All-that-is, as it is! One becomes aware of the perfection of the Divinity within the very life on is currently living. One becomes aware that nothing is missing, and that indeed everything is perfect, whole and complete.

Life on this planet is indeed illusory. The Cathars have often been accused of putting themselves above others. They were called: "The Pure Ones," and indeed what most never understood, nor tried to understand, is that the Mystery Schools, were striving for purity. The White Flame is the Eternal Diamond Fire of the Divine, and incorporates all other cosmic colour fires or rays. The White is the Diamond Pure Ray. The highest calibre diamonds are flawless and pure. Any flaws will show up.

It is vital to be aware that while here on this planet in a physical form, there will be darkness and there will be light. Whether consciously there, displayed in the Sun or Moon by night, they are but two different poles of the same magnet. One cannot cut the magnet in half, and expect it to function. It needs both the positive and negative poles, yin and yang, masculine and feminine.

If one attempts to cut half of one's self, half of the world, out of the equation, then suffering, pain and disease are created, whether personally or collectively. The more one tries to deny the shadow, the more it will rise up to counterbalance the light. The more darkness tries to shut out the light, the more the light will penetrate the darkness and light up what needs to be lit.

Judgment leads to distortion. It judges only the one side of the coin, and forgets the other half, which is always present, always there. All are simultaneously present at exactly the same moment!

The more one tries to live in a one-sided world, the more the other side will make its presence felt. It will spurt and rise up, and immediately manifest itself, until a balance point is reached!

The scales will tip up and down until equilibrium is attained, which opens the path to Higher States of Being, when one transcends the polarity consciousness, and starts tapping into the higher state. One can then literally access any information, and experience the Divine and Divinity, internally and externally at a very high level, even spanning dimensions, in a high altered state. One connects to the Higher Mind, the Telos, the All-Knowing, the All-Seeing, the All-Being, and it is this transcendental state, which accesses the innate soul knowledge, and that of all things.

This is the path of Enlightenment which all initiates sought. Within the Mystery Schools there were different paths that initiates could follow. Mary Magdalene chose the path of the high Transmitter Soul, that of Prophetess, Teacher, Seer. At the same time, also the path of the Brotherhood and Sisterhood of the Rose, the Serpent and Sacred Grail. This encompassed training in the sacred sexual rites, the highest form of Alchemy, and one aspect of this, is the Hieros Gamos,[3] or the Sacred Marriage, which she shared with her Beloved. Few understand, however, that such sacred marriage is not just of the flesh, it is the merging of souls. The soul energy merges, which forms the Sacred Fire of Creation Itself, and is transcendental.

Esclaremonde de Foix was indeed the Cathar Bishop. When the Crusade was at its highest and most brutal, she was shielded, and a man took on the burden of leadership. Yet, he was her equal, and she was not submissive to him. In fact, she was the Hierophant. It was under her leadership that a school for girls, women and widows, opened in Dun. Later the Catholics would follow her example, and start convent schools.

She was not only highly educated, but indeed a high initiate of the inner secret teachings of the hidden Mystery Schools.

In my own remembrance, Sissi, her niece, was trained in the same Mystery Schools from the age of five onwards, in secret places in the Pyrenees. They were totally concealed and sealed off during the genocide, and will remain hidden until such time as the Gospel of Love is returned to Humanity.

Men within the ranks of the Cathars followed the same initiate path. There were always an equal number of men and women within the highest ranks. The Cathar's Inner Circle, followed the secret teachings of Mary Magdalene, and all the Mary's before her. Mary, being a title, of the High Priestess, and not a name. Many of these Mary's travelled between the Mystery Schools, as did the men. There was a constant exchange between the 7 Mystery Schools, and the High Initiates knew each other through secret signs and symbols.

The Templars, the inner High Initiates, had the same access, although they later added in many of their own interpretations and rites. The inner core though was the same, with women in its ranks.

Many of the top ranking Cathars and Templars, found refuge elsewhere. Some in Portugal, Scotland and Ireland, some merged with the Teutonic Knights. Some were given safe-haven in other European countries.

My experience of the Cathars walking chained and singing unto death on the stake at Monségur, opened within me the understanding that the last of the Cathars had attained the highest state of Gnosis, where they were already in a transcendental state, the state of Oneness, where there is just pure love and gratitude. There is no fear of death, but rather a knowing that the physical vessel will just be discarded, as the soul ascends into it primordial first creation – the soul light body.

The Inquisition and Crusaders at that time, bought into the false doctrines and power plays of the Church. Most were motivated by greed, and by what they could get from joining in such slaughter.

I did a lot of research on the de Montfort family, after Simon de Montfort's rise to fame and fortune, and interestingly, his grandson and namesake, married the King of England's sister. He also displayed the

---

3   *Hieros gamos* or Hierogamy is a sexual ritual that plays out a marriage between a god and a goddess, especially when enacted in a symbolic ritual where human participants represent the deities. Wikipedia.

ruthlessness his own grandfather had exhibited, and rose to great power – only to be disgraced and slaughtered in the most devastating manner. What you sow, you reap, even over generations. The Divine Law of Cause and Effect is exact.

Yet, in reality even the darkness served. For they counterbalanced the immense Light of the Cathars. Both the light and dark served – opening the path to Gnosis, not in their lifetime, as the church sunk further into false rule and darkness, but ultimately this led to the Renaissance.

In truth, the Light of the Cathars never dimmed. It may have been forgotten, yet their legacy lived on. I so often stood in churches in France, and found their symbols and figures everywhere. They were subtle, but also right under people's noses, telling the story of Mary Magdalene and the Cathars, in hidden symbolism. It was as if someone somewhere wanted the world to know the truth for indeed the unspeakable had happened in Southern France, and somehow these secrets had to be exposed and paradoxically one can best hide the truth in plain view!

All souls who were involved in Cathar times, have returned. Some will remember. Some will not. Some will just be drawn to the region, without reason, and know that their soul is connected there.

Certain people are riding on the bandwagon, creating all kinds of groups, and trying to outdo each other; however, the truth will only reveal itself to those who truly seek. For the greatest of all truth is found inside oneself, in the soul, and not outside of self!

"Know thyself!" The soul indeed knows it all! The soul is Divinely centred. It is Cosmic. When the soul becomes aware it can access Heaven and Earth, and span dimensions, it is not bound by space or time. It is infinite, with infinite knowing and the ability to grow into ever greater levels and frequency bands of enlightenment.

This is what the Templars and Cathars knew, and had access to. It was never through the doctrines of the Catholic Church, intent on brainwashing the masses, and keeping them under their control, but rather in the higher states of being, one accesses from deep within oneself!

Such is the inner knowledge they had.

In addition to this, they knew and practiced the principles, the doctrines, and the knowledge of the Gospel of Love.

The full volumes of the Gospel of Love, will be returned.

At the moment it is still sealed off.

By the year 2034 it will be the living River of Love and Life for all Humanity.

* * *

CHAPTER 10

# The Gift of Love: The Mystery of the Rose, the Serpent and the Holy Grail reveals itself

The truest remembrance is that of the soul. The soul has neither past, present, nor future. It simply records all the experiences energetically in all lifetimes and parallel lives, throughout the Universe, and thus all the knowledge and experiences the soul has had, are stored for infinity.

When incarnated here, the soul adopts a physical vessel, a certain persona. The soul is not the vessel, or the persona. The soul is intrinsically linked to its Soul Group, and to the Divine. It cannot ever be separated from the Greater Whole, the Greater Omniverse Creation.

When we remember past lives, we are recalling a single experience of the soul. It is not the entire soul – it is but a fraction which incarnated, and thus such memories are fractal. They are incomplete. They do not define the soul, yet they form part of the soul's initiation into ever higher evolutionary states of being, as it sojourns through the Galaxies, Star Systems and Universes.

During my journey, as I literally spanned dimensions, and worked on so many historical timeframes simultaneously, I was reminded that time does not exist. However, within the great energy matrix fields, everything is connected. My soul memory banks opened, and I could tap into the energy fields to download whatever I needed, and release what needed to be released.

During those times when I had to liberate so much trapped pain and trauma from the landscape, I simply allowed my Higher Soul Self and Higher Guidance to take over. I became the Seer, the Seeing and the Seen. All else faded into no-thingness. There was just pure, blinding white light. I had to merge with the White Flame of Purification, in order to do the work.

It was only when I returned home, that I realized the magnitude and immense scale of the work that had been done in France. Those two months of travelling, retrieving, releasing and opening up, had taken its toll on me, in ways I hadn't anticipated. In the next four years, I had to work through soul memory banks of suffering and agony which had been triggered, in order to allow them to dissolve.

In moments of great ordeal and challenge, the soul often withdraws into a state of non-being, in order to cope with the intensity. I frequently felt I was in a bubble, especially when dealing with collective hardships. The collective somehow became the bubble which when resolved, released the souls, as all that energy was transmuted into the highest form via the White Flame of Purification. Although I had released this, by entering into a greatly altered state, I still had to work through it within my own soul memory banks. It was really showing me, just how deeply the collective woundedness of Humanity impacted the individual soul as well. In truth one soul is the many. The many are the one.

Reflecting on this, a well of gratitude rises, for indeed, through it all, with what had been released and reopened, the energy grids in France were regenerated to allow the Fires of Illumination to be anchored in there. Since the Fall of Avalon, and even before this in the Lion Kingdom, the Fires of Illumination from the 7th Central Sun, via Sirius, had been blocked and closed off. Now, the Fires could expand again, and open the gateways for massive dimensional shifts. Indeed, since 2016, there have been concentrated modifications, which will escalate in the next 12 to 21 years. We are stepping increasingly into the 5th dimensional state, and the shift will accelerate into the 7th, the original dimension of the First Creation, Elysium.

Avalon is rising, and its submerged parts will re-emerge in the next few years as the ice on the poles melt even further, and the Earth changes accelerate. Indeed, land masses will rise in some places, and others will sink. Offshore of Brittany and the west coast of France, parts of Avalon will arise. A massive Stonehenge-type monument will be found, far bigger than the one in Britain, as well the submerged pyramids. The same will be found offshore of Ireland, to the west.

I had to do intense remote energy work in September 2018 in Ireland, to open the energy lines from Carnac to Ireland once more, and from Monségur to Ireland and beyond that, as all parts of Avalon are rising.

We will recall how to work with the spiraling energy fields and sound technology. Teleportation will become the norm, as scientists are already teleporting information instantly from location to location, across the Earth. It is a profound remembrance, as the dimensional shifts are opening up the higher mind of Humanity, and with it the technology will return, which is indeed ancient and not new at all.

The story of Mary Magdalene, will continue in my next book, chronicling my tours of Greece (particularly Delphi) and Egypt, as I have now been called to physically walk the same initiation paths that she did. Mary Magdalene was a high Priestess of the Highest Order, and she decided to complete her ministry in her country of birth, even after she and Yeshua (Jesus) parted ways, as he chose to return to Persia and India in his later years. It was her fearlessness in proclaiming the truth, and her deep devotion to her soul mission and calling, which brought her into direct confrontation with those misogynists who wanted to expunge women completely from the Church, and recorded history. After her death, this is exactly what happened. Mary Magdalene was a true Gnostic, and one deeply committed to the higher paths. Her calling was rooted in Alchemy, and in truth her own sacred marriage with her beloved was physical, yet also of the spirit, mind and soul. He could never have done the miracles without her. She was his equal.

Mary's ministry, and the manuscripts and scrolls she brought with her to France, from the Essenes, Delphi and Egypt, were secretly hidden away by the Guardian and Keeper families of Southern France. These were the 3 families that I have already mentioned in previous chapters. The Essenes had a Prophetess named Judith, within their midst, a few years before Mary Magdalene arrived in Israel. Judith was a High Priestess, Teacher and Prophetess. She foresaw the time that the Essenes would be persecuted, and the fall of Masada.[1]

She prophesied that the most important teachings of the Essenes had to be safeguarded and hidden away, so that the knowledge they held as one of the Mystery Schools would not fall into the wrong hands.

Judith foresaw the arrival of Mary Magdalene and accordingly, when she arrived with Yeshua (Jesus) and joined the Essenes in Israel, the community recognized her as the one she had prophesied would come. Mary Magdalene was then carefully initiated into the content of the manuscripts and scrolls. With the subsequent arrests, and when the Essene community itself came under attack, she took it upon herself to help smuggle out the manuscripts and scrolls, using her own family connections (one of whom was Pontius Pilate's wife) and thus, when she arrived in France, these manuscripts and scrolls were already there, waiting for her.

She ensured that they would be safeguarded within the Mystery Schools, of which she was a member. Some were held within her own school, outside Rennes-le-Château, and some were burnt in the fire when the school was attacked, but the most important of them were not destroyed. They were kept elsewhere.

The three families who were the Guardians and Keepers of the Sacred Information and Secret Teachings, which later became Catharism (or rather were hidden under its banner) included the Count of Foix, the Count of Comminges, and the Viscounts of Béarn (de Moncada family), all forming the nucleus. Their strongholds were high in the Pyrenees Mountains, and their family ties spilled over into what is now Northern Spain and Southern France. They took oaths of secrecy to defend the sacred texts.

I remember at the age of 12, when the Albigensian Crusade[2] was initiated, I was summoned by my father, Ramon Roger, the Count of Foix, to take an oath that I would do everything in my power to smuggle out the manuscripts and scrolls that he held in his vast library (spread over his holdings, not just in Foix, but also in Monségur and other locations), and that I would be willing to lay down my life if need be to safeguard and protect them, even unto death. I fulfilled that pledge.

During this time, I was deeply involved with The Templars, and later with the Grand Master of the Templars in particular, in smuggling out the documents. We carefully selected which to send first, which ones to hide within certain cave systems, and which ones to smuggle to the Templar headquarters in Portugal, where they were assembling their own considerable collection.

During the intense persecution of the Cathars, many other European countries were appalled at the events taking place, and secretly assisted the Cathars through the Templars.

The Templar Grand Master, assigned a special unit of men to me, some scholars and scientists, and some armed men ,and we worked day and night to smuggle these documents and other sacred items, originating from the time of Avalon, and even before this, and all pertaining to the Mystery Schools, to safety. I could outride any man in that lifetime, and rode bareback.

---

1 Masada (Hebrew: מצדה metsada, "fortress")[1] is an ancient fortification in the Southern District of Israel situated on top of an isolated rock plateau, akin to a mesa. It is located on the eastern edge of the Judaean Desert, overlooking the Dead Sea 20 km (12 mi) east of Arad. Herod the Great built two palaces for himself on the mountain and fortified Masada between 37 and 31 BCE. According to Josephus, the siege of Masada by Roman troops at the end of the First Jewish–Roman War ended in the mass suicide of 960 people. Wikipedia.

2 The Albigensian Crusade or the Cathar Crusade was a 20-year military campaign initiated by Pope Innocent III to eliminate Catharism in Languedoc, in southern France. Wikipedia.

Times became desperate. The Inquisition put out an alert for me, because they had been foiled in their attempts to locate and imprison my Aunt Esclaremonde, ordained leader and Bishop of the Cathars. Conjointly there was an ancient vendetta between my father, the Count of Foix, and the Bishop of Urgell, over a land dispute, and my father was consequently imprisoned.

I met with the Grand Master of the Templars, just before my death. He was indeed, at that time, reaching the end of his tether. Even though the Templars had done their utmost to assist me, I still had extremely important Mystery Schools documents to smuggle out, and consequently I would have to go near Urgell to retrieve these and take them across the border into the de Moncada territory, where I would be safe.

My cousin the Grand Master Guillaume, had become my lover during these desperate times, even though I was much younger, and we now shared that special love which grows when two souls have a common mission and bond. It was thus with tears running down his cheeks, that he told me, although he had done what he could, and given it his all, he was unable continue the work. He would assign his most trusted men to me, who would be willing to give up their lives, if needed to protect me and the documents we carried. He could not do more than this, as he had been called to a meeting at the Templar holding, next to the River Aude. In fact, he already knew that he would be betrayed, and was riding to his death, for some of the order had been secretly influenced by the Pope to turn against their own.

So, I rode out with five of his most trusted men-at-arms, and we managed to retrieve the documents, and to reach the De Moncada territory. However, there was a tremendous downpour, so we could not return via our planned route, and had to retrace our steps into Urgell territory. During our last night's stay in a relative's home, someone betrayed our presence, and we were arrested at the site.

During the subsequent confrontation with the Bishop, I was accused of being a Cathar, and the daughter of his enemy, and condemned to be burnt at the stake, while the Templars were released as free men. They refused to leave and this proved to be my saving grace, for had they not done so, I would have been repeatedly raped and sacrificed. These men refused to let me out of their sight, and thus it was with these five Knights' Templars that I was secretly burnt in the Bishop's Palace in Urgell, with the Bishop and his priests, singing the psalters, bibles in their hands!

Interestingly, in that moment when the flames first started to consume us, I had shifted into a much higher, altered state, where I was hovering over my body, and witnessing events, and was no longer in my physical form. I was in an elevated state, a transcendental state, as I had been trained. In such a state, no pain is felt, in this light body state, one is no longer stuck in the physical vessel. Such was the blessing and loving Grace we received!

The Grand Master Guillaume, met his death when he entered the Templar Holding on the Aude river. He was the Templar I had to release, who had his throat cut and body thrown into the fountain. He also knew that he was riding to his death, having been betrayed by a faction of his own men.

In truth, that lifetime has served me, for not only did I return to France, and perform intense healing work there, but in a higher sense, I also set many thousands of souls free from trauma and pain, after many hundreds and thousands of years. It has taught me not to judge. For in truth the darkness serves as much as the light.

What the Inquisition and Church so desperately wanted to annihilate, was never destroyed. So many manuscripts which had been smuggled out, found their way into Europe and elsewhere, and helped to inspire the Renaissance. Some still need to be rediscovered, and will start making their appearance in the next few years. One will be the extensive volumes of the Gospel of Love.

The Gospel of Love, is indeed a compendium of all the most secret teachings of the Ages. Every single word in those scrolls was carefully chosen to epitomize and capture the energy of Pure Divine Love. It is a celebration of the Divine Feminine, who holds the Cosmic Heart, and eternal Flame of Love.

It is a celebration of unconditional love, of the greatest of all Divine Powers, the Power of Love. It is the all-embracing love. Love which embraces both shadow and light, yin and yang, and indeed brings all into the eternal One – the Union, the transcendental.

It is a guidebook for souls who wish to walk the highest pathways of love. It is the songs of songs, where sacred marriage is celebrated with intimate union of two souls reaching transcendent oneness through the merging of their energies, their fires, thus igniting the sacred fires in this mystical union, as they step into the role of co-creatorship with the Divine.

The Gospel of Love, is even more than this!

When it is rediscovered, Humankind will indeed find the energetic keys and codes to step into the 7th dimensional state once more!

It is the most sacred of the sacred.

Within the Gospel of Love, the sounds of Creation are found. These were used by the Cathars in their healing sessions, and indeed stem from the First Creation. For if one chants these sacred sounds, the Universe vibrates and expands, and this gives one access to the primordial sound keys and codes of the First Creation.

It is only through the immense power of Love, that any soul can access the highest states of Illumination. One cannot access such a state via any other channel, and thus the most sacred state, is that of transcendental Love. Love all-embracing!

There is just Love – all else is illusion.

The Omniverse pulsates and radiates out Love. Pure unconditional love.

On this planet, love is still conditional. I will love you, if …

The Divine Love, Loves. It places no limits, no conditions.

It is!

The greatest of all teachings of the Mystery Schools in France, and elsewhere embraced this All-Knowing, the All-Seeing, the All-Being of Love!

The Power of Love supersedes all others.

Such is the lasting legacy of the Cathars, Mary Magdalene, and the hidden secret teachings of the Mystery Schools.

My journey to France was not only a journey of remembering, and deep soul healing, it also served to heal and connect the Spinal Column of the Earth to the most ancient of energy centres in the Womb of the Earth, which is France. The next journey will be that of reconnecting the navel of the Earth, Delphi, with that of France, and then back to Egypt, and the Spinal Column of the Earth.

I had to re-open the Crystal Pyramids in the Pyrenees, and the Sun Portal in Versailles, and that of Carnac and the Crystal Pyramids offshore of France. My work has been done, yet it continues.

Through these years my heart has expanded. The Power of Love is the driving force of my life.

So many souls who were involved with me in France, during the time of Avalon and the Cathars, have found me again for Soul Readings. Through this, I have been able to reconnect them to their own souls, as I was being blessed, and I am grateful that I could render such service to Humanity, as I have also done in many other lifetimes.

My greatest wish is that the Gospel of Love be returned to Humanity, and that the highest illumined state of Pure, Unconditional Love becomes the ultimate state of Being.

\* \* \*

# Epilogue

When I was called to go to France, I had no idea what would be waiting for me. It was in so many ways a healing journey for me, so that the old soul wounds from my lifetime as Sissi, who risked her life to smuggle out manuscripts and people with the Knights Templar and who was then burnt at the stake with the five Knights Templar. I was seeking answers and I found more than just answers, I found the untold story of Avalon and all the energy centers I was asked to reactivate.

France was a healing homecoming for my soul, which I eventually comprehended at the close of last year, when the remaining Cathar memory banks were cleared. I first had to go to Greece and Egypt, so that the circle could be completed.

Monségur is forever in my heart and soul, and the very last of my lifetimes there was dealt with in 2021. I hope to be able to return one day, to make it up to the castle. I only understood now why I never could go up there, until that last memory bank came to the fore and I could lay the ghosts to rest.

Monségur will indeed rise again like a shining beacon in the New Earth, and so will all the souls who were ever initiated there, and who still bear the secret knowledge within their own souls.

Mary Magdalene remained present in my life and therefore I was called to go to Greece and Egypt, and to follow in her initiation journey into the Mystery Schools there. My next books will be the continuation of her story, bringing all the strands Avalon, The Lion Kingdom and Elysium together. For it was in Egypt that Mary Magdalene first met Yeshua and then accompanied him to Israel, as High Priestess. In my encounters with her and the guidance given to me, there was always a reference to the Book of Love, which she brought with her from Israel and the Essenes, to Southern France. It contained 144 000 volumes and it was smuggled out along with the pure Essene teachings.

I have been told that the Book of Love will be returned to humankind with the advent of the New Golden Age. This coincides with Mary Magdalene, as Avatar and Ascended Master, now returning to anchor in the Feminine Christ. Consequently, there will be a return to Balance with Yeshua, who holds the Masculine Christ and the restoration of the Power of Love, which goes beyond words and description.

When in France, Mary Magdalene was constantly bringing me to the deepest knowing that the Book of Love would be returned to humanity, in all and every form and way, as it holds the infinite Divine Feminine Powers of Love, which those who are called to serve in the High Priesthood of the Feminine Divine have always practiced and were initiated in.

It activates the highest Feminine Intuitive Powers, as well as the Sacred Heart, the Holy Chalice/Grail.

What is happening is the full return of the Feminine Christ, which Mary Magdalene is now wholly anchoring in. With it the New Golden Age, the Age of Love is here, and with it the Heart centre is opening in the highest degrees.

With Mary Magdalene now fully anchoring in the Feminine Christ, and Yeshua, who holds the Masculine Christ, harmony, unity and balance is being restored in the greatest degree. Immense healing is now flooding in via Mary Magdalene, of the collective trauma of persecution in all and every form, alongside the healing of the deepest fears and wounds of all souls on planet Earth.

The Holy Grail was never an object, nor a treasure – it was the full opening of the Sacred Heart and the Sacred Womb and Sacred All Seeing, All Hearing, All Knowing, the Divine Feminine holds with the pure White Flame. It is the Sacred Rose, the Infinite Rose, which is held within the Sacred Heart of the Divine Feminine and the Feminine Christ.

The Feminine Christ holds the transcendental Love, the Transfigured Love, which goes far beyond the physical, and holds immortal and infinite love, which is ingrained in the soul fire and thus is eternally present. It is a Love which goes far in excess of words, or expression. It simply is!

Mary Magdalene's presence is immensely powerful, yet, immeasurably feminine and her love is truly transcendental. She works with the Feminine Trinity, the Divine Feminine, the Holy Sophia and the Holy Shekinah, and together they hold the Sacred Arks of the Covenant, and whenever they appear, so does the Seraphim.

She will often touch your heart centre, and when she does, you will feel your heart expanding like never before. It is beautiful opening now of the woundedness within you. It is releasing incredibly old patterns of pain and suffering, and especially as said, persecution of any kind in any lifetime. Much of this is like old stuck energy still held in our energy fields, which is now simply dissolving through her touch. When this transpires, you will just have tears flowing, as a deep forgiveness of self and others arises, along with a very deep healing. A healing which goes beyond words.

If you were an Essene or a Cathar or Templar in other lifetimes, or persecuted in any way (often burnt innocently as a witch or branded as such), simply ask her to touch your heart centre and request this healing. Do this when you can be alone, quiet and still and then enter the inner sacred temple of your own heart centre and call her in and ask!

Mary Magdalene, during her last lifetime on earth was being prepared for her return as the Feminine Christ, and accordingly descended in order to heal our wounds and trauma, and pain. She needed to experience the deepest anguish of the Feminine, the worst persecution, to be able to assist us now all to heal.

She knows our deepest wounds, our deepest trauma. And yet, through it all, she holds the Power of Divine Love, which is omnipresent.

I will never forget how, in a little village church in France, she appeared to me and anointed me, with Yeshua. Such love, such a powerful presence and initiation, as well as an anointing, stays with one forever more.

Mary Magdalene will assist you in so many ways to release old, stuck emotional energy, which you may not even be aware of. She will work with you to connect deeply to your own feminine core, to reveal the deepest love which is there inside.

Frequently, when we were hurt or experienced deep pain, especially more so if you are overly sensitive like me, we were inclined to store this in our emotional and our physical bodies, as we needed to cope with life. Typically, we tended to put bastions around our hearts so that we would not feel such intense hurt or pain any longer. This becomes stuck energy in our bodies.

Recently I experienced her dissolving this energy in the deepest ways. I cannot even put into words what this meant to me, for I could at last forgive in the most earnest ways, all that transpired in other lifetimes of persecution, which was carried over into this lifetime when I experienced more of the same kind of involvements, and suffered through more of the same. A deep healing of the Masculine energy took place, whereas before I thought I had cleared it all.

Mary Magdalene works with deepest alchemy and thus alchemizes the old stuck energy into the highest Christ Light and Love.

Her message for you today, is that working with the Divine Mother White Flame in the last few month, has prepared you now for far greater work and a far higher calling and purpose than you could even imagine.

She will open you to ever greater levels of love, which were previously inaccessible. As the old you progressively dissolves, so does the ego, and all that is left is the deepest depths of your soul. The Truth of who and what you in truth are.

All pretence is gone. The persona is gone. There is only the Purity of your soul shining through as you live your highest truth, and stand in your full power of your highest Mastery.

With Yeshua, she anchors in the balance between the Masculine and Feminine again. She creates harmony and unity in all our relationships. In order to dissolve old anger, pain and bitterness, there is often a tumultuous breaking open of the heart centre. All that muck needs to be released. A broken heart is a heart that can be mended and created anew, and thus can be healed. As long as we refuse to open our hearts, we cannot be healed in the deepest sense.

To me, the fact that Mary Magdalene was deeply remembered, especially in Southern France where she had her ministry, and kept alive in their churches and openly so, indicated that although the church branded her a prostitute (largely due to Simon Peter's hatred and jealousy of her), they firmly held her in their hearts, and remembered the truth of her. This faith in her was sustained, despite the greatest genocide ever in those areas where people held the teachings pure.

She stands here before you today, looking deeply into your eyes, heart and soul, and she asks you to forgive, even as she had to forgive. She, who had always loved Yeshua and as High Priestess fulfilled her soul calling and purpose, and healed and taught alongside him, always knew his greatest sorrow, heartaches, and deepest love, as she was one with him. This is why she was the one who held him and kept vigil for him when he went through the resurrection process. A greater love has never been known. After that to then be persecuted by her own ilk, and having to flee to her country of birth, was always a great sorrow to her. She also lost her Mystery School, as it was attacked and burnt down by a mob of angry men who followed Simon Peter, which forced her to withdraw into the caves in Southern France, to complete her mission.

Yet she never ceased healing, she never ceased bringing her message to the people, and it was especially the women and children who followed her, as she was held in the love of the Ancient Mystery Schools which already existed in France, as she always was one of them. She has left her footprints of her heart and soul all over Southern France, and it was her teachings and those of the Mystery Schools there that were preserved by the Cathars and the Templars. This is why so many of the Cathars, even when on the stake and burning to death, still joyously sung the Ancient Chants and Songs she had taught them, shedding their physical form with love and joy.

She brings healing to our most intimate relationships, with Yeshua, for it is here that our utmost healing lies. So often the sexual energy was misused and abused, and used to enslave, to bind, to conquer, to manipulate, etc. As the Divine Masculine heart opens, so does the Power of Love. Many times, men were forced to be and become what they never were in truth, ordered to use brute force, only to suffer the consequent guilt and shame for what they had done. Yet they were told that it is manly to kill, and a man never cries. So often, in their bewilderment and lostness, and so frequently with their inability to speak from their hearts and soul and live from this place, their own minds overrode their hearts, which thus hardened. Society reinforced this through false teachings that denied the heart and made a God out of the mind.

As this deep healing of the Masculine and Feminine is occurring on all fronts, let us open our hearts and souls to true forgiveness. Let us allow ourselves to be healed by the Masculine Christ and the Feminine Christ, and allow them to bring us into the deepest healing within. The Woundedness.

Let balance be restored.

Invite them to heal you; and invite them to heal your relationship with yourself first and foremost, and then your relationship with others. Allow them to dissolve all the false belief systems, the ancestral belief systems, the false programming of education and society and the media. Let it all dissolve.

Seek quietude. Stillness. Go out in nature and then simply ask that Yeshua and Mary Magdalene open your heart and soul and assist you by opening your deepest wounds to help them to dissolve and to heal. Let all resistance and judgements go. When tears flow, let them flow. They are healing tears.

To me Mary Magdalene epitomizes forgiveness and Loving Grace, yet also that of the Power of the Divine Feminine and more than this, the Power of Love. Unconditional Love.

You may call in Mary Magdalene any time you wish to. You may ask her to guide and teach you and to heal your deepest woundedness.

She will so often appear as a teacher, and will always gently guide you to the deepest truths, the highest purity, enabling you to truly step into your own highest soul self, and to fulfil your purpose and mission here on earth.

She is love in the deepest and most profound way. She has been with me all my life.

Since France she has been with me constantly. I followed in her initiation footsteps from France to Delphi in Greece to Egypt, and will one day complete it by going to Israel.

To me it has been a journey of soul, a deep remembrance of the Power of Love, and forgiveness, healing and reconnection with so many aspects of my own soul.

I hope for you too, as you ask her to fully merge with you and be your mentor and guide, as she opens you up to ever greater levels of love and being loved and living life as the Master you in truth are. You will remember and this book will trigger many soul memory banks and the keys and codes of all who read it.

I thank all of these brave souls for returning, as together we ascend into the New Earth and co-create the New Golden Age with love!

I wish to thank Kristina Lundgren for travelling with me through France, and for being there for me in so many ways. I will never forget how, when we were being led to places and finding jigsaw puzzle pieces, she would say: "I love playing Sherlock Holmes with you!" With her ability to speak French, to translate, and her knowledge of Southern France and the people and places, Kristina proved to be invaluable, and so was her love. Thank you, Kristina. This book is as much yours, as it is mine.

I thank all of those who attended the seven seminars in Cuiza. You will be forever in my heart and I will never forget our journey and experiences at Monségur.

I would like to thank my chief editor Jill Charlotte Combes for her immense editing work, and for her willingness to share my life journeys. Without her offering to start editing my work a few years ago, my books would never have seen the light of day. She is a guiding light in my life. Thank you, Jill, for all that you are, as you are!

Thank you, Janet Vollmer, who helped with the essential final editing of the books, and who attended my seminars in France. Thank you, Janet, for your insights and suggestions, and for all the effort you put into the book. I so appreciate it!

I thank Vanessa Wilson and her Quickfox team for their expertise and service excellence, and all the effort they made in the formatting and production of this book.

For all who have shared my soul journey in one form or another, and all whom I met in France: you will be forever in my heart and soul.

So much Love to all who read this book and shared my journey with me.

**Judith Küsel**

* * *

# Additional Information

## Sun Discs

"I was taken to a monumental Temple of the 7th Galaxy of the 7th Central Sun. There in the centre, suspended in mid-air, was a splendid, rotating Sun Disc! It was spinning and humming, with a vast core of pure liquid white-gold. It was pulsating and alive, and was a massive energy hub. Human language is so primitive and limited, and it is difficult to describe in words, but it was like a gargantuan, intelligent and very powerful energy force field. It was alive and conscious! It literally seemed to be spitting fire from deep within it – with an explosive, fiery energy that reminded me of the Sun. As far as this relates to the Tree of Life, I believe that the Spinal Column of the Earth is the Tree of Life. So, it contains within its 33 vertebrae, all knowledge, technology and the Super Consciousness Energy Fields, for they are all linked.

Many people talk about the grid ley lines, or Web of Light. These were laid down at the time of Atlantis, and therefore are much younger than the original energy grids and fields, which were laid down when the Earth was created. So, this grid certainly exists – those who practise dowsing can tap into it quite easily, and it mostly aligns with the Sun and Moon. However, a third component has been forgotten, namely the Sun Discs, which were used by the Ancients. Huge, golden ones were placed in their temples to remind them of the Central Suns.

The Sun Discs did not incorporate the 12 signs of the Zodiac, but rather the 12 original Central Suns, as each of them hold a certain key encodement to the higher states of Enlightenment, and thus Cosmic Consciousness. They all slot into one single Central Sun Super Consciousness Energy Field, which the numbers 12 and 13 always play a central role in unlocking.

Many are only aware of one single Central Sun, but you cannot reach the advanced states of evolutionary enlightenment, or Super Consciousness, without an understanding of the 12 Master Central Suns. They hold the keys and codes to All of Creation – everything that is held, created and operational within the Central Suns.

The Ancients knew the Sun Discs were not there as adornment, or for ceremonial purposes. They were actually giant computers that tapped into the vast knowledge and Super Consciousness Energy Fields of the Great Central Suns. Their inner workings were like those of a clock. As each central spoke clicked, mechanisms would open a portal to a certain energy field, as held within the disc. This would unlock the knowledge contained therein.

There are two forms of Sun Discs: There are the massive ones, like the one I described from the 7th Temple of the 7th Galaxy of the 7th Central Sun. This was one huge, intelligent energy field, and it incorporated knowledge from the whole Cosmos.

On Earth, at the time of Elysium, these were housed in the Temples of the Central Suns. You will find a description of one that I had to reactivate, later in this book. These gigantic Sun Discs worked on the principle of rotating clockworks, with internal slots where smaller Sun Discs were kept. These could be detached from the major ones. They then served as smaller field information discs.

The keys and codes to access these are ingrained, or programmed, into some souls who have worked with them before and are now here to return the Fires of Illumination to the planet.

Yet, these can only be accessed if one is ready to retrieve the information, and able to easily shift into higher dimensional states, for they are held in the 7th dimension or octave of consciousness, pertaining to the 7th Central Sun.

The closest correlation I can think of is a DVD disc, but they are much larger and rotate, at an incredible speed. They hover over your head and then download information you require or want to retrieve, directly into your higher heart/mind.

I believe that this is what the medieval artists later depicted by painting halos around the heads of saints, for indeed the Sun Discs do that. They work directly with the All-Seeing Eye of Horus, and therefore the higher mind and heart. Later versions of these, retrieved from some ancient sites, are much older, more primitive prototypes that preserved the general shape and outline of the first Sun Discs, or those still found in the 7th Temple.

The Sun Discs act like energy storage – solar disc devices that store the powers of Illumination, and all the secret knowledge of Illumination from the 12 original Central Suns within them. The Sun Discs have smaller discs within, which work on the blinding White Ray Energy. When the keys and codes are activated within these discs, smaller etheric energy discs are released, which then connect with the brain/higher mind of the High Priestess, and will download the Illumined texts, knowledge, technology of Light energies, and the keys and codes of Illumination. This was the ultimate download that enabled this Soul to be able to tune into the 12 Central Suns. Each Sun, in turn, is the configuration of whichever of the 12 Master Sun Discs it downloaded. So, the Suns of Illumination and Wisdom are amplified and activated in immensely powerful ways.

This is only given to those who will use this energy and technology and knowledge of Illumination in constructive ways, within the parameters of the Divine Cosmic Laws."

(Excerpt from *Why I was Born in Africa: The Previously Unrecorded History of Elysium and The Lion Kingdom*, by Judith Küsel)

## The Spinal Cord

"Deep inside the African continent, the most ancient and important energy centers are buried, and the portal that contains this higher knowledge and understanding is the Lion Portal. The Lion People guard this portal, as the Sphinx is guarding the south.

It has been purposefully hidden and forgotten by humankind, yet the Giza Pyramids point to Sirius and Orion, and most importantly to the Lion People, via the Sphinx. The Sphinx is guarding not only the Lion Portal, but the spinal cord of the world. This spinal cord is not found exactly on the 33° longitude line, for that was calculated by men with limited knowledge and inaccurate calculations. The spinal cord of Earth is aligned to its axis, and thus holds the whole planet upright, as does the spinal cord in the human body.

It is divided equally into 33 energy centers. The Lion Portal activates the keys and codes within each of these centers. No person can grasp the importance of this, but we have to comprehend that some of these 33 energy centers were moved out of alignment because Earth was hit by asteroids and comets almost simultaneously, so ending the First Golden Age of Elysium. First there was fire, then volcanic eruptions, with huge twists and turns of the Earth's crust. Then came floods, as the planet was thrown out of its orbit.

As mentioned already, the 33 energy centers of the Earth's spinal cord reflect the human spinal cord. To understand this, we must first look at it:

Each vertebra contains within itself an energy wheel, which emits crystalline energy. It looks like a spider's web, perfectly reflecting the Web of Light around the planet. When they spin within each vertebra, they radiate colour and sound. The coloured strands look like fractal energy strands of light. Each vertebra connects to each of the Earth's vertebrae, so connecting our spinal cords with the spinal cord energies of Earth and the Web of Light. Indeed, this is such an intimate connection as all life forms function as One entity.

In essence, each vertebra forms a tiny MerKaBah energy field, and when all are fully activated, functioning and flowing, the MerKaBah energies of the spinal cord connect as one, in a form similar to a lightning rod, or magic wand. The double and triple helix vortex energy fields are then established. This rod provides the base energy field around which the kundalini can form, so that multiple serpent strands wind around it.

When all 33 vertebrae are fully activated, this brings the upper pyramid situated in the skull into alignment, and connects the pineal and pituitary glands, forming the upper pyramid in the body, with the lower pyramid based in the coccyx area. The Spinal Column then becomes a 'lightning rod 'literally able to connect 'as above, so below,' acting like a powerful antenna.

The spinal cord forms the lightning rod, the 'magic wand', so to speak, with the kundalini energies moving up and down the rod, in a double-helix, or serpent-like form. If the spinal cord vibrates inside the rod, and the kundalini forms flames outside of this, the three together then become a mighty energy conduit and transmitter that emits incredibly high frequencies

When all the spinal cord energies are fully activated, their frequency band becomes amplified and the 99 and 999 number sequences spring into motion. This allows the complete entity to tune into the Higher Cosmic Sound Frequency Fields of the Cosmic harmonic frequencies, which reverberate throughout the entire Cosmos.

When the Earth's spinal cord energies are once again fully reactivated, the planet's light body, which will already be forming around its spinal cord (like our own), will be fully activated, and the full sound vibration will lift it into the 5th dimensional state. All life and life forms on Earth will simultaneously be elevated. That means our spinal cord energies will be fully activated and tuned-in to vibrate at that frequency band."

(Excerpt from *Why I was Born in Africa: The Previously Unrecorded History of Elysium and The Lion Kingdom*, by Judith Küsel)

## Crystal Pyramids

"At this time, the great Crystalline Pyramid or energy grid, was put in place around the whole planet to artificially control climatic conditions and to shield the planet from the rampant cosmic storms and upheavals. It also acted as a barrier to prevent hostile elements from interfering with the experiment, or from landing their own craft there.

The Crystalline Pyramid Grid formed a series of portals to the space stations underground, through which spacecraft could come and go as they wished. These Crystalline Grid lines were also amplified by the Crystal Pyramids that were connected to them. All of them working together, helped maintain Earth's state of balance. So, not only were climatic conditions stable here, but the grid also acted as a natural energy source that could be tapped into by all beings. This helped the smaller craft operate more effectively, and scientists could travel from one end of the planet to the next within seconds. They could actually use these lines to fly on, and thus the mythological gods remembered in the collective human psyche were literally able to fly!

At that time, the Crystalline Grid also enabled the scientists to communicate at will with all the other galaxies and constellations, as well as the Divine Source. All beings were at-one. So, everyone could communicate freely with their loved ones wherever they were, and keep up to date with happenings elsewhere, via the interlinking motherships' communication systems, which were connected to the energy systems of each of the constellations, universes, and other planets in this solar system.

In time, this became part of an even more important scientific innovation and power supply, which we will examine later.

The scientists created massive underground tunnel systems that linked the inner world, Agartha, to the outer world and also knitted the underground space stations and crystalline chambers together. These chambers were the fertile cultivation ground for imported crystals, as most of their technology worked with the crystalline energies and energy fields.

They laid down a vast Super-Conscious Energy Field Matrix in and around the planet, which worked like a giant hard drive, recording everything that was happening on and inside the Earth. It was tuned directly into the 7th Central Sun of Illumination.

It was created to work in tandem with the entire energy system, forming a planetary communication network and technological hub where they could recharge their craft. They could also teleport and communicate instantaneously.

As the scientists and those first creators worked at creating their masterpiece, some fell in love with their own Creation. Indeed, the more they worked on and with her, the more they developed the yearning to settle on the planet's surface.

By this time, they had erected the first 12 Crystal Pyramid Temples, and massive diamond-shaped electromagnetic portals. They established crystalline structures – the first observation centers, to monitor how the new life forms developed.

The inhabitants called themselves the Sun People and transmitted the Solar Logos rays of the great Central 7th Sun. Their craft could not only circumnavigate the planet, but were amphibious and could be used on sea, land, and in the air.

They built the original Crystal Pyramids and vast city complexes in labyrinth forms, and also built stone circles and other megalithic sites, which were aligned to the Sun and Moon and the constellations from where they had originated and they all communicated with each other and the Crystalline Grids and the Spinal Column of the Earth. They worked from precise measurements, attuning these sites to the inner and outer Webs of Light, the Earth energy centers and the tonal chord of the Earth, as it is cosmically tuned into the Cosmic Music of the Spheres. During that time period, the Earth's vortex energy was inside such circles, and this in turn fed the energy grids used for their housing, work, and various other purposes.

The minor pyramidal structures were conduits of the vortex energy and were tuned in to the harmonic frequencies of the planet. Each one was aligned to the sound of the major Crystal Pyramid Temple of its region. This formed a vast harmonic tonal chord, reflecting Earth's tonal chord, which in turn aligned with the Cosmic tonal chords and the music of the spheres.

As above, so below!

The first 12 pyramids were essentially centers of higher learning; teaching; knowledge; wisdom; prophecy; sciences; technology; higher healing; ceremony and magic; love, and of the Sun and Moon.

The High Priest regarded himself as the embodiment of the male aspect of the Divine, and the High Priestess of the Divine Feminine aspect of God. Together they worked and functioned as One and performed certain sexual rites, as the sexual energy in itself is the experience of the God force energy, when it is properly channelled and directed. It was thus a conduit for harnessing certain energies, to become a creative force.

The 12 High Priests and 12 High Priestesses were associated with each of the 12 Crystal Pyramid Temples, which had a High Priest and Priestess reigning over the temple and county they administered. The men were mainly the administrators, while the women were the transmitter channels (prophecy and channelling), and in charge of the sexual and other rites of passage and initiations. They were also the Higher Healers and the creative ones. Men had the ability to invent and strategize. The women created what the men had visualized. The two worked in tandem in balance and harmony.

They not only acted as the custodians and administrators of the 12 Regions of Elysium, but they also held the secret keys and codes. In essence, the Temple of the White Flame was the power base of Earth, and its High Priest and Priestess had final jurisdiction and decision-making powers. They reported directly to the Central High Command of the Intergalactic Federation of the Great White Brotherhood. They had enormous responsibilities, and only the purest of the pure were considered worthy of holding such a position."

(Excerpt from *Why I was Born in Africa: The Previously Unrecorded History of Elysium and The Lion Kingdom*, by Judith Küsel)

## The Temple of the White Flame

"The first 12 pyramids were essentially centers of higher learning; teaching; knowledge; wisdom; prophecy; sciences; technology; higher healing; ceremony and magic; love, and of the Sun and Moon.

The first era, when the planet opened up for settlement, took place when the land masses joined together. It formed a type of hamlet, with a series of islands interlinked and interspersed with lakes and rivers, arranged in a colossal spiraling pattern in the shape of a labyrinth. It was constructed using sacred geometry.

This entire area formed an enormous and impressive vortex energy circuit that is currently being reactivated. In those first days, the Temple of the Diamond Ray, which was also affiliated with the Temple of the White Flame, as the White Flame represents the diamond ray, was in the centre of the islands and lakes. It was here, at this great temple complex in the form of a labyrinth that a massive vortex energy source was laid down. It was also here that the first ever Earth settlement developed!

It could be described as being part of a university complex, as Intergalactic Federation scientists gathered there and were experimenting with life and life forms on the outer rim of the planet, to monitor just how this form of energy could be used in different and far-reaching ways.

One of the applications was a momentous type of vortex, synergistically aligned so that the whole complex could be lit up, and spacecraft refuelled and revitalized by this energy. It was therefore an experiment of great significance, as it was from here that vortex energies in the other regions of the planet were created. They all started working as one within the Web of Light.

Within the Crystal Pyramid of the White Flame, another smaller pyramid was housed, or rather incorporated, which held the 13th Master Codes and Keys for the planet. It was directly linked to the 13th Master Key Codes of the Divine Halls of Records. These were administered by the 12 Elders surrounding God's throne, holding all the keys and codes of all of Creation. One can describe it as the mainframe brain, or mind of the whole Cosmos, as it holds all the records of everything ever created.

The High Priest of this Temple held not only the 12th Crystal Skull, but also the 13th. His counterpart, the High Priestess, held the 12th and 13th Crystal Keys, and together they held the 13th Master Code.

In essence, then, the Temple of the White Flame was the power base of Earth, and this temple's High Priest and Priestess had final jurisdiction and decision-making powers. They reported directly to the Central High Command of the Intergalactic Federation of the Great White Brotherhood. They had enormous responsibilities, and only the purest of the pure were considered worthy of holding such a position.

They held the complete balance of the Masculine and Feminine energies; the ultimate keys and codes for the eternal existence of life and all life forms in the entire Cosmos and on the planet. They were considered the Illumined Ones, the Chosen Ones. They were specially assigned to act as Guardians or Keepers of the sacred and sanctified.

It was considered the Divine Mother Flame, and therefore it held the Creative Force of the Divine Mother herself, in perfect balance with her Divine counterpart, the Male Principle of the Divine.

Once a year, or whenever major decisions had to be made, the 12 High Priests and Priestesses gathered at the Temple of the White Flame, with their Crystal Skulls, keys and codes, so that the 12 flames could be reunited in one single flame – the 13th Master Key Flame. This was considered the most sacred and sanctified of all gatherings, and therefore all underwent stringent purification rites before being allowed entry to the island. Such was the holiness of the place.

This was the Golden Age of Elysium, the Garden of Eden, and the first beautiful and profound Creation – 7th dimensional, prospering and at peace.

People were content and happy, and lived their lives peacefully.

Elsewhere in the Cosmos, however, vast thunder storm clouds were looming. They would reach even the outposts of the Heavens and cast their long shadows on to planet Earth and on our Solar System …"

(Excerpt from *Why I was Born in Africa: The Previously Unrecorded History of Elysium and The Lion Kingdom*, by Judith Küsel)

## The Secret Legacy

**Atlantis and Lemuria**

Before you embark on an epic journey through France with me, it is essential to pause for a moment as we travel further back in time. Actually, we need to go back to the time of Atlantis. What happened there clearly indicates what was later to be suppressed in France, and even shamefully persecuted. At the same time what was suppressed, provides the very key to the ascension into the New Earth, and resurrection to a totally new way of life.

Intrinsically linked to all of this, are the Isis Mystery Schools, and their continued survival through time and space, with the Fall of Humanity at large from the 7th Dimensional state, the 7th Heaven into the 3rd, lower than the Animal Kingdom. Nevertheless, the Mystery Schools survived throughout all of these upheavals, largely due to the continued dedication to the highest service rendered by two Soul Groups, namely the Shining and the Illumined Ones, who incarnated time and again, holding the light steady for Humanity.

They agreed to hold the sacred knowledge within their own souls, so that no matter what happened to them during an Earthly sojourn, this knowledge would never be lost. Thus, they assumed the role of Sages, Prophets, Teachers, Architects, Engineers and Astronomers, resurrecting themselves lifetime after lifetime, after severe devastation and destruction, sowing the seeds of knowledge wherever they went, holding the most sacred knowledge sacrosanct within their own, mostly secret schools or inner circles. This was necessary, as they knew full well that this knowledge was like a two-edged sword – what was done with it could either make or break one, and either uplift or destroy Humanity.

The Golden Age of Atlantis existed in a lower octave in the 5th dimension. It was a glorious age when all lived in unity and harmony, and the Atlanteans were at peace with the androgynous Lemurian civilization which existed simultaneously and had arisen, when Avalon fell.

When the Atlanteans opened their stellar borders to allow other alien races to settle there, they opened the door to the same faction that had begun the Wars of the Heavens, the Black Magi, who infiltrated their minds, taking control of Atlantis. They implanted control boxes into their populace, transforming them into robots who were controlled remotely.

The High Priesthood of Atlantis stood firm, and thus became a target. The Black Magi then turned their attention to the androgynous Lemurians, spreading cunning lies about sexual energy and intercourse among them, and invented a machine to split their form into separate male and female bodies. Undoubtedly, this caused immense trauma and pain to those who allowed this to happen, as they could no longer unite with their other half, no matter how hard they tried. Thus, they weakened the Atlanteans, then enslaved them, causing the destruction of Lemuria.

The High Priesthood was under siege, so they fashioned invisible shields around their temple's complexes, but the Sages and Seers foresaw the total destruction of Atlantis, and the Great Flood. They thus knew they needed to safeguard their knowledge, and began to do this by inserting it into energy fields, sun discs, and secretly prepared chosen sites, where they could live underground until the flood subsided. Some did leave the planet by spacecraft, to return later. So, the Isis Mystery Schools went deep underground again, establishing small colonies of new life in remote areas to continue their work and safeguard their legacy, and managed to survive the floods, with their knowledge base intact.

Then the great wars of destruction of Atlantis by the Black Magi began, which was unprecedented. The Atlanteans created robots which eventually turned against their own masters and killed them. As events unfolded, the Atlanteans were remotely mind controlled, and slaughtered, as crystal atomic lasers came into play, which caused vast landmasses to tear off and sink under the sea. They then bombarded the temples, but the invisible shields kicked in, so the laser beams boomeranged right back at the enemy.

In the process the Atlanteans nearly destroyed Earth, necessitating the Intergalactic Councils to intervene, and in the aftermath of the Wars of the Heavens, they proclaimed that no planet, galaxy or star system would ever be destroyed again. Thus, huge comets and asteroids intervened, and hit the planet, contributing to the Great Flood. In fact, the Black Magi would have blown Earth up, for they had the means to do so, and amongst them were exactly the same souls who had in fact, blown up the planet between Jupiter and Mars during the Wars of the Heavens.

**The Legacy of Atlantis**
Consequently, there was a fall from Grace, a fall from Unity and Oneness, and in addition, separation from the Divine Source, from one other and from our own soul selves!

Indeed, negative patterns that had been created in Atlantis then became the greatest challenge that Humanity as a whole needed to transcend: Duality had been created, both within and outside of themselves.

A sense of meaninglessness and hopelessness reigned, along with a profound recall of the Golden Ages of Humanity, the First Paradise of Elysium, The Lion Kingdom, Avalon, etc.

This was accompanied by the suppression of Patriarchy, for it was in Atlantis that women were first persecuted, because the Black Magi were deeply afraid of their intuitive powers, and they dreaded the Power of Love even more!

The Fall into the Third Dimensional State and the Rise of Patriarchy:

As chaos and destruction now reigned on the Earth, those who managed to survive had to establish a civilization afresh. Survivors could be found living together in pockets all over the globe, and this phase is remembered by all indigenous people. Yet life had become a struggle for existence in a hostile environment, as Earth had changed drastically. An ice age began, with survivors just managing to stay alive, living inside caves and other areas that had somehow managed to remain intact.

Thus, the Shining and Illumined Ones returned to remind Humanity of the basics of civilization, and the Isis Mystery Schools rose up, now bearing different names and guises over time. Hitherto, the innate knowing was always held within the souls of the Shining and Illumined Ones, who incarnated time and again, and who were so often persecuted and misunderstood, or hated because of their purity, and for standing in their truth. Yet they never gave up, returning at this time to see Humanity through the Dying of the Old Earth (on the 5th July 2020) and the birth of the New Earth, the start of a totally new epoch with a new Humanity rising. Indeed, this is what they have been ceaselessly working towards over thousands of years.

In the procedure one also needs to understand that in the beginning, in the first 7th dimensional civilizations, vocal cords were not used for communication, and there was no written language. There was no need for one. One communicated telepathically, storing information in energy fields and sun discs. All Universal creations, and all events and creations under the Great Central Suns, are recorded energetically. When this is applied through your own soul and tapped into, a written or spoken language is superfluous. The Universal Language of Light, is indeed a symbolic one that creates sacred geometric patterns of sound, understood universally, for the Universal codes are read through sacred geometry, and sacred mathematics and numbers, energy and energy fields.

All those who are remembered as "gods" in mythology and in later accounts, were but those who held this sacred or superior knowledge, and could apply it. To the newly rendered 3rd dimensional humans, these souls seemed to have superhuman powers and knowledge, thus appearing God-like. In fact, they were advanced beings who came to teach Humanity.

The most sacred teachings were stored in the Mystery Schools which rose again, in Mesopotamia, India, the Himalayas, the Kahunas in the Pacific, the Sages in Africa, with different branches in Ancient Egypt, in France, in Greece, in Spain, in the Pyrenees, within the Celtic Druidic Communities spanning Europe, Britain, Ireland and the Middle East, including Jerusalem, Harran and other places. One of the highest and most hidden was in the Ural Mountains, in what is now Romania, and some are still there in the etheric. Others were in South America, in Mexico and North America.

**The Inner Secret Schools**

One cannot understand the ultimate truths or knowledge of Mary Magdalene, Joan of Arc, the Cathars and Templars, who all belonged to the Mystery Schools as High Initiates, without knowing that within any such groupings, you always had the ordinary congregants, and lay people, who were separate from the inner group. They attended ceremonies, and sermons as simple folk, who often contributed towards the external running of the groups. For instance, the Cathar faith had many weavers in their ranks, who were not even aware of the inner Mystery School in their midst. This also applied to the Templars, who were loosely structured on the same principle. There were highly esoterically trained, educated priests in their ranks. The fighting was done by the military wing – another branch of the order, who were not highly initiated.

Within this context then let us also understand that Mary Magdalene was born in France, into a high Jewish noble family who held property both in Southern France (as did many Jews, King Herod among them), as well as in Israel. Her family were Essenes, who had a secret branch in France. For it had long been foreseen by the Essene prophets, that they needed to preserve their teachings and knowledge there, as they had forecast the destruction of Jerusalem, and the scattering of the Jewish people.

I will not go further into her history here as this is written down elsewhere, but suffice to say, that she certainly was a high initiate and High Priestess in her own right, with access to the highest inner teachings. She brought these back to France, and they were incorporated into the French Mystery Schools, which were already in existence. Her support base arrived as soon as she landed in France. Moreover, her teachings, additional knowledge and the Ancient Book of Love, were incorporated into the Mystery School at Monségur, which had smaller branches all over Southern France.

The Essenes themselves were part of the Mystery Schools of Alexandria and Heliopolis in Egypt. Such great Greek Philosophers as Plato, spent thirteen years studying in the Mystery Schools in Alexandria, as had his own Grandfather Solon. This Mystery School incorporated the Ancient Mystery Schools of Egypt, which went back thousands of years, right back to the time of Atlantis, and earlier to the Lion Kingdom. Indeed, the Sphinx holds much of this information on energetic levels, and in sun discs.

Now there is a third component here, which includes the branches of the Egyptian Mystery Schools, who apart from the Essenes, also incorporated the Mystery School of Delphi in Greece, and Haran, as well as Ephesus. Certainly, the Egyptian Schools were one with the schools in what is now Iraq (indeed Ur, where Abraham is said to have originated, held an Ancient Mystery school, of which he was a high initiate), plus those of India, and the Tibetan ones in the Himalayas.

Thus, we can see an intricate network of sages, holding the secret teachings. The Essenes belonged to an extended group of wisdom keepers, and one needs to understand this. John the Baptist trained in these teachings, as much as Yeshua did.

Interestingly, other branches of the same mystery schools were found in Britain and Ireland, with the most significant one on the Island of Iona, and another one in Scotland, near Edinburgh.

All these schools had a common thread – they all practised certain rites, and held specific knowledge, as they were the same Mystery Schools and branches which Isis had brought into form and being, millions of years ago.

Mary Magdalene belonged to the Age-Old High Priesthood Secret Mystery School, thus was known as a High Priestess in her own right. Yet, she brought to France certain scrolls and knowledge from the School of Alexandria and the Essenes, which incorporated the Highest Teachings of the Divine Feminine, as originally taught by the Goddess Isis in the Gnostic Tradition, which then became the teachings or the experience of the Holy Sophia. Again, the same concepts but in different disguises.

Since she was already under pressure and intense persecution, even in France, the knowledge she brought with her went underground, to be incorporated into the Mystery School Teaching in France.

This proved to be vital, as Mary Magdalene had foreseen that women who held any form or rank would be severely oppressed and thus it was vital to safeguard the information.

She was certainly proven right. In the aftermath of the emperor Constantine declaring the Roman Catholic Church to be the state religion, the Gnostics (who incorporated the Ancient Mystery School Teachings) were brutally victimised, and their books and scrolls were burnt. Next came the attack by Christians on the Library and Schools in Alexandria, and many priestesses and teachers were stoned to death.

As women were then denied any form of rank or position in the Catholic Church, they had to retreat underground to protect the Ancient Teachings and Secrets.

Within this context, the Cathars and Templars, with St. Bernard of Clairvaux, all held the same secret teachings, with access to the same knowledge as the High Initiates, and thus they were the next to be targeted by the Roman Church, who wanted to annihilate them, for the secret wisdom they held, mainly driven by the lies of the church they upheld.

In the next part of the book, my own journey through France unfolds, with the knowledge that I literally had to release intense trauma and pain, as the greatest genocide of a people, especially women, occurred in Southern France, and thus the Cathars had to bear the brunt of the Catholic Church's attempt, to annihilate them, in order to stamp out the Truth.

I have done many soul readings, in the meantime, of souls who were Cathars during that time, and the horrors committed by the Inquisition, knows no bounds.

Yet, the souls have returned. Indeed, the soul lives on!

And the Laurel Wreath is rising again, as was prophesied.

The truth is rising again.

At this most crucial time, when the Old Earth has ceased to exist, and the New Earth has been born, the secret knowledge of the Cathars and Templars, is definitely most relevant.

Now every soul, who chooses to transfigure into the new embodiment and new form, is required to go through exactly the same rites of passage and illumination, they taught and practiced.

So many are constantly seeking for the Hidden Treasure of the Cathars, digging for it in the Pyrenees, when in truth, this treasure was something completely different.

Here lie the central keys.

The Power of Love returns!

# The Druids and the Three High Orders of the Druids

1. The High Order of the Alchemists.
2. The High Order of the Bards.
3. The High Order of the Mystic Rose, Serpent and Grail.

**1. The High Order of the Alchemists**

To even be allowed into this order which was open to everyone as an acolyte was considered a great accomplishment. The general Druid training from the early years of life up to the age of 17, was pretty much the same, involving successfully passing initiations, which determined in which of the three orders one would spend the rest of one's life, as a Druid Priest or Priestess.

To some degree, young girls and women were subject to a different set of initiations and rites of passage, because in these Druidic Orders, knowledge of the highest uses of the sexual energies was imparted early on. So, on reaching puberty, with its first physical manifestation, there were already the first initiations to be mastered. (I will furnish more detail regarding these rites and inner teaching later.)

Suffice to say, that what is now identified as White Tantra, and in the Gnostic content, the Hieros Gamos, was known to the Druids, and practised in the highest degree. It involved the uses and directives of igniting the Sacred Fires during sexual union, and simultaneously awakening and using the so-called Serpent Energies (known in the East as the Kundalini Energy). So, tuition included knowledge of how to direct and to amplify this energy, and the use of the spiralling Energy of the Goddess herself was essential. It was the self-same energy found in the Crystal Pyramids, the Crystalline Pyramid Grids, directly linked up with the Lightning Rod energy within the Spinal Column, and planet Earth. The higher the initiate, the better they knew how to direct them, and in these very altered and higher states, they were able at will, to manifest or de-manifest, to co-create, and even change forms. (I will come to this later in more detail.)

Additionally, the Alchemical Knowledge of this High Druidic Order, worked with the intricate and hidden secret knowledge of the inner workings of Mathematics and cosmic mathematical formulae, as well as the higher uses of Phi and Psi (the latter is the female counterpart of the Phi, which we have forgotten). It was knowledge of how to fuse seeming polarities, and opposite poles into one single energy field, directing them with the heart-mind. One had to feel into what one wished to manifest and create, and then direct it through the picture in your mind.

Shapeshifting was an inherent process within, and the Druidic Alchemist knew how to shapeshift into any chosen form, becoming the very energy field they were working with, by dissolving into it. When they became as one, they shifted into whatever they wished to create, manifesting this into form, then detached themselves from this energy field, again assuming their original form and state.

Many Initiates died in the process of dissolving into the energy fields. Here one is reminded of when Jesus in his conversations with Nicodemus, in the New Testament, states that unless one was prepared to die and be reborn, one could not enter the gateway to Heaven. The Druidic High Orders knew the hidden secret meaning of this in their alchemical work - if you could not step past your own negative ego, you could not work miracles or wonders.

Another important component of the alchemical training, involved the uses of the Hidden Fingers of God, the YOD (YOD means Finger of God), the Sacred Geometries, the Fire Letters, and Symbols of the Divine. (The Divine I refer to is the Godhead, incorporating the Divine Masculine and Divine Feminine as One.) Sacred geometry with sacred mathematics, was the higher esoteric knowledge of the manipulation of sacred geometries, with sacred math and formulas, using this to create with. This entailed the use of certain number sequences, and sacred geometrical forms (each one works with symbols, which in turn work with maths and numbers within sacred formulas that the Divine used to invent certain aspects of Creation). Consequently, certain sacred patterns repeat themselves throughout the Cosmos and all of Creation.

There was a third component in the Highest Mastery – Physics, so by applying sexual rites, and the hidden meaning and knowledge of physics, including energy fields, matrix and Super consciousness energy fields, plus the spiralling Serpent energy, one could literally change the face of Creation!

Of course, this could only occur within the set rules of the Divine Cosmic Laws, which stood for all eternity. The acolyte knew that they could face death as the penalty, if they contravened the laws at any given time, so they dared not tamper with them, but rather observed them. For within the Divine Laws, lie hidden secret structures, order and harmony, which are inherent cosmically. If contravened, one could destroy oneself, and create chaos and destruction. So, when an acolyte did try to go against the teachings, and these inherent Rules or Laws, they usually died, most frequently from their inability to resume their physical form, or to retrieve their original soul form, after allowing themselves to disintegrate into energy fields.

You will now understand why the High Druidic Orders were so strict in the training and initiations, for the content worked with here as Master Alchemists was extremely powerful and potent. You absolutely had to gain mastery over yourself first, before mastering the energies, energy fields, matter or non-matter being worked with!

Physics included the skilled art of creating with all forms of the elements, and the expressions thereof, visible or invisible, including metaphysical training, as it was essential to be informed about the physical, as much as the invisible, to be in a position to receive the highest insights and understanding of exactly what was being worked with.

Alchemy in its highest form, is not so much concerned with transmuting lead into gold, as it is the transformation of one form of energy into a completely different one. Hence it was crucial to master the Fires of Transmutation, a Fire Energy available cosmically for those who call upon it, as it could transmute all matter and even energy, into a totally different and much higher vibratory form!

Herein lies the greatest of all the secret knowledge of the High Druidic Orders, their ability to literally change any form of matter into something else, transforming any form of energy into a much higher and more potent energy form. Indeed, they could teleport such energy instantly, over vast distances.

Later this would be remembered in the character of Merlin, the Magician, but in truth all those in the High Orders of Druids bore the title of Merlin or Merlinda. It had prefixes, plus their soul name, so they were addressed as Merlin A-Ha-Thu-An-Ru-A-Ra, the latter the given name, or Merlinda Gui-A-Ve-Ra-Ve-Ay-A-Ru-Ra.

The Druidic Symbols of the highest degree always incorporated the 7th Central Sun of Illumination, the Caduceus (Serpent energy, plus Lightning Rod), the spiral and serpent, the five or six-pointed star, the Triangle (pyramid), and so forth.

With each successful initiation, these symbols were either tattooed on the upper regions of the left arm, or sometimes under the breast, and they wore them as arm bracelets, torques, and sometimes as circlets around the head, denoting rank, and the level of initiation. The higher the degree of the Initiate, the more serpent heads would rise from the circlet or crown, signifying having passed the ultimate initiations. So, one reached the highest form of enlightenment by mastering the Serpent energy (kundalini and the spiralling energy). Sometimes a globe or disc would be added to this, which indicated the High Priesthood or High Priesthood, anchoring in the 7th Central Sun of Illumination, as a transmitter channel for the highest degree of knowledge, technology and wisdom.

The High Order of the Alchemist was the first of the Three Orders. Sometimes initiates, if called to do so, could be initiated into all three Orders, which was the exception rather than the rule, for to even obtain the degree of Priest or Priesthood in these Orders was a feat in itself, and only those of the highest purity ever made it to the top. Purity here would incorporate truth, integrity, and absolute dedication to render the highest possible service, in the highest possible way. The Pure Ones literally meant the highest initiated ones, for the purer one's intent, the more one stood in one's truth, and the more one could do and be no other than that.

Later, it was this order which would be most challenged on truth and integrity, and this ultimately proved to be their downfall.

**2. The High Order of the Bards**

The High Order of the Bards were the sound engineers, working with the highest sound vibrations and frequencies, in all their forms and expressions. In addition, they were Custodians, Keepers and Guardians of the Highest Knowledge of the Druidic Orders, also Storytellers, Minstrels (Troubadours), Musicians, Singers and Stewards of the Creative Soul – art, music, ceremonies, rituals, worship, and secular activities. Using Sound vibrations, they were also Higher Healers in their own right, familiar with its inner workings, able to tune into the Cosmic Music of the Spheres, and they knew the Light code invocations, the Love Vibrations, and how to heal through the voice and chanting.

The High Order of the Bard started Epic Storytelling with Music and Sound, activating keys and codes within all who listened, often triggering soul memory banks, and activating those deeply dormant within the soul. Using sound, they worked with the spiraling energy of the pyramids and Pyramid Grids, the Lightning Rod of the Spine and the Earth, fine-tuning the Spinal Column and their energy centres using the Ankh, as a tuning fork.

One must remember that in those days, people did not communicate through the voice, but telepathically. The voice was used as an instrument for chanting, singing, and often as a vibratory instrument to the highest degree.

It was known that if one chanted the vowels even for an instant, one could directly tune into the highest Divine cosmic vibrations, and the primordial Paradise vibrations, healing landscapes, people, etc. just by chanting them. Chanting the vowels also opened the third eye, the inner hearing, seeing and knowing, and if chanted in a circular, or spiralling fashion induced a deep trancelike state, allowing direct access to the Divine Heart, and an experience of the outpouring of Divine love in vibratory forms. It was known that chanting vowels also calmed the mind and mental bodies, and healed the emotional one. So, in the chanting they also used the Light Language codes, and some of the most ancient Paradise sounds (Paradise meaning the First Creation of the Divine Sound Vibration). They were even able to project this sound over huge distances, communicating over continents to the ends of the Earth, and back again!

The most highly trained of these Bards, communicated across the solar system and the Milky Way Galaxy in this way, and could tune into Sirius, the Pleiades, and Andromeda, as well as some other Galaxies. So, one could say that they knew and used the gateways of sounds and inter-stellar communication systems in ways we have completely forgotten about!

The Bardic Order placed great importance on the use of stringed instruments in their daily rituals, especially the lyre and Harp, some gongs, bells, high-pitched percussion instruments, and the hand-held drum. Interestingly it was in Avalon that the Bagpipe, the Uilleann Flute, and other such Celtic Instruments originated, chiefly because of their pitch, and definite vibratory tones. Many Irish instruments today reflect this to some degree, and are still used.

The human voice was not just used in chanting, but also in a ceremonial sense, as people knew how to project their voices, and to use meditative sounds to reach highly altered states. Round-songs were sung, blending male and female voices, into what I can only describe as Celestial sounds, combined with the instruments, and this created an amazingly altered experience, putting one in direct contact with the Divine, and enabling an experience of the Divine in ways which were not otherwise possible – it was pure magic in a higher sense!

In addition, they also recorded the entire history of the planet in vibratory energy fields, for example the way in which they created the standing stones, Stonehenge, the dolmens, etc., as an expression of vibratory rock gongs and instruments which tune into planet Earth's frequencies and its own soul song. When they were played correctly, they could amplify sound energies over vast distances. In this case they used a type of Alpine Horn, as well as whistles, bells, bagpipes, the Uilleann flute, the harp and lyres, and the human voice.

If you look closely at a dolmen, you will find that every single rock has its own sound, and plays its own tune, and when struck with the white gold wand, they vibrate and emit sound. Each stone was struck by a priest and priestess which resulted in the most sublime sounds, combining earthly and heavenly vibrations together in a celebration of sound, which woke up Humankind and all the Earth to a much higher vibratory level.

In this way they ensured human-beings and all the world vibrated to a single heart and soul song, thus singing in unison, and vibrating as one heartbeat, and one soul song. They were in tune with one another, and the rest of the Cosmos!

The High Order of the Bards were truly extraordinary in that the men and women of this order used their gifts in the highest possible service, thus bringing a high degree of Unity Consciousness and Unity vibrations and frequencies to all – not just to other people, but also to the animals, the plants, the trees, etc. So many of their most sacred ceremonies were held in sacred oak, yew, and birch tree groves, where the elements and elementals could join in the music and chanting, and the general high altered states of pure at-Oneness with all the Cosmos, and the rest of Creation.

They held White-Gold, the highest of the alchemical metals, as their symbol, and many of their finest instruments, including the Ankh, were created with it. Their cities were white-gold and thus called the Place of the Bards. (I had to reopen such a city when I was in Brittany, France.)

The High Bardic Order fulfilled very varied roles in the greater context of Avalon, as musicians and singers, who possessed a genius for creating the highest vibrations and frequencies of musical sounds. They often walked amongst the people, fine-tuning their souls, to bring them harmony and Unity Consciousness. Sometimes they introduced plays, so the various roles could showcase their musical genius. They fashioned Epic Poems, using the hidden vowels and Light language keys and codes to ignite within the listeners the Highest Knowledge, knitting heart and mind energies together, in the music they created, which incorporated various harmonies to open the heart and soul. (Much further in the future, the Minstrels and Troubadours of this High Bardic Order would assume this role, especially in Southern France, but we will come to this later.)

Then there were those who specialized in the sound frequency vibrations of rock gongs, and the standing stones, the circular spiralling sound energies, containing the earth songs and vibrations, and cosmic harmonies and the music of the spheres. They could project sound frequencies and vibrations over vast distances (like the satellite systems today, but they did not use such technology). It was done purely through the knowledge of vibratory energy fields, working with the Crystalline Energy Grids to "throw" sound.

I use the word "throwing" for want of a better word – sometimes they would create what looked like huge humming balls of light and sound vibrations, visualising in their mind's eye clearly where they wished to direct them, then throwing them, and they instantly hit the target and did their work. Today this might seem like magic, but in fact it was just the knowledge of energy and vibratory sound energy fields. (The Aborigines in Australia remembered the Song Lines and went walkabout to visit the sacred sites underground. Most places were considered holy and sacred, and only Shamans were allowed access to them. There the rituals of sound vibrations would be played out as remembered. The Didgeridoo is one such high vibrating percussion instrument, which, when accompanied by certain rattles and singing, induced the full activation of the Song Lines once more, and reconnection with Mother Earth.)

The Temples of Sound were circular and spiralled upwards, or they were within the Crystal Pyramids, where sound chambers were made from pure quartz Crystal in the different colour hues. Thus, colour and sound combined in the higher healing techniques in the fine-tuning of the physical and all 12 bodies, as well as the soul.

The High Order of the Bards were totally focused, a highly specialized order working with the highest vibrations, sound frequencies and energy systems. They could teleport the densest and heaviest of matter, dissolving it into feather light material, and teleporting it exactly where it needed to be manifested into form again. Vast megalithic blocks were precisely cut at the quarries with the help of sound vibrations, frequencies and technologies, then dissolved into featherlike substances, teleported and placed exactly, according to plan, to slot in, and manifest into form again. Machu Picchu and other sites give testimony to their immense knowledge of sound engineering.

The same techniques were used in Higher Healing, in their worship services, music, singing and even dancing. In their worship services, they also knew the 72 Names of God and the Goddess (the Divine) – sometimes chanting these 24 hours in succession, or in groups of chanting choirs. The reverberating effect was like a giant cathedral of sound resonating and echoing back through the spiralling energy systems.

They knew the higher uses of the YHVH and the primordial vibrations, and of the hidden secret sounds and the sound technologies as held within the 7th Central Sun.

This High Bardic Order was one of the most powerful, because they interacted with the populace of Avalon more than the others, and were highly respected, but also accessible. They were on the front stage, the most visible actors on the great collective stage of Avalon, due to the role they played in unifying them through singing, their musical abilities, their advanced knowledge of the sacred maths and geometries hidden within music and musical scales, vibrations and frequencies, and the power of the spoken word. (This was not speech as we know it now, but using vowels in the Light Language keys and codes.) These vowels, when spoken or sung, or even repeated, were one of the most powerful enlightenment tools. They also worked with Sun Discs and the Sun Dial Knowledge to the highest degree, which were known to open certain faculties held in the third eye, namely the All-seeing, the All-hearing, the All-tasting, and the All-knowing, the All-experiencing.

There are certain degrees of sacred Mathematics, Geometries, and Physics, which, when used in conjunction with sound vibrations and frequencies, produce the highest states of Enlightenment, where all faculties of the Higher Mind and Higher Heart/Soul are opened to the supreme degree, and this is the state, when one can literally move the proverbial mountain instantly! In those higher states one can also access the highest of the High – pure states of the highest ecstasy, which were utilized by the High Priest and High Priestesses of this Druidic High Order, to co-create what they wished to manifest into form, and what they wished to teleport, transport, and change the patterns and forms of. We cannot even imagine this, but in truth, if this knowledge is diligently applied, within the framework of cosmic laws, one can literally create anything, manifest, or dissolve, or change patterns even of the programming of the human cell and the DNA structures, including removing energy blockages, etc.

Music and sound speak the language of the soul – the High Druidic Order of the Bards had attained the highest degree of Mastery in the art of using sound frequencies and vibrations in every form, thus utilizing this knowledge in ways we cannot even dream of now.

### 3. The High Order of the Mystic Rose, Serpent and Grail

This High Order belonged to the High Order of Aysis-Ra-A-Ru-A-Ra, and therefore was the most secret and sacred of the three. It often included those from the other two Druidic Orders, but in truth stood apart, as the Highest Mastery one could obtain – Enlightenment in the Highest Degree.

It was Aysis herself who had created this High Order, when she reigned supreme in the Lion Kingdom, and she created the Crystal Pyramid Temples in the Pyrenees, and the first Mystery Schools held therein. They belonged to her, more than to her consort Osiris-Ra-A-Hu-Ra, although his teachings and contribution to the Highest Rites of the Divine Masculine stood on a par with hers. Osiris at that time gave his full support and blessings, as the founder of the Divine Masculine portion of this High Order, although he did not lay its foundations. In truth this High Order leaned more towards the Goddess, than towards Osiris, but was then oriented towards the Divine, the Godhead, thus the Trilogy, the Divine Masculine, the Divine Feminine plus the Sacred Fire ( known as the Holy Spirit to some, but in truth it is called the Supreme Sacred Fire.) When all three are present, this forms the Godhead, the Supreme Deity, and The Divine Source.

The training here was totally focused on the sacred Sexual Rites, which worked with the Kundalini Energies, and the supreme union between the Divine Masculine and the Divine Feminine, to create the Sacred Fires, and thus the highest states of Enlightenment themselves. This was a co-creative state, and during such a high degree of union, one knew how to project the energy and then, through the amplification of the Spiraling Energy emitted throughout the Crystal Pyramid Temple, in which the highest rites were performed, this could be used to the maximum degree of co-creatorship. Indeed, one could create miracles in this way.

However, the training for this purpose was the most stringent testing, and only the purest of souls ever made it to this degree of purification – thus many never made it, for they lacked the degree of discipline, focus, truth and integrity that this High Order demanded. It brought out the God in the Male, and Goddess in the Female to the highest degree, but it also worked with the full knowledge and understanding of the Sexual Energy force, as a Creative force in itself, not for self-gratification, or orgies, or any sexual sport or misuse, but only for the highest degree of service work together.

The Serpent was used by this Order as a symbol of the Highest Degree, for it was the serpent-like coil they wished to create (Kundalini, as it was known in the East), so High Initiates wore a Gold or Silver Serpent bracelet on their left arm. They had a Rose tattooed under their left breast, and the Caduceus tattooed just above the entry to their private parts. They wore the circlet with sun discs, and within that disc was the Caduceus (the serpent and staff, or rod), the Rose and the Chalice.

Now the Chalice in this case, was a symbol of the womb, but more than this, it was symbolic of the highest degree of Enlightenment attained. The ultimate state of Being, where one traverses the Super Consciousness Energy Fields, masters them and then transmits this into Co-creative acts.

The woman was the Transmitter of the energy, with the man, and through them both, into Being. She was the one who helped him create the miracles he wished to create with her, and vice versa. Without her, he could not do this. Neither could she do it without him, both were needed in order to materialize what they wished to create, into physical form or manifestation.

However, there was another option in this Order, the possibility to choose another degree of Enlightenment, which did not require a sexual partner, in which the rites were performed alone. The Highest Female Initiates could then experience Immaculate conceptions, by uniting with the Cosmic Divine Masculine Energy itself, and thus bearing a miracle child. The degree of mastery this took was a chosen path of highest service, often remembered in the collective consciousness as the immaculate conception of the Virgin. In truth it was only the highest initiates from this Sacred Order who could attain this state, after intense training and inner initiations!

The Rose depicted the Thousand Petals of the Heart-Rose, for the heart-energy centre connects directly to the Soul. There are two other roses with a thousand petals, hidden elsewhere in the body – one over the sexual centre (vagina and clitoris) and one over the Third Eye/Throat Centre, and therefore they all function as a single unit.

When fully activated, this opens the Higher Transmitter channels, connected to the Higher 4 Roses, held with the Bridge of Light, causing the Spinal Column Rod to grow from the crown, with the potential to extend to the 354th degree of Divinity, when fully activated. At the 354th degree, the Divine Feminine Roses, the three and one are fully activated, and the soul in question becomes a full and very powerful Transmitter Channel for the Mystic Rose aspects of the Divine Feminine.

The Chalice or Sacred Cup, holds the Holy or Sacred Fires, and the Transmutation Fire, that same alchemical fire, but now amplified and expanded, with the Fires of Illumination, from the 7th Central Sun. These initiates were highly trained to tap into the Fires of Illumination, in the highest sense, to the highest degree. The Highest Transmitter Channels often became Oracles (especially in later Delphi and the high Pyrenees) and were given the gift of

Prophecy, and immense foresight. This meant that during such rites, they were able to move into the highest All-knowing, All-seeing, All-being state, thus retrieving extremely powerful information, which they transformed into higher teachings, or incorporated it into some manifested form, for the higher good of the Collective.

During the most sacred and profound union, the highest faculties of both the Male and Female lit up to the extreme. They literally became the Divine Masculine, Divine Feminine and the Sacred Fire, and could direct the energy fields in any way they wanted. They knew how to merge the Kundalini (Serpent) Energy, with the Lightning Rod (Spinal Cord Energies), and the Rose/Grail/Fires of Enlightenment, co-creating in very powerful ways. These rites were often performed before mass gatherings of the Rainbow Tribes, and the High Councils, directed at amplifying the energies to facilitate shifts, and to uplift the whole.

The Brotherhood and Sisterhood of the Rose, Serpent and Grail (Sacred Chalice) in the inner planes, are of the Supreme Service Orders, incarnating cosmically where the greatest incentive, or need for Enlightenment, or the Fires of Illumination exist.

Some of these souls have served Humanity in immensely powerful and selfless ways, and some belong to the High Brother and Sisterhood of the White Flame.

They are known for their utmost purity, and their commitment to reincarnating for many lifetimes since Avalon, the Lion Kingdom and Elysium, holding the Fires of Illumination steady for all of Humankind. They often led Humanity through the most intense periods of darkness, and more. (I will come back to this at a later stage.) For now, suffice to say, those ordained into this third and secret Order, were the Highest Initiates, and on the highest possible path. However, it demanded the utmost dedication and selfless service, and within this work, the negative ego had no place.

These initiates were hand-picked, some were Twin Flames with eternal soul contracts and bonds. They thus knew they were destined for each other, to unite for the highest service possible, which would knit them together, like nothing else could.

Thus, training and the initiations were restricted to sacred and secret places, where the other Druidic Orders were barred. This was mainly to maintain the energies there at the highest degree of purity, as these sites had direct energetic links to the 7th Central Sun and the Fires of Illumination. Initiates knew how to identify each other, via the symbols placed etherically into their auric energy fields, and encoded in their souls. They will recognize each other cosmically, through many lifetimes, parallel lives and Universes, and do this work here and cosmically, wherever they are summoned.

They are extremely highly evolved souls of the highest calibre, so were subject to the most stringent initiations of all the Orders, but once ordained into the highest ranks, they often stood unshakable and unmovable in the highest truth and integrity, and never divulged their secrets or yielded, even in the face of the severest persecution later on. For they were aware that this knowledge could be abused to the extreme in the wrong hands.

Sexual energy does not need a physical body to express itself. It can be present in many other forms, and therefore as with all energy and energy fields, it can be expanded and projected, and is one of the highest pathways of Enlightenment, providing a glimpse of what the Divine Source is like. One then experiences Divine Sexuality, Ecstasy, Divine Creativity, and this Divinity is expressed at a much higher level, when two become as One.

There are many higher expressions and uses of Divine energy, and the Sexual energy force, which originally was fully understood as a sacred and sanctified Divine gift, when used correctly, in the highest possible service. When it was awakened in puberty, the sexual energy force was carefully and meticulously nurtured, and brought into its full maturity at 60, for the most sacred of rites, becoming a higher Pathway to Enlightenment itself.

It has a very deep mystical component, for here one delves into the deepest mysteries of Creation itself. It was through the merging, of the Divine Masculine with the Divine Feminine, that Creation was manifested and given birth to. It is through the merging of both, that the Divine Godhead, the Divine Source which holds the Trinity within it, moves and creates, and expands into infinite Beingness.

There is a much deeper and hidden component here, which only the highest initiates ever aspired to delve into. For one had to be an initiate of the highest degree, before this could become a means of exploring the Divinity within, the highest alchemical knowledge, the deepest depths of transmission, and the highest merging with the Godhead and all Creation.

During moments of intense union, in that highly altered state of All-Being, one could traverse the Heavens, literally tapping into any information or hidden knowledge of the 12 Central Suns, stepping into the highest degree of the All-knowing, All-seeing, the All-being.

Thus, all the stringent initiations, all the immensely tough purification rites, proved worthwhile, for it is only when one's vibrational frequencies, and ability to dissolve into these immense Divine Super Consciousness Energy Fields were very high, the All-Being itself, was it possible to retain the human physical form.

If all of these had not been mastered, with constant upgrading of the 12 bodies, and the Higher Soul Self, one simply could not hold form.

Why? This was because one stepped into a much higher dimensional vibratory and frequency state, rising several octaves of energy, due to the sacred union.

One was not just creating the bliss and the ecstasy of merging the Divine Masculine and Feminine, and projecting and using of the Kundalini or Serpent spiralling energy, one was also dissolving into the Super Matrix Conscious Energy Fields, which embrace the All-knowing, All-seeing, All-being As One.

Not only did one need to stay consciously aware to such an extent that one could co-create within this field, but one had to direct this energy into whatever one wished to access or to create!

In fact, many attain this state of higher bliss, and then allow it to dissipate, for they cannot hold the frequency band, and fear of death is inherent here. This had to be overcome to such an extent, that if one disintegrated completely, you could go through a rebirth of the soul and body, resurrected into a higher altered state!

One was in the World, but not of it.

One was body and flesh of the physical embodiment, but at the same time able to transcend this.

Moreover, one worked with the Sacred Fires, which transmute, and change the energetic form. Thus, one state is transmuted into a no state, void, no-thingness, and then is reborn, or re-emerges or is re-formed and re-structured, into a much higher state.

Those who practised these rites to the highest degree, emitted such radiance and blinding Light, that they often literally blinded people with their presence. This was a consequence of having transcended the physical embodiment to such a degree, that they could literally traverse the heavens and teleport themselves anywhere in the Cosmos, at will. They could manifest into form instantly whatever they chose to, and transform the state of anything they chose to.

This Sacred and Secret Brotherhood and Sisterhood of the Rose, the Serpent and the Grail, are not bound to the Earth. The souls belong to this Order in the Inner Planes, and often for eternity. They have so often served to the highest degree, and taken on the collective pain of Humanity, in order to hold the Light and Love vibrations steady. Some took on immensely challenging lifetimes, to uphold the highest degrees and principles, even when under fire.

However, we will get to their story as Avalon's history unfolds.

Druids were also known as Magicians by the populace, and the title Merlin and Merlinda became synonymous with Magic and High Magic, and the supernatural arts.

The title of Magician was added to that of the Druids, and the three High Orders, but in truth it was an immensely high degree of Mastery and Knowledge of the Energy and Energy Fields, and the manipulation, transcendence and reinvention of these fields.

It is good to deeply comprehend this, for, in order to understand the subsequent history of Avalon, and then later that of France, one must grasp this to the greatest degree.

So many false accusations, so many untruths, so many fallacies have been scattered around, that one must gain this understanding from the deepest knowing inside of the soul, forgetting all the false history, all the false doctrines and all the falsehoods of those who wished to keep Humanity prisoner and bound in darkness.

Suffice to say that these three High Druidic Orders, formed the backbone, the Spinal Column of Avalon.

Even the High Kings and High Queens, had to bow to their instructions and wishes.

## The High Kings and High Queens of Avalon

As much as the High Druidic Orders held the power behind the scenes, the administrative powers were in the hands of the High Kings and Queens – the kingdom was divided into 12 regions, each with their own High King and Queen.

They synchronized their decisions and administrative actions with the High Druidic Councils, and the High Druids were represented on the High Royal Councils. There were 12 of these Councils, each assisting the High King and High Queen of the 12 regions, with the 13th Council being the overruling one, so the Highest King and Queen had the decisive vote, or the overall decision-making powers.

Interestingly, it is from here onwards that we have the Celtic Race as a whole to deal with, as well as all the 12 Main Celtic Tribes and Tribunal Councils, with each of them representing the High King(s) and Queen(s), as well as the High Druidic Orders.

The Royal Lineages went via the Female lines as, interestingly, it was the female who chose her consort. This was related to survival, as after the Fall of the Lion Kingdom, some Druidic Lineages were forced to intermarry with the Royal Lineages to keep the hereditary lines pure, and on the same vibratory rate as before. This concerned their own highest state of evolutionary consciousness, having to hold the Light and the Fires of Illumination steady during times of immense war and destruction, and they led their people to lay the foundations for Avalon, in the midst of the dying Lion Kingdom.

Thus, this link between Royal lineages and the Druidic Lines flowed into one single unified stream. However, the average person still had access to the highest Druid Mystery Schools. Parents could have soul readings done by the High Priestess of the Alchemical Druidic Order, so babies with a special soul purpose and calling to be trained in these orders were easily identified, and admitted into the schools at five.

With the Celtic Tribal Community, the whole concept of being free people was celebrated, as well as the infinite forms of unity. Each Tribe had their own distinctive sacred geometrical patterns, with the spiral appearing everywhere, to depict the spiralling energy they all had the access to, from the humblest to the most Illustrious.

Indeed, whether King or Queen or free man or woman, there was kinship here which went far deeper, with infinite loyalty towards their tribe and fellow humans. There was a bond of unity which interlinked them all, so there was a general sense of belonging, forged in brotherhood and sisterhood of the highest soul connection.

Thus, the *Anam Cara*, the Soulmate of the Celtic Lore was that of the kindred spirit, the soul companion – the infinite knowing you were walking with someone on the same soul path as you. It is in a higher sense a deep sense of homecoming. *"According to the Celtic spiritual tradition, the souls shine all around the body like a luminous cloud. When you are very open – appreciative and trusting – with another person, your two souls flow together. This deeply felt bond with another person means you have found you anam cara, or Soul Friend/Mate. Your anam cara always beholds your light and beauty, and accepts you for who you truly are. When you are blessed with anam cara, the Irish believe, you have arrived at that most sacred place – home."* (John O'Donahue)

In the aftermath of such destruction, it was this close degree of kinship needed to recreate the unity, which was the glue that brought them closer together, kinship between families, tribes, and with the greater Humanity.

Running through everything was a very deep respect for Mother Earth, for Nature, for the plant, tree, animal and elemental kingdoms, alongside a deep respect for the Guardians and Keepers, and the sacred groves were never entered before requesting permission from the Invisible World.

As Druids identified the more sacred energy vortexes and sacred sites on Earth, they declared them sacred and sacrosanct, earning the people's respect. The sacred oak, yew, and birch groves were considered places of worship, and places to connect with the invisible realms just as much as the visible.

Crops were never planted without asking permission to plant and harvest there, requesting assistance from the elementals, the fairies, gnomes, sprites, working with them with the natural rhythms. Being familiar with the inner workings, resulted in healthy food crops, high in nutrients. The people only took what was needed, and shared everything with their helpers from all domains.

As for medicinal plants, they knew of their sacred geometrical patterns, and the exact use of herbs, plants, trees, or fungi for medicinal purpose, calling in the Guardians and Keepers, elementals and Earth Angels to assist in maintaining optimum health for all, including the ecosystems, creating more harmony, greater abundance and prosperity for all.

Those who governed were just as well-versed and educated in the visible as the invisible, which was so necessary, as they traversed both with equal ease and familiarity.

Avalon became a truly magnificent and magical place. The People, nature and Earth, were in balance and harmony, and therefore peace reigned between tribes, and the High Kings and Queens. Any disputes arising were immediately and efficiently dealt with by the High Councils, so a very highly evolved race emerged, from which stemmed the later Celtic Races.

Avalon gradually expanded its borders, incorporating much of the previous Lion Kingdom, and facilitating the glorious blossoming forth of the Ancient Mystery Schools in the Orient, the Balkans, Greece and what was left of the Lion Kingdom in small pockets in the region of what is now Alexandria in Egypt, and also parts of what is now Iraq.

This extended into India, Nepal, the Himalayas, into the islands of the Far East, inclusive of Indonesia, the Philippines, Bali, parts of the islands of Japan, parts of Australia, Africa as well as the Americas, as said (including islands).

They used amphibious craft on land, in the ocean and air. The larger craft could traverse the heavens via the Milky Way Galaxy and the planet belonged to the Intergalactic Councils and the Intergalactic Fleet, consequently in some larger cities there were spaceports for the huge Intergalactic craft.

Avalon was also in close communication, and interacted with inner Earth Agartha, with that great interchange in their Mystery Schools, and there were immense interactions with Inner Earth and between the High Druidic Councils, High Kings and Queens the High Councils.

This was a flourishing civilization with high technologies, using the Crystal Pyramid Spiraling Energy, the Crystalline Pyramid Grids, the Lightning Rod of the Earth, the Tree of Life knowledge, combined with the vast Illuminating Fires of the 7th Central Sun, and thus all were in highest alignment with the Divine Laws.

The kinship between the tribes knew no bounds, and although each were attached to their own tribe, High King and High Queen, as well the Druidic Orders, there was still a deep respect and understanding of the principles of free will, and the free spirit within each soul was nurtured to blossom from an early age. This free spirit, embodied by the Fool in the Tarot, was understood as necessary to discover ever greater and higher ways to reach evolutionary consciousness. So, old barriers of thinking, acting and being were broken, and all were encouraged and allowed to follow the calling of their soul, to use its inherent knowing, allowed to pursue such for this inevitably led to new discoveries, new frontiers opening up, and new and higher ways of service.

It was because the individual soul's uniqueness, gifts and talents were nurtured and allowed to bloom into Being, that everyone felt validated to the core and therefore the Unity consciousness grew, as each soul slotted into the greater whole perfectly, with contentment.

In Avalon nothing was deemed impossible – there were always new and higher concepts, technology, and knowledge to be mastered, and new frontiers to be broken into. It was this pioneering spirit, which truly enabled the High Druidic Orders, and even the humblest of souls tending the land, at-one with Nature and the elementals, to span dimensions and activate vast energy fields, manipulating and ordering them into being and physical manifestation. They possessed the simple knowledge of vast conscious and intelligent energy fields, used in magnificent ways to change their forms, to transmute matter into non-matter, and to re-create it into something totally new.

When all blossoms into expanded beingness, from the smallest and seemingly insignificant, to the greatest of the great, then all benefit. For in truth all are necessary for the greatest God-Creation. All Avalon knew and lived this, applying the Divine laws of "what is within, manifests without, what is above, is reflected below, and what is below is reflected above." They married Heaven and Earth, the Cosmos and planets, galactically, their conscious awareness expanding beyond even the 7th dimension, as some of the most highly evolved of the souls, could even traverse the 12th.

Avalon, in its heyday, was the most splendid example of what the Human Race could attain, when it was in unity and harmony with itself, and allowing everyone the freedom to be.

They had no need to separate, to judge, to cut down, to control, or to manipulate, which was awe inspiring, but at the same time, a shadow started to fall from nowhere so they were becoming more fragile and vulnerable.

The greatest legacy of Avalon was their thorough and complex knowledge of energies and energy fields, their activation and the use of the Kundalini (serpent) Energy, in manipulating, changing and working with vast energy fields, and redirecting and co-creating with these energies, changing patterns and forms.

Their knowledge of Alchemy spanned time and space, and expanded cosmically, drawing on the powerful Fires of Illumination from the 7th Central Sun, working with the massive Sun Disc Dials and Sun Discs, the Kundalini (serpent) Energies, Fires of Transmutation and the Sacred Divine Fires. It was through their use of the Elements of Fire, Water, Air and Earth in the Cosmos, that they could literally command whatever they wished to manifest instantaneously.

Their knowledge of Sacred Sexuality within the Sacred Sexual Rites of Sacred Alchemical Marriage, was understood to the highest degree in connection with co-creation, and an experience of the Mystical. Through practising these rites, they worked High

Magic, evolving and expanding the soul into its highest Soul expression and manifestation. This was the highest degree of Son and Daughtership of the Divine, co-creation which required the highest degree of commitment and sheer inner strength, power, resilience, truth and integrity. These attributes could not be faked, for the powers used could co-create for the greater and higher good, but could also could be misused for destruction.

Since the Fall of Avalon, Humanity has never been able to regain this type of knowledge and its application nor this degree of conscious awareness. For this existed in the 7th Dimensional state.

As Mu was rising in the west, Avalon shone with its White/Gold/Platinum Sun of Illuminated Consciousness, High Technology, High Physics, High Maths, High Sacred Geometries, Unity and immense power.

It represented the highest accomplishment of Humanity, in the aftermath of the terrible wars and destruction of the Lion Kingdom.

Yet, there was an Achilles Heel which was to be exposed, and interesting one the most enlightened of High Kings in Avalon's Golden Age, was called Archilles.

## Before The Final hour

In that moment all was silent. She sat there, but a shadow of her once beautiful, sunny self. She felt as if her life-force was slowly draining away. It was not just her physical wounds, caused by a severe beating, she had had enough of those from Bernard to know the effects on her body, it was the soul wounds that were wearing her down now.

She was lying in the highest cavern, deep in the Pyrenees Mountains, her love for them had drawn her back into the safety of their presence, where she always found solace and healing. She lacked the strength to even try and contact the Wise Ones to ask for help and healing. She felt as if her life had been worthless – she had seen too much, been through too much, and had lost everyone and everything she loved. Here she was, a mere 27 year-old, feeling more like a hundred!

Would the nightmare ever end? Maybe the gods begrudged those who had experienced too much happiness, who had tasted the nectar of love, the sweetness, the touch. Flashes came. The face of her beloved father – how much she missed him and his infinite love and wisdom in such times as these.

When alive, he had often taken her to places of great holiness and sanctity to her people, and had always instilled in her the notion of bravery, to stand tall in the face of challenges, and to never, ever give up hope!

She remembered how, in the midst of the terrible war and the massacre of her people with thousands burnt alive at the stake, all in the name of God, how eyes and tongues had been cut out of those lucky enough to escape with their lives, how man's inhumanity to man had haunted him.

Often in times of great tragedy, she would find him in the early hours of morning standing on the castle ramparts he was trying desperately to defend, with tears rolling down his cheeks. His was the heart of the poet, the eternal philosopher, the one whose love for music, for song, for wisdom and learning, had led him to collect manuscripts and precious books from all over the ancient world. His was the dashing presence that made the ladies of Languedoc desire him (although he was very alienated from her mother), and whose poems and songs had won him the heart of one of the most beautiful ladies in the land, the She-wolf, Lupo's mother

In his day he had been sought after in the Royal Courts, being a companion to Louis of France, and Richard the Lionheart, on the Crusade to the Holy Land. Richard his great friend and mentor, Count of Narbonne, had competed in troubadour bouts as that was his true calling, and one he loved. He came from the same ancient and respected lineages as them, the royal families of Atlantis.

She remembered how this calling had to make way for the constant cries of war, in a desperate attempt to save his people against all odds. Not just his people, but also their ancient traditions, their ancient root beliefs from the Ancient Ones, the High Priests and High Priestesses of Atlantis, from the great Divine Source, since time immemorial.

The Pyrenees Mountains held the ancient secrets of the Wise Ones, the Ascended Masters, and tremendous sources of power lay in the wonderful pyramids and crystal caves. It was in ancient teachings and knowledge of astronomy, of alchemy, and of sacred geometry. It was in all that was forbidden and had been lost in the mists of time by the Church of Rome, who were after this knowledge with a vengeance. Grasping Priests, who wanted to enrich themselves, not only from the rich spoils of Languedoc, but also to seize the secrets of her people … secrets which were only known by a select few, and were zealously guarded!

It was to her that he turned, to safeguard them. It was to her that he gave the Keys. It was to her that entrusted his most valuable collection of manuscripts – to safeguard these for all time and eternity.

She did this, with the full knowledge that it could cost her very life – she was aware of this from the beginning. Ever brave and fearless, she had embarked on the quest with an innate recklessness that had often led her into trouble. She could out-ride anyone on her magnificent stallion (a gift from the Emir of Moorish Spain to her father) and the fact that she knew every part of her beloved land, served her at such times.

She knew the ancient secret entrances to the great inner cities and caves. She had the protection of the Ancient Ones, who helped and guarded her at all times – as did the ancient Oak groves of the Pyrenees, which were sacred to her people, and acted as secret portals to the hidden world they defended. Yet, even those had been overrun by renegades, by Cathar Believers trying to escape the wrath of the Inquisition – who after the final war was lost and her brother was finally forced to give up the fight, had moved in with a ruthlessness that had stunned even the most battle-weary and hardened.

Often Esclarmonde, her younger half-sister and a trained healer, had her hands full in nursing these people – some half-starved and frost-bitten. Cécile and Lupo, when he had time to help her, as he himself had his hands full to keep the Inquisition at bay, had rescued many of these souls, fed and given them shelter, and ensured they moved higher up in the mountains, to inhospitable regions and caverns, where they lived in great colonies, on a meagre diet of wild berries and any food that could be found in those high altitudes.

The biting cold was chilling her bones, and she had a bare minimum of supplies with her. She had finally managed to outwit Bernard and his soldiers, in escaping from the Comminges Castle keep, where he had held her since the birth of her son. When he discovered that the child, also called Bernard, was not his, as he was born with the dark hair of his real father – dark hair was unknown in their family – he immediately accused her of having a child fathered by Sancho.

The fact that she had been pregnant when she was abducted and forced to marry, never crossed his mind. She had passed the child off as premature, after he had raped her! As she had turned her knife on him and nearly killed him, he locked her up in the keep, and beat her on every occasion, as much as her pregnancy allowed. She had fought back like a tigress, making things worse, and eventually he drugged her one night – and forcefully had a chastity belt put on her, a humiliation and added injury, to an already insufferable situation.

However, her secret appeal for help to Lupo was answered, and he nearly killed Bernard in the process for having mistreated his half-sister. Subsequently, Bernard had taken another lover and left her alone. In the interim, she regained enough strength with the help of trusted servants and a horse, to flee to these mountains.

She managed to unsaddle it – normally she rode bareback, but the servant had supplied the saddle and with the chastity belt hurting her, for she was but a bag of bones at this moment, it proved to be a blessing. She entered the cave, and was enveloped in its warmth. At last, she found the hidden tools for making a fire, and to her total surprise, found fresh food and she gulped down some dried raisins, and even found wine. This warmed her a bit, and there was fresh straw for her horse, and also some for her to sleep on.

To her surprise, she also found a dagger and a sword hidden in one of the secret places, and immediately recognised it by the design as one of her father's! That astonished her, and as tears ran down her cheeks in gratitude to the unknown hands helping her, she cuddled up to her horse, and with the added warmth of the fire, fell into an exhausted sleep …

The next day, a Wise Ancient One found an unconscious Cécile in the cave and immediately help was summoned. Gentle and kind hands then lifted her into a barge, and she was taken deep into the ancient heart of the mountains, to the Ancient Ones' Abodes. For three weeks there was a titanic battle for her life. When they stripped her, they discovered her wounds from the beatings, and saw where the belt that dug into her flesh, which was rotting in the places where it had chaffed.

With great love and ancient healing methods they tended her, yet the scars of her soul went deep. Cécile gave up the battle for life, hanging between two worlds, and only by great power of will and many prayers to the Divine Source, the great I AM WHO I AM, the soul was reminded that it had not completed its mission, and had to return to Earth.

As Cecile finally came back, it took more inner healing for her to assume some semblance of herself again. It was the sheer love and devotion, the inner Light that brought her back to herself. During this time, she mostly slept, and was given herbal potions, and ray treatments to facilitate healing.

She kept calling for Sancho and her children, the three had been taken from her, and the youngest she had had to leave behind. She kept seeing her father, and as she rambled on, concerned onlookers used all their powers to keep her from slipping away into her own inner world.

Her half-sister was summoned from Albion, and Esclarmonde, who loved Sissi more than life itself, helped to soothe and calm her. Lupo was also summoned, and seeing what state his half-sister was in, he had great difficulty in not killing his brother-in-law with his bare hands! This scene would be embedded in his mind forever, and later nearly caused him to kill this man. It was only by the intervention of Sissi's son, Roger, Count of Foix, that Bernard's life was saved! It was then decided that Lupo should go to Castile and Leon, to get hold of Sancho – as he had been summoned to help his uncle at the court there. Lupo departed, promising to bring Sancho back with him.

It took three months of dedicated healing for Sissi to finally heal. As her body grew stronger, so did her mind. As the shadows fled, she regained her unquenchable spirit, and with it the will to live. During this time, she felt the presence of her departed father very near to her. She also received great help from one of the great Ascended Masters who resided there, and with his help her soul started to awaken, and he told her of her sacred mission – a soul contract that had been made before she was born, to bring Light into the world.

Throughout this time Sissi had profound visions, finding a deeper connection to the Divine Source, more than ever before. Although her sunny nature broke through, it was a far more mature and wiser soul that emerged. Her inner strength came to the fore, and with it a radiance that shone through her – giving her an other worldly appearance.

It enhanced her beauty which had returned. As she gained weight, and her figure returned to normal

– she had a breath-taking beauty, even greater than before.

Soon she was riding in the hidden valleys on her beloved horse, bareback as usual. She was given a beautiful white horse by the Master, forging an immediate bond with him, and this horse was fleet of foot and seemed to fly. She called him Pegasus, and he was her pride and joy!

From Esclarmonde she heard news of her children, and knew they were all well and taken care of. Her daughter in Ireland was well looked after at the Court of her cousin, and was thriving in the Royal Household. Her eldest son was being cared for by his father in Castile, and was already learning to read and write. He was greatly loved by Sancho's uncle, the King, who adopted the boy as his own.

Her son Roger had been taken away by her brother Bernard Roger, to be the next Count of Foix, and he seemed well and happy enough. Bernard had taken a new wife, who was caring for the child.

Bernard of Comminges, the youngest, was already proving to be a handful, so he was sent to Bernard's half-sister, news which jolted Sissi, as this sister had been the wife of Arnaud de Montfort and had two daughters by him. He was the son of the Butcher, Simon de Montfort. Yet, she had still been a teenager, and had been forcefully married off, and her heart was good enough. Sissi made peace with that, knowing that the boy was better off there, rather than with his brutal father, and the soldiers at his court.

Esclarmonde returned home, and Lupo came back on his own, without Sancho, who could not come as he was on business in Italy and would come when he could. He brought a pile of love letters and poems that she devoured. She reread them until they were fragile, she wrote letters back, and to her delight soon enough answers came.

The Ascended Master had explained to Sissi that Sancho was her twin-flame and thus the love-bond between them was eternal, hence her father had turned a blind eye to her affair, as he had understood this. Also, Sancho's lineage was even more ancient than theirs, and thus the blood within their children was in a way the blood of the Ancient Ones – special and sacred to her people.

For the first time Sissi understood why she always felt such great love and devotion to Sancho. That he felt the same about her, was expressed in his letters. Although he had reunited with his sickly wife, the marriage was unhappy, and their child was also weak. It was the only child that they could have, something he was greatly relieved at, as his wife had nearly died in childbirth. Sissi was silently relieved about this too, although she knew in her heart that she had no right to be feeling that.

It was during this time that Sissi received further instructions into the ancient secrets. She was given keys to these secrets, and access to the magnificent ancient chambers and the underground cities. What she saw and experienced changed her forever, as she understood the immense importance of keeping these Ancient Ones and their secrets safely hidden from the grasping hands of the Inquisition.

News of atrocities reached them, and often the Ancient Ones would save entire groups of Cathars and their families from being burnt at the stake. Some were incorporated into the Ancient Ones' chambers – but only those trusted not to reveal their secrets. Others were simply helped to escape via a network of underground tunnels that emerged on the Atlantic and Basque coasts. They were then secretly shipped to Ireland, Scotland, Italy, and further afield. With it went many of their secret manuscripts and other sacred items – such as the Gnostic Gospels, etc.

They were helped by the Knights Templar, who secretly provided the ships, and transported the treasures that these people harboured. In many ways their beliefs were similar, and there had always been a great love and understanding between the Cathars, the Templars and the Ancient Ones, in safeguarding these secrets.

Many Cathar secret manuscripts and treasures found their way into the Templar Castles and Keeps, and thus these same Templars helped many Parfaits to disappear to far-off places.

Sissi in the meantime, had regained her strength, and was helping now where she could. She often went in disguise, so as not to be recognised, often donning peasant clothes so that she could blend in with the people.

She was reconciled with her brother Bernard Roger – as he had heard from Lupo what had happened to her. He allowed her to take whatever she wanted from her father's Libraries and provided armed guards, wherever he could. He had aged considerably during this time, with the toll of the constant war, and the wounds sustained, playing havoc with his body.

Sissi was reunited with her son Roger, and he took to her, as they were very much alike. He had the dashing good looks of his father, blended with the beauty of his mother, and his hair was the golden red-blond of his grandfather, after whom he had been named. Yet they could never meet openly, as the danger of being discovered by the Inquisition was ever present.

At last, out of the blue, Sancho arrived – older, but very much the same, and it was one of those summers when time stood still. They were at last reunited, and their love for each other grew more and more intense, with the maturity that had been lacking before. Others left them alone, as they moved higher up in the mountains both knowing that time would not allow them to be there forever.

When summons came for Sancho to return home, Sissi bid him farewell with a breaking heart, and with it came a foreboding that she would never see him again, and she said as much to him.

As she stood in the shadow of the ancient oak groves, and watched him disappear in the mist, tears were pouring like a waterfall down her cheeks. Only the Ancient Ones recorded how true this premonition would prove to be, for Sissi was called into action again, and this time her mission to save her people, and the secrets of the ages would prove to be her greatest test, and it was with all her heart and soul that she dedicated herself to the task of safeguarding the secrets – the promise she had given to her father, ever present in her mind.

As the news arrived of unimaginable atrocities being committed, all in the name of God, she had no other option than to pick up her sword of Light, and move into action.

It came much sooner than anyone would have ever anticipated … even the Ancient Ones.

\* \* \*

# Book list

**Part 1**

Chapter 1, page 35: Tom Kenyon, *Mary Magdalene Energy Meditations: Alchemical Practices to Elevate and Balance the Serpent Power Within*. 2006. Sounds True Incorporated.

Chapter 2, page 39: Polybius, *The Histories*. 264–146BC.

Chapter 2, page 40: Antoine de Saint-Exupéry, *The Little Prince*. 1943. Reynal & Hitchcock

Chapter 7, page 87: Graham Robb, *The Ancient Paths*. 2014. Picador.

**Part 2**

Chapter 1, page 91: Diodorus Siculus, *Bibliotheca historica*. 60–30BCE.

Chapter 1, page 91: Graham Robb, *The Ancient Paths*. 2014. Picador.

Chapter 1, page 91: Timagenes, *Universal History* and a *History of the Gauls*.

Chapter 9, pages 147 and 148: Juan Garcia Atienza, *The Knights Templar in the Golden Age of Spain: Their Hidden History on the Iberian Peninsula*. 2006. Destiny Books.

Chapter 9, page 149: Judith Küsel, *Why I Was Born in Africa: The Previously Unrecorded History of Elysium and the Lion Kingdom*. 2017. Judith Küsel.

Additional information, page 187: John O'Donahue, *Anam Cara*. 1996. Harper Collins.

# Index

**Symbols**
3rd Crusade, 101
3rd dimensional state, 29
3 Standing Stones, 81
5th dimensional frequency band (of Atlantis), 29
5th dimensional state, 141, 159, 170
7 Crystal Pyramids, 36
7 Crystal Pyramids of Sound Alchemy, 79
7 pyramids, 55, 60
7 Sacred Islands, 60
7 seminars, 20, 123, 128
7 Sun-gates, 60
7th Central Sun, 7, 8, 28, 30, 32–5, 39, 51, 52, 60, 62, 81, 135, 159, 168, 169, 171, 179, 182–4, 188
7th Central Sun of Illumination, 7, 8, 30, 33, 39, 51, 52, 62, 171, 179
7th dimensional, 9, 12, 17, 75, 80, 162, 173, 175
7th Dimensional Lion Kingdom, 142
7th dimensional state, 9, 17, 75, 141, 162
7th Dimensional Vibrational Frequency, 8
7th Dimension of Avalon and Lemuria, 29
7th Galaxy, 168, 169
7th Heaven, 8, 52, 60, 62, 173
7th Heaven on Earth, 60
7th Temple, 169

7th Temple of the 7th Galaxy of the 7th Central Sun, 169
9th dimension, 10
12 Central Suns, 168, 169, 185
12 Crystal Pyramid Temples, 171, 172
12 High Priestesses, 8, 132, 135, 172, 173
12 High Priests, 8, 132, 135, 172, 173
12 Main Temples, 8
12 Master Central Suns, 168
12 Master Galaxies, 7, 8
12 Master Sun Discs, 169
12 Regions of Elysium, 172
12th and 13th Crystal Keys, 173
12th Crystal Skull, 173
12 Tribes, 8, 141, 142
13th Master Key Code, 172, 173
13th Master Key Flame, 173
72 Names of God and the Goddess, 181
100-year war between France and England, 74
333 (codes), 28
777 (codes), 28

**A**
Aborigines – Song Lines, 181
Adonis, 71
Africa, 7–11, 17–9, 26, 28, 33, 51, 56, 60, 80, 98, 123, 144, 149, 151, 169–73, 175, 187, 194
African continent, 33, 169
Agartha, 8, 9, 29, 108, 110, 119, 171, 187
Aimery, 109, 111

Albigensian Crusade/Cathar Crusade, 99, 153, 160
Alchemical Druidic Order, 186
Alchemical Mystery School, 23, 52, 118
Alchemist, 112
Alchemy Powers, 60
American, 22, 142
Anam Cara, 187
*Ancient Book of Love*, 163, 176
Ancient Keys and Codes of Enlightenment, 151
Ancient Megalithic Sites, 12
Ancient Mystery School/s, 22, 99, 123, 151, 152, 176
Ancient Mystery Schools of Egypt, 98, 176
Ancient Ones, 24, 28, 30, 36, 38, 40, 76, 110, 111, 116, 119, 144, 190–3
Ancient Sun Path, 12, 98
Ancient Supercontinent, 141
Androgynous, 141, 174
Andromeda, 7, 52, 60, 180
Anglo-Boer War, 80
Angoulême, 93–5
Ankh, 179, 181
Anne of Brittany (daughter of Margaret of Foix), 69, 73
Anointing at Bugarach, 130
Anointing – Jeanne, Mary Magdalene, Anne of Brittany, and others, 73
Antarctica, 17, 19, 26–8, 32, 55
Antoine de Saint-Exupéry, 40, 194

Arc de Triomphe, 41
Archangel Azrael, 64
Arcturus, 108
Atlanteans, 98, 174
Atlantic Ocean, 10, 13, 39, 75, 79
Atlantis, 7, 10, 13, 17, 29, 39, 56, 98, 110, 141, 142, 168, 173, 174, 176, 189, 190
Aude river, 23, 95, 96, 118, 137, 161
Avalon, 7, 11–3, 17, 19, 24, 28–31, 35, 38, 39, 51, 60–2, 68, 75, 78–80, 87, 90–2, 98, 103, 105, 107, 110, 119, 123, 141, 142, 150, 152, 154, 159, 160–3, 174, 180–2, 184, 186–9, 194
Aysis from/of Sirius, 10, 17
Aysis – Consort of Osiris Ra-A-Hu-A-Ra, from Sirius/Lyra/Andromeda, 60
Aysis Mystery School, 99, 106, 107
Aysis Queen Bee (Fleur de Lys), 60
Aysis-Ra-A-Hu-A-Ra, 60
Aysis-Ra-A-Ru-A-Ra, High Order, 182
Aysis-Ra-A-Hu-A-Ra, Queen of the Serpent/Spiralling Energy, 60
Aysis The Sun Goddess, 60, 66
Azores, 33

**B**
Bards, 87, 113, 180
Battle of Orleans, 73
Bear Constellation, 7, 52
Bearn, 102, 109
Belgium, 11, 17
Bérenger Saunière, 123, 126
Berenguela de Montcada, 148
Bernard of Comminges, 112, 116, 192
Bernard Roger, now Count of Foix, 112, 192, 193
Bi-locate, 11
Bishops Palace, 18, 140
Bishops Palace in Urgell, 18
Black Forest, 98
Black Madonna, 105
Black Magi, 30, 174, 175
Black Sea, 91, 98
Blois Castle, 68–71, 74
Bogomil Elders, 104
Bogomils, 104, 152
Bourbon lineage, 113
Bridge of Light, 183
Britain, 10–12, 17, 52, 60, 79, 98, 141, 159, 175, 176
Britany, 73
Bugarach, 130, 131, 135, 136

**C**
Caduceus (serpent energy, spiralling energy, Lightning Rod), 48, 49, 61, 73, 74, 78, 178, 179, 183
Canary Islands, Tenerife, Madeira, 33, 34, 94
Candelabras (Jeshua, Mary Magdalene, Joseph of Arimathea), 134, 136
Cape Town, 26–8, 31–3, 94
Carnac, 11, 18, 20, 24, 28, 29, 31, 34, 35, 51, 75–81, 84, 87, 90, 91, 93–5, 106, 119, 132, 159, 162
Carnac Stones, 20
Catalonia, 18, 146, 148, 149
Cathar Crusade/Albigensian Crusade, 99, 153, 160
Cathar Hierophant, 152
Cathar High Priestess, 103
Cathar Hymn, 108
Cathar Prophecy, 100, 144
Cathar Prophets, 105
Cathar(s), 12, 24, 99, 100–10, 113, 116, 132, 135, 144, 147, 148, 150–7, 160, 161, 163, 164, 175, 190, 192
Cathar Treasure, 102
Catholic Inquisition, 147
Cave of Apollo, 56
Cécile de Foix, 13, 18, 24, 36, 40, 73, 92, 109, 111, 114, 142
Celestial Fairies and Gnomes, 8
Celtic Druid(s), 11, 12, 91, 175
Celtic Druidic Communities, 175
Celts, 12, 17, 24, 31, 87, 97, 98, 110, 123, 141, 142
Central High Command of the Intergalactic Federation of the Great White Brotherhood, 172, 173
Central Sun/s, 7, 8, 28, 30, 32–5, 39, 51, 52, 60, 62, 81, 135, 159, 168, 169, 171, 175, 179, 182–5, 188
Central Sun Super Consciousness Energy Field, 168
Chalice, 62, 63, 64
Chalice and Grail – sacred womb of the Goddess, 60
Chartres, 18, 20, 30, 31, 34, 35, 56–9, 61, 62, 65, 68, 70, 71, 74, 77, 80, 95, 119, 141
Chartres Cathedral, 59, 60, 62, 63, 66
Château des Duc de Joyeuse Hotel, 23, 117, 118
Chosen Ones, 173

City of the Bards, 76, 90
Cloak of invisibility, 83
Co-creation of Earth, 8
Collioure, 146
Comminges, 102, 109, 111, 112, 116, 149, 160, 190, 192
Cosmic Consciousness, 168
Cosmic Hierarchy, 55, 82, 83, 87, 142
Cosmic Music of the Spheres, 171, 179
Cosmic Mystery Schools of Sirius, 10
Couiza, 23, 103, 137
Council of 12, 106
Count of Comminges – Bernard V, 109, 160
Count of Foix – Ramon Roger, 18, 97, 99, 101–4, 109, 112, 114, 148, 150, 152, 160, 161, 191, 192
Count of Foix – Roger-Bernard II, 109
Crystalline Energy Grids, 8, 84, 108, 171, 181
Crystalline Light Webs, 8
Crystalline Pyramid Grid, 18, 170, 188
Crystalline Star Grid, 28
Crystal Pyramid of Gold, 35
Crystal Pyramid of the White Flame, 172
Crystal Pyramids, 8, 9, 17, 18, 30, 31, 34, 36, 39, 51, 52, 62, 79, 103, 106, 110, 119, 123, 127, 130, 141, 162, 170, 171, 177, 181
Crystal Pyramids in the Montségur Pyrenees, 51
Crystal Pyramid Temple, 8, 171, 172, 183
Crystal Pyramid Temple of The White Flame, 8
Cygnus, 7, 52

**D**
Dark Ages, 39, 98, 150
Delphi, 11, 24, 51, 79, 98, 99, 151, 152, 155, 159, 162, 166, 176, 183
De Moncada, 104, 109, 111, 148, 160, 161
De Moncada family, 104, 148, 160
Devil's Peak, 26, 27, 28, 33
Didgeridoo, 181
Diodorus Siculus, 91, 194
Divine Cosmic Laws, 169, 178
Divine Counterpart, 48, 49

Divine Feminine, 7, 13, 30, 62, 64, 65, 97, 126, 133, 162–4, 166, 172, 176, 178, 182–5
Divine Halls of Records, 173
Divine Laws, 12, 153, 178, 188
Divine Masculine, 60, 165, 178, 182–4, 185
Divine Mother Flame, 173
Divine Sexuality, Ecstasy, Divine Creativity, 184
Divine Source, 7, 171, 174, 182, 184, 185, 190, 191
Divine Universal Laws, 108
DNA structures, 182
Dolphins, 8
Druidic Alchemist, 178
Druidic Headquarters, linked directly to branches in Versailles, the Pyrenees, Delphi, Vancouver New York, parts of Britain, Scotland and Ireland, 79
Druidic Symbols, 179
Dun, 109, 110, 111, 156

**E**
Earth, 7–13, 16, 17, 20, 21, 26–30, 32, 35, 38, 39, 51, 52, 60–2, 80, 108, 121, 141, 142, 146, 152, 154, 157, 159, 162–4, 166, 168–75, 177, 179–81, 185, 187, 188, 191
Earth – "The Crown Jewel of Creation", 8
Egypt, 10, 18, 25, 27, 30, 60, 98, 99, 112, 113, 135, 152, 159, 162, 163, 166, 175, 176, 187
Egyptians, 24
Eiffel Tower, 41, 48, 49
Elemental Kingdom, 8
Elementals, 8
Elixir, 60
Elysium, 7–9, 11, 17, 18, 28, 32, 39, 60, 110, 123, 149, 159, 163, 169, 170–74, 184, 194
Elysium – 12 Regions, 172
Elysium – Golden Age, 170
Energy fields, 11, 12, 18, 21, 25, 32, 34, 38, 39, 41, 43, 50, 52, 58, 77, 78, 80, 82, 85, 93, 98, 108, 114, 119, 124, 130, 141, 154, 158, 159, 164, 168, 170, 171, 174, 175, 178, 180, 181, 183–6, 188

Energy lines, 11, 17–19, 26, 27, 32–5, 42, 43, 45, 47, 50, 74, 75, 77, 78, 80, 85, 87, 90, 92, 94–6, 114, 115, 119, 126–8, 159
Epic Poem of Parsifal, 101
Esclarmonde, 13, 109, 110, 112, 190–2
Esclarmonde de Foix – Cathar Bishop, Hierophant, 13, 109
Essenes, 24, 99, 100, 105, 151, 152, 159, 160, 163, 176
Europe, 8, 10, 12, 17, 24, 30, 34, 60, 98, 148, 153, 154, 161, 175
Eye of Horus, 169

**F**
Fires of Illumination, 25, 29, 34, 36, 60, 96, 97, 99, 100, 103, 107, 133, 136, 159, 169, 183, 184, 186, 188
Fires of Transmutation, 179, 188
First Creation of the Divine Sound Vibration, 180
First Crusade, 103, 148, 149
First Paradise of Elysium, The Lion Kingdom, Avalon, 174
Fisher Kings, 148
Foix Castle, 102, 103, 109, 114, 153
Fool in the Tarot, 188
Founder of the Templars, Hugo de Payen, 19
France, 7, 10–12, 17–22, 24–40, 44, 47, 50–2, 58, 59, 65, 68, 74, 87, 90, 92, 94, 96–100, 102, 106, 111, 113, 117, 121, 123, 126, 128, 130, 133, 137, 141, 142, 144, 146–52, 154, 157–67, 173, 175–7, 181, 186, 189
French Revolution, 24, 40, 43, 44, 57

**G**
Gallizenas (Gaulish maidens), 87
Garden of Eden, 173
Gauls, 24, 31, 56, 70, 91, 142, 148
Germany, 11, 101, 105, 112, 154
Giza Pyramids, 27, 169
Gnosis, 133, 151, 155, 156, 157
Gnosis – Highest State of Equilibrium, 151
Gnostic Monastery, 135
Gnostics, 176
Goddess Aysis, 46, 60
Goddess site, 45, 49, 119, 133
Goddess Sophia, 48, 49

Goddess statues, 46, 85
Goddess Stone, 81, 82
Goddess Temple Site, 59
Goddess vortex energy, 48
Gold, conduit for the serpent energy, energy enhancer, a way of prolonging life, 61
Golden Age of Atlantis, 174
Golden Age of Elysium, 170, 173
Golden Ages of Humanity, 174
Golden circlet, 77
Golden City of the Bards, 90
Golden torques, 77
Gold Lines, 32
Gold or Silver Serpent, 183
Gorge de Galamus, 143
Gospel of Love, 99, 106, 120, 121, 150, 151, 154, 156, 157, 161, 162
Graham Robb, *The Ancient Paths*, 87, 91, 194
Grand Master, Guillaume, 24, 25, 161
Grand Master, Jacques de Molay, 151
Great motherships, 7, 8
Greece, 10, 11, 30, 60, 98, 113, 152, 159, 163, 166, 175, 176, 187
Green and Gold Crystal Pyramids, 119
Green-golden fire, 33, 60
Green-golden river of fire, 34, 35
Green-gold light, 35
Group tour to Monségur, 117
Gruissan, a little gnome, 144
Guardians and Keepers of the Sacred Grail, 149
Guardians and/or Keepers, 22, 26, 30, 31, 32, 76, 77, 100, 111, 105, 106, 110, 124, 132, 144, 148–50, 153, 160, 173, 179, 187

**H**
Halls of Records, 39, 173
Halls of the All-Knowing, 39
Halls of Wisdom, 39
Hermes, 48
Hidden Fingers of God (YOD means Finger of God), 178
Hieros Gamos, or the Sacred Marriage, Sacred Fire of Creation Itself, 156, 177
High altar, Chartres Cathedral, 64
High Bardic Order(s), 12, 96, 181, 182
High Brother and Sisterhood of the White Flame, 184

High Druidic Council, 141
High Druidic Order(s) – Alchemy Mystery School Branch 7 Crystal Pyramids of Sound Alchemy, 35, 62, 79, 90, 98, 99, 107, 149, 152, 178, 179, 182, 186, 188
Higher Cosmic Sound Frequency Fields, 170
Higher Mind – the Telos, the All-Knowing, the All-Seeing, the All-Being, 156, 182
Higher teaching, 184
Higher teaching and learning centres, 52
High Initiates – Isis and Osiris, the Essenes, Egyptians, The Oracle of Delphi, Mary Magdalene, Cathars, Troubadours, Esclaremonde de Foix, Cécile de Foix, Templars, Joan of Arc, Marie Antoinette, 156, 175
High King of the Lyran People, 10
High Magic, 52, 186, 188
High Magic or Wizard Schools, 52, 186, 188
High Order of Aysis-Ra-A-Ru-A-Ra, 182
High Order of Melchizedek, 30
High Order of the Bards, 75, 82, 150, 177, 179–82
High Priestess, 10, 34, 60, 73, 77, 81, 103, 105, 106, 110, 151, 156, 160, 163, 165, 169, 172, 173, 176, 186
High Priestess of the Lyran People, 10
High Priesthood of Avalon, 17, 19, 110
High Priest of the Lyran People, 10
High Queen of the Lyran People, 10
Hildegard von Bingen, 154
Himalayas, 10, 51, 99, 175, 176, 187
Hippolytus, 91
Holland, 10, 11
Holographic energy pattern, 81
Holy Grail, 24, 101, 114, 133, 158, 164
Holy Sophia, 164, 176
House of Béarn, 104
House of Leon, 104
Hugo de Payen (also known as Hugo de Bagá, Hugo de Baganis, Hugo de Pinos, Hugo de Payons) – Founder of the Order, 19, 104, 111

**I**
Ile de la Cite, 50
Ile St. Louis, 50
Illumined Ones, 10, 96, 173, 175
Immaculate conception of the Virgin, 183
India, 112, 159, 175, 176, 187
Indian Ocean islands – Mauritius and Reunion, 33
Inner World of Agartha, 119
Inquisition, 97, 101, 102, 105, 107, 108, 112, 114, 120, 121, 144, 147, 148, 153, 156, 161, 177, 190, 192, 193
Intergalactic Council(s), 8, 174, 187
Intergalactic craft, 8, 187
Intergalactic Federation, 7, 10, 52, 172, 173
Intergalactic Federation of the Great White Brotherhood, 172, 173
Intergalactic Fleet, 7–9, 187
Inter-Stellar Energy Grid, 28
Iona, 11, 176
Ireland, 10–12, 17, 51, 52, 60, 79, 98, 105, 112, 141, 154, 156, 159, 175, 176, 192
Ireland – to open the energy lines from Carnac to Ireland, 159
Isis, 10–13, 24, 25, 27–30, 32, 113, 127, 142, 173–6
Isis Mystery School(s), 173–5
Island of the Swans, 47, 49

**J**
Jean-Antoice Injalbert, 48
Jean Formige, 48
Jeanne d'Arc / Joan of Arc, 13, 20, 24, 40, 68–70, 73, 74, 93, 132, 135, 146, 175
Jean of Foix, 73
Jesus, 20, 24, 99, 118, 121, 123, 127, 132, 134, 135, 144, 147, 159, 160, 178
Jesus – "The Teacher of Righteousness of the Essenes", 99
Jewish settlements, 99
John the Baptist, 105, 106, 152, 176
Joseph of Arimathea, 134
Juan García, 147
Jules-Felix Louten, 48
Julius Caesar, 31, 39, 91, 98
Jupiter, 7, 9, 52, 174

**K**
Keys and codes, 19, 35, 40, 55, 80, 83, 106, 107, 116, 124, 133, 162, 166, 168–73, 179–82
Keys and codes to/of all Creation, 168, 173
Keys and codes of Divine Love, 107
Keys and codes of Enlightenment, 19, 151
Keys and codes of Illumination, 40, 169
Keys and codes of Longevity, 60
keys and codes of Love, Power and Wisdom, 107
Keys and codes of sacred union, 107
King Baldwin II, 149
King of Aragon – cousin to the Count of Toulouse – Count of Foix, and Viscount of Béziers and Carcassonne, 97, 111, 113, 146, 149
King Pedro of Aragon, 104
Knights Templar, 67, 103, 104, 111, 112, 138, 147, 148, 163, 192, 194
Kristina Kahnlund, 20, 40
Kundalini, 27, 34, 35, 170, 179
Kundalini and the spiralling energy, 35, 178, 177, 179

**L**
Labrador, 22
Languedoc, 99, 109–11, 121, 148, 149, 160, 189, 190
Langue D'Oc, 97
La Rochelle, 94, 95, 142
Lemuria, 13, 29, 51, 110, 141, 173, 174
Lemurian Civilization, 51, 174
Leopard man, 28
Liberty, Equality and Fraternity, 57
Light Bearers, 29
Light Language, 25, 35, 141, 180, 182
Light Language keys and codes, 180, 182
Lightning Energy Conductor, 8
Lightning Rod (energies, spine and of the Earth), 60, 62, 177, 179, 184, 188
Lion Kingdom, 7–12, 17, 18, 24, 28–30, 32, 35, 38, 39, 51, 60, 61, 79, 92, 98, 105, 113, 119, 123, 127, 141, 142, 144, 152, 159, 163, 169, 170–74, 176, 182, 184, 186, 187, 189, 194

Lion Kingdom Complex, 113
Lion People, 9, 28–30, 98, 169
Lion Portal, 169, 170
Loba, 109, 110
Louis XIV, the Sun King of France, 31, 52, 53
Louvre, 24, 45, 47, 53, 128, 146
Love Courts, 101, 107
Lupo, 102, 109–12, 189–93
Lupo de Foix, 109
Lyra, 7, 9, 52, 60
Lyran(s), 9, 10, 11

## M

Machu Picchu, 181
Madeira, 33, 94
Magician, 179, 186
Malta, 11, 27, 28, 32, 34, 51, 56, 95
Margaret of Foix (mother of Anne of Brittany), 73
Marie Antoinette, 24, 30, 43, 44–6, 50, 52, 53, 146
Marie of Orleans, 73
Marie, the Countess of Mirepoix, 104
Mars, 9, 52, 174
Mary Magdalene, 13, 20, 22, 24, 35, 40, 66, 69, 73, 92, 97, 98–100, 105–7, 113, 117, 118, 123, 125–8, 130, 132–6, 142–6, 151–7, 159, 160, 162–6, 175, 176, 194
Mary Magdalene's Mystery School, 22, 117, 123, 128, 130
Mass genocide of Occitania, 97
Master Alchemists, 178
Master Architects, 9, 30
Master Galactic Races, 7
Matriarchy, 11, 60, 61, 92, 141
Mauritius, 26, 33, 83
Mediterranean (and Sea), 10, 11, 17, 28, 32, 60, 95, 98, 106
Megalithic (and Sites), 9, 12
Melchizedek and the High Order of Melchizedek, 30
Mercury, 7, 52
MerKaBah, 170
Merlin A-Ha-Thu-An-Ru-A-Ra, 179
Merlinda Gui-A-Ve-Ra-Ve-Ay-A-Ru-Ra, 179
Merlinda(s), 11, 12, 179, 186
Merlin(s), 11, 12, 20, 30, 52, 179, 186
Mer people, 33
Middle East, 10, 11, 119, 148, 151, 153, 175

Milky Way Galaxy, 7–9, 52, 180, 187
Monségur, 10–12, 18, 19, 29, 34–6, 74, 87, 99, 102, 103, 107, 109, 111–24, 127–31, 149, 156, 159, 160, 163, 166, 176
Mother Earth, 8, 21, 38, 61, 121, 154, 181, 187
Mother Mary, 20, 64, 105
Motherships, 7–9, 171
Mu, 13, 51, 141, 189
Multi-dimensional
  forms, 75
  journey, 58
  space, 13
Mystery School, 10–3, 22, 24, 28–30, 35, 39, 52, 60, 70, 79, 92, 98–100, 104–7, 116–8, 123, 124, 127–30, 133, 135, 142, 149, 151–6, 160–2, 165, 173–6, 182, 186, 187
Mystery School of Mary Magdalene, 123, 127
Mystery Schools of Alexandria and Heliopolis in Egypt, 176
Mystery Schools of Isis, 10, 13
Mystic Rose, 60, 93, 177, 182, 183
Mystic Rose initiation, 93
Mystic Rose of Enlightenment and Illumination, 60

## N

Napoleon, 46, 98
Nepal, 187
Neptune, 7, 52
New Jerusalem, New Golden Age, 106
Norway, 10, 11, 17, 79

## O

Occitania, 96–104, 107, 108, 148–50, 154
Octopus Sun Gate, 55
Old Earth, 175, 177
Oracle, 24, 99, 151, 155, 183
Oracle – a Prophetess or a Seer, 151
Oracle of Delphi, 24, 99, 155
Order of the Knights Templar, 111
Orion, 7, 9, 10, 52, 169
Orkney Islands, 11
Orleans, 18, 20, 31, 34, 35, 59, 60, 68–70, 73–7, 80, 95
Osiris, 10, 11, 17, 24, 29, 60, 182
Osiris-Ra-A-Hu-A-Ra – SUN GOD, 60

## P

Pacific, 10, 13, 29, 175
Palace of Justice, 42, 43
Paris, 10, 11, 17, 20, 38–49, 58, 60, 74, 140, 141, 146
Patriarchy, 30, 123, 142, 174, 175
Pegasus, 52, 192
Phi and Psi, 178
Philippa de Moncada – House of Béarn, 104, 105, 109–11
Phoenicians, 98
Piri Reis Map, 151
Place of the Bards, 76, 181
Planetary Councils from other planets in this solar system: Jupiter, Venus, Saturn, Uranus, Neptune, Pluto, and Mercury, 52
Pleiadeans, from Sirius and Orion, 9
Pleiadeans, the Master Botanists of the Fleet, 8
Pleiades, 7, 52, 180
Plettenberg Bay, 36
Pomponius Mela, geographer, 87
Pont de Bir-Hakeim Bridge, 47
Pontius Pilate, 98
Pontius Pilate's wife, 152, 160
Pope Gregory, 104
Portugal, 11, 17, 34, 35, 51, 52, 60, 94, 95, 105, 150, 151, 156, 160
Power of Sound, 11, 12
Priest-Scientists, 7
Primordial sound keys and codes of the First Creation, 162
Prophecy, 100, 144, 184
Pure Ones, 155, 179
Pyramid Grids, 9, 25, 28, 39, 52, 177, 179
Pyramid Temple(s), 8, 171, 183
Pyrenees, 10–12, 22, 24, 29, 31, 34, 36, 51, 60, 73, 74, 77, 79, 80, 87, 92, 96, 99, 102, 104–6, 110, 112, 113, 115, 119, 123, 127, 130, 139, 142, 144, 146, 148–50, 154, 156, 160, 162, 175, 177, 182, 183, 189, 190
Pythagoras, 99, 149, 152
Pythagorean philosophy, 91

## Q

Queen of France, 74

## R

Rainbow Tribes, 184
Ramon Roger, the Count of Foix, 99, 101, 104, 105, 109–11, 114, 150, 160
Raymond IV of Toulouse, 149
Raymond Roger, the Count of Foix, 18
Rennes-le-Château, 22, 30, 35, 123, 126, 127, 135, 136, 160
Reunion, 33, 45
River Seine, 42, 44, 45, 47, 49, 50, 60
Robben Island, 26, 27, 28
Roger-Bernard II, 109
Roland, a Frankish military leader under Charlemagne, 97, 148
Romans, 12, 31, 91, 98, 142, 148
Rose quartz, 35

## S

Sacred Astronomy, 141
Sacred Chalice, 62, 107, 184
Sacred Cup, 183
Sacred Geometry/Geometrics, 8, 9, 53, 80, 91, 98, 104, 141, 172, 175, 178, 189, 190
Sacred Geometry, with the sanctified number sequences and mathematics, 80
Sacred Mathematics, 8, 9, 107, 141, 175, 178
Sacred Name of the Divine – Yod Hay, Vod Hay, 80
Sacred sexual union, 34
Sacred tones and sounds, 8, 9
Sahara Desert, 27, 28
Sainte-Chappelle, 43
Sanctified number sequences, 80
Sancho Fernando Jaime de Leon, 111
Saturn, 7, 52
Scandinavia, 11
School of Metaphysics, 52
Scotland, 10, 17, 79, 156, 176, 192
Secret Keepers, 105, 153
Seminar participants, 124
Sena in the British sea, facing the coast of the Osismi, 87
Sentinel Rock, 83
Sentinel Stone, 80–2, 84
Serpent energy, 48, 61, 178, 179
Serpent energy, Chartres and Versailles, 56
Serpent mound, 62, 79, 80, 141
Serpent mound, Orleans/Blois, 59
sexual energy, 22, 62, 165, 172, 174, 184
Shapeshift, 11, 12, 80, 84, 178
Simon de Montford, 111
Simon de Montfort, 147, 156, 192
Simon Peter, 165
Sirius, 7–11, 17, 51, 52, 60, 62, 159, 169, 180
Sissi, 36, 105, 109, 110–14, 142, 146, 148, 156, 163, 191–3
Socrates, 48, 49
Solar, Galactic and Universal Energy Fields and Systems, 154
Solar Logos rays, 171
Solar system, 7, 8, 52, 171, 180
Song Lines, 181
Song of Roland, 97
Soula, Place of the Sun, 103, 114–16, 121, 122
Sound frequency technology, 77
Sound keys and codes of Creation, 162
South America, 17, 51, 175
Southern France, 17, 40, 52, 92, 96, 97, 100, 123, 137, 142, 144, 147–9, 152, 157, 159, 160, 163, 165, 166, 176, 177, 181
Spain, 10, 11, 17, 18, 27, 52, 60, 97, 98, 109, 110, 111, 123, 139, 141, 147–50, 160, 175, 190, 194
Spanish Moors, 99, 104, 105, 148, 150
Sphinx, 169, 176
Spinal Column (of the Earth), 8, 18, 27, 30, 39, 51, 52, 80, 162, 168, 170, 171, 177, 179, 183, 186
Spinal Cord, 169, 184
Spiraling Energy, 8, 9, 11, 25, 27, 29, 30, 33, 35, 75, 116, 151, 159, 179, 183, 188
Spiraling Energy, as held in Delphi, 151
Standing Stones, 12, 20, 24, 25, 28, 29, 31, 78, 80–5, 98, 180, 181
Star Energy Grid of the Stargate (Stellar Portals), 29
Star Energy Grid of the Star Gate (Stellar Portals), 29
Stargate, 28, 29
Star Gate, 79, 80, 81, 84, 85, 87
Statue of Liberty, the Paris Replica, 47–9
St. Bernard of Clairvaux, 105, 177
St. Bernard of Comminges, 116
St. Dominic, 147
Stellar Gateway Portal in France, 30
Stellar Portal, 31
Stellar Portal in the West at Carnac, 31
St. Julia de Bec, 20, 40, 113, 122
Stone circle, 20, 30, 31, 33, 39, 80, 141, 171
Stonehenge, 30–3, 35, 51, 55, 80, 141, 159, 180
Sun Centres buried – Malta Delphi, Giza, New York Gulf of Mexico Brazil, 51
Sun Disc(s), 11, 12, 17, 21, 24, 25, 27, 28, 30, 31, 33, 39, 51, 55, 60, 70, 168, 169, 182, 188
Sun Gate at the City of the Goddess Olympia, near Malta, 56
Sun Gate at Versailles, 56
Sun Gate Complex, 51
Sun Gate linked Lemuria and Mu to Avalon, 51
Sun King of France (Louis XIV), 31
Sun Path Lines, 77
Sun Paths, 12, 16, 17, 39, 40, 91, 98
Sun People, 171
Suns of Illumination and Wisdom, 169
Sun Temple, 30, 34, 52, 55, 119
Sun Worship at Versailles, 31
Super-Conscious Energy Field Matrix, 171
Super Consciousness, 18, 32, 168, 183, 185
Super Consciousness Energy Field, 18, 32, 168, 183, 185
Supercontinent, 8, 9, 10, 141
Super Matrix Conscious Energy Fields, 185
Super race, 10
Susan Kerr, 66
Swan King and Queen, 35, 47

## T

Table Mountain, 26, 27
teleport, 11, 32, 80, 84, 171, 179, 181, 182, 185
Telluric energy center(s), 8
Templar and Cathar Cross, 132, 154
Templar Castle, 130, 131
Templar crosses – Nova Scotia, 151
Templar Grand Master, 105, 160
Templar Holdings, 51, 140
Templars, 12, 13, 19, 23–5, 30, 35, 64, 92, 101, 104–6, 111, 112, 114, 116, 121, 123, 130, 133, 137–9, 143, 144, 147–53, 156, 157, 160, 161, 165, 175, 177, 192, 193
Templars Kibbutz, 152

Templar State, 105
Templar Treasure, 101
Temple domes – liquid crystal tubes – cylindrical feature of massive sound chambers, 80
Temple of Solomon, 149
Temple of the Diamond Ray, 172
Temple of the Sun God, 51
Temple of the White Flame, 10, 172, 173
Temples of the Sun, 38
Tenerife, 33, 34, 94
Teutonic Knights, 105, 154, 156
*The Ancient Paths* – Graham Robb, 87, 91, 194
The Chalice, 183
The first triangle – Blois Chartres, Foix, Monségur, Versailles and Paris, 74
The Great Flood, 29, 174
The High Altar, Chartres Cathedral, 63
The High Order of Bards, 52
The High Order of Mystics, 52
The High Order of the Alchemists, 177
The High Order of the Mystic Rose, Serpent and Grail, 177, 182
The High Order of Wisdom, Metaphysics and Science, 52
The Knights Templar in the Golden Age of Spain, 147
The Place of the Bards, 76
The Shining Ones, 10, 173, 175
Third Crusade, 99, 100, 101, 104

Thousand Petals of the Heart-Rose, 183
Tom Kenyon, 35, 194
Toulouse Airport, 146
Tower of Babel, 55
Transformer Crystal Pyramids (7), 31
Transmitter Channel, 183
Treasure of Delphi, 99
Tree and Flower of Life, 60
Tree of Life, 107, 152, 168, 188
Trickster, the Joker, the Fool, 38
Troubadour Courts of Love, 12
Troubadours, 24, 96, 130, 148, 150, 179, 181
Tuileries Gardens, 24, 146
Tuning fork (Ankh), 179
Tuning fork (spinal column of Earth), 8
Twin Flame, 34, 116, 118

**U**
Uilleann pipes and bagpipes, 75
Ultimate Illumined State, 108
Unity consciousness, 105, 127, 152, 188
Universal Divine Laws, 12
Universal Language of Light, 175
Ural Mountains, Easter Islands, Peru, 51, 175
Urgell, 18, 112, 116, 121, 148, 161

**V**
Vannes, 87, 90–4
Venus, 7, 52

Versailles, 18, 20, 24, 29–35, 43, 45, 47, 49–57, 60, 74, 79, 80, 95, 119, 141, 162
Viscountess of Beziers and Carcassonne, 150
Voltaire, 57

**W**
Wars of the Heavens, 8–10, 52, 174
Web of Light, 7, 168, 170, 172
Wedekinsh, 48
White Flame, 8, 10, 12, 155, 158, 159, 164, 165, 172, 173, 184
White Flame – Eternal Diamond Fire of the Divine, 8, 10, 12, 155, 158, 159, 164, 165, 172, 173, 184
White Ray Energy, 169
Why I was born in Africa, 7, 8, 18, 26, 33, 149, 194
*Why I was Born in Africa: The Previously Unrecorded History of Elysium and The Lion Kingdom*, 169, 170, 172, 173
Winston Churchill, 80
Wizard School, 52
World War I, 142

**Y**
Yeshua, 107, 130, 136, 159, 160, 163, 164–6, 176